THE BEST OF

—— THE ——

WORD FOR YOU TODAY

365 DAYS OF STRENGTH AND GUIDANCE | VOLUME 6

BY BOB GASS

The Best of The Word for You Today, Volume 6

International Standard Book Number: 978-0-578-08975-1

Copyright© 2011 by Celebration Enterprises
Roswell, GA 30075

DEDICATED

TO: ....

FROM: ....

DATE: ....

— HOW TO —
GET THE MOST OUT OF THIS DEVOTIONAL

SET ASIDE A DEFINITE TIME
EACH DAY TO READ IT.

Ask God, "What are You saying to me?"

IS SOMEONE YOU KNOW HURTING?

Give them a copy. It could change their lives.

ARE YOU IN BUSINESS?

Give it to your clients and customers.

DO YOU WORK IN A HOSPITAL...A PRISON...
A REHAB CENTER...OR A RETIREMENT HOME?

This devotional is the perfect tool
for reaching people with God's love.

WHY USE SO MANY TRANSLATIONS?

For two important reasons. First, the Bible was originally written using 11,280 Hebrew, Aramaic, and Greek words, but the typical English translation uses only around 6,000 words. Obviously, nuances and shades of meaning can be missed, so it is always helpful to compare translations.

Second, we often miss the full impact of familiar Bible verses, not because of poor translating, but simply because they have become so familiar! We think we know what a verse says because we have read it or heard it so many times. Then when we find it quoted in a book, we skim over it and miss the full meaning. Therefore we have deliberately used paraphrases in order to help you see God's truth in new, fresh ways.

INDEX OF ABBREVIATIONS

*All scripture references are from the
King James Version, unless otherwise noted.*

AMP	Amplified Bible
CEV	Contemporary English Version
GNT	Good News Translation
GWT	God's Word Translation
NAS	New American Standard
NCV	New Century Version
NIV	New International Version
NKJV	New King James Version
NLT	New Living Translation
NRS	New Revised Standard Version
PHPS	The New Testament in Modern English
TEV	Today's English Version
TLB	The Living Bible
TM	The Message

OLD TESTAMENT

Genesis	Ge	Ecclesiastes	Ecc
Exodus	Ex	Song of Solomon	SS
Leviticus	Lev	Isaiah	Isa
Numbers	Nu	Jeremiah	Jer
Deuteronomy	Dt	Lamentations	La
Joshua	Jos	Ezekiel	Eze
Judges	Jdg	Daniel	Da
Ruth	Ru	Hosea	Hos
1 Samuel	1Sa	Joel	Joel
2 Samuel	2Sa	Amos	Am
1 Kings	1Ki	Obadiah	Ob
2 Kings	2Ki	Jonah	Jnh
1 Chronicles	1Ch	Micah	Mic
2 Chronicles	2Ch	Nahum	Na
Ezra	Ezr	Habakkuk	Hab
Nehemiah	Ne	Zephaniah	Zep
Esther	Est	Haggai	Hag
Job	Job	Zechariah	Zec
Psalms	Ps	Malachi	Mal
Proverbs	Pr		

NEW TESTAMENT

Matthew	Mt	1 Timothy	1Ti
Mark	Mk	2 Timothy	2Ti
Luke	Lk	Titus	Tit
John	Jn	Philemon	Phm
Acts	Ac	Hebrews	Heb
Romans	Ro	James	Jas
1 Corinthians	1Co	1 Peter	1Pe
2 Corinthians	2Co	2 Peter	2Pe
Galatians	Gal	1 John	1Jn
Ephesians	Eph	2 John	2Jn
Philippians	Php	3 John	3Jn
Colossians	Col	Jude	Jude
1 Thessalonians	1Th	Revelation	Rev
2 Thessalonians	2Th		

FACING THE NEW YEAR WITH COURAGE!

Be strong and courageous.
DEUTERONOMY 31:6 NIV

Without courage you're not living, you're hiding! Courage is what moves you forward; it's the muscle that makes your faith work. Faith by itself can be nothing more than a set of beliefs. Courage is what activates your beliefs. Every Promised Land has "giant" problems, and you have to face them and defeat them before moving in and taking up residence. Notice three things in Deuteronomy chapter seven, that God said to Israel about taking the Promised Land: *(1) "Your God, who is among you, is a great and awesome God"* (Dt 7:21 NIV). Be assured, God is greater than anything you'll face this year! *(2) "Will drive out those nations before you"* (v. 22). God will go ahead of you. He will do for you what you cannot do for yourself, but you've got to show up for the fight. *(3) "Little by little"* (v. 22). Whether it's conquering your Promised Land or your character flaws, you can't do it all at once. So God works with you in one area after another. Life is not one big battle and then you march in the victory parade. No, it's a series of small, daily struggles required to defeat the enemies of your spiritual growth.

Twenty-three chapters later God is still telling Israel to be courageous. That's because courage is like oxygen; you can't survive without it. Courage is not the absence of fear, it's the conquest of it. Courage means doing it afraid—until you're no longer afraid. It means—trembling your way to confidence! God promised to go *with* them and *before* them. Who does God walk with and work with? Who does He go ahead of and fight for? Those who show courage!

HAVING WHAT IT TAKES TO SUCCEED

The Lord gave him success in everything he did.
GENESIS 39:3 NIV

To succeed at anything, there are four things you must have: *(1) Morals:* What are you willing to do in order to get where you're trying to go? You can't get there just any kind of way; you must have boundaries. Now, all of us have broken the rules at some time. But thank God we had rules to break! We were able to realign ourselves because somebody had pitched a tent on where "right" is. Today folks don't seem to know or care where "right" is. *(2) Methods:* Your methods are your road map. A goal without a plan is like a road to nowhere. First the goal, then the plan, and then the process. Adopting this simple three-step formula helps you understand that you won't just leap into the middle of your dream, or get there overnight. There are methods that must be employed—and stayed with! *(3) Means:* When God gives you a vision, look for His provision. If you can't find it, either your timing is off, or what you want differs from what God wants for you. God's provision may come as an idea that hits you suddenly, or a thought that takes root and grows in you over time. Certainly, God's provision will always involve the help of others, so walk in love wherever you go. *(4) Management:* Jesus said: "To whom much is given, of him shall much be required" (Lk 12:48 AMP). Some people think it's "over" when God gives it to you. No, it's just beginning! And guess what your biggest management challenge will be? Yourself! That's why the Psalmist prayed: "Order my steps in thy word" (Ps 119:133).

THINGS TO REMEMBER WHEN YOU'RE ANOINTED

Not by might nor by power,
but by my Spirit, says the Lord.

ZECHARIAH 4:6 NIV

Any time God anoints [empowers] you, keep three things in mind:

(1) To be anointed is to walk alone. When God uses you to do great things, people assume you're strong so you don't need anything. They don't realize that underneath it all is a small, frail person who's half-scared-to-death, and who's as amazed by it as they are. And when nobody ministers to you, or you act like you have it "all together," you become an easy target.

(2) Without God's anointing you're in trouble! It happened to Samson: "Then [Delilah] called, 'Samson, the Philistines are upon you!' He awoke from his sleep and thought, 'I'll go out as before and shake myself free.' But he did not know that the Lord had left him. Then the Philistines seized him" (Jdg 16:20-21 NIV). God stepped back and let Samson see that it was not he doing it, but the Lord. And those who lead forget this at their peril!

(3) The anointing makes the difference. Take the sling out of David's hand and the stone out of Goliath's forehead and what are they? Worthless by themselves! So if you're waiting for God to give you exceptional equipment before you decide to get into the fight, you're not going to experience great victories. God's "strength is made perfect in weakness" (2Co 12:9). The way to know you're truly anointed is when God takes substandard equipment and performs supernatural feats. And that only happens when you say, "Lord, I don't see how You could do this through me." Then God gets the glory. And His reputation—not yours—is what it's all about!

SANDCASTLES

All the things I had toiled for...I must leave...
to the one who comes after me.
ECCLESIASTES 2:18 NIV

Max Lucado writes: "A little boy is on the beach. He packs the sand with plastic shovels into a bright red bucket. Then he upends the bucket and a sandcastle is created.

"A man is in his office. He shoves papers into stacks and delegates assignments. Numbers are juggled, contracts are signed, and a profit is made.

"Two builders—two castles. They see nothing and make something. And for both the tide will rise and the end will come. Yet that's where the similarities cease. For the boy sees the end while the man ignores it. Watch the boy as dusk approaches. As the waves near, the wise child begins to clap. There is no sorrow. No fear. No regret. He knew this would happen. He is not surprised. And when the great breaker finally crashes upon his castle and his masterpiece is sucked into the sea, he smiles, picks up his tools, takes his father's hand and goes home. The grown-up, however, is not so wise. As the wave of years collapses on his castle he is terrified. He hovers over the sandy monument he protected. He blocks the waves from the walls he has made. Salt-water soaked and shivering he scowls at the incoming tide. 'It's my castle,' he defies. The ocean need not respond. Both know to whom the sand belongs...and I don't know much about sandcastles. But children do. Watch them and learn. Go ahead and build, but build with a child's heart. When the sun sets and the tides take—applaud. Salute the process of life, then take your Father's hand and go home."

SEEING GOD IN YOUR EVERYDAY LIFE

When...he turned aside...God called to him.

EXODUS 3:4 NKJV

It was business-as-usual for Moses the day he noticed the burning bush, an event that wasn't uncommon in the hot desert. Except this time the bush *kept* burning. And "when... he turned aside to look, God called to him." You'll have some of your greatest spiritual experiences in the midst of your everyday life—if you're open to a divine interruption.

In Luke chapter ten, Mary ministered to Jesus' *divine* nature while Martha ministered to His *human* needs. But Martha's "kitchen agenda" made it almost impossible to interrupt her, while Mary was so heavenly minded she'd probably have forgotten to turn the stove on! Now, it takes both to achieve a balance. But if Jesus has to choose, He'll take foot-washers over master-chefs every time. That's because one of our primary focuses should always be praise and worship (expressed appreciation), resulting in greater intimacy with God.

Are you so busy working on your "to-do list" that it would take fire from heaven to get your attention? A well-known pastor writes: "You can be in the midst of a common moment, only this time the activity is filled with the presence of God. When in the middle of your harried day you notice something unusual...your first reaction might be, 'I'm too tired to investigate...I'm not going to disrupt my life.' Yet in that moment you may have the opportunity for a unique encounter with God. When you see the unusual in the midst of the mundane, don't continue business-as-usual. God may have ordained that moment to be life-changing for you and those around you."

HOW TO PRAY FOR OTHERS

Grace, mercy, and peace from...Jesus Christ.
1 TIMOTHY 1:2 NKJV

Paul prayed for three things to be given to those he loved. So when you're not sure how to pray for others, what better example than this one where he asks God to give Timothy:

(1) Grace: Peter says, "God, who gives all grace, will make everything right. He will make you strong...support you and keep you from falling" (1Pe 5:10 NCV). This word grace implies "all of God you'll ever need to handle whatever you're facing." That's worth praying for, isn't it? *(2) Mercy:* A large publishing house has a machine that automatically mails reminders to its readers that their subscriptions have expired. One day it malfunctioned and a rancher in a remote Colorado town received 9,734 notices! So he drove for miles to the nearest post office, mailed in his check, and wrote, "Send me the magazine. I give up!" That's how it is with God; He keeps sending us notices! The Bible says: "Because of the Lord's great love we are not consumed, for his compassions never fail. They are new every morning; great is your faithfulness" (La 3:22-23 NIV). *(3) Peace:* "All who listen to me shall live in peace and safety, unafraid" (Pr 1:33 TLB). What a gift to know that God's peace can sustain you through the worst situations. And the kind of peace He gives is different from what the world offers (See Jn 14:27). At best, it offers us temporary relief. But: "The peace of God, which transcends all understanding, will guard your hearts and your minds" (Php 4:7 NIV). So the next time you're praying for someone, ask God to saturate them in His grace, mercy, and peace.

BRING YOUR RED UMBRELLA

Ask...in prayer, believe that you have received it,
and it will be yours.

MARK 11:24 NIV

When severe drought hit a small farming community in the Midwest, a local church called a prayer meeting and everybody showed up. Crisis has a way of getting our attention! As the pastor stood before his packed church he noticed an eleven-year-old girl sitting in the front row, beaming with excitement. Lying next to her was her bright red umbrella poised for use. The beauty and innocence of this sight made him smile as he compared the faith of this child with that of the rest of the people in the room. You see, the rest of them had just come to pray for rain—she had come to see God answer!

One of the dangers of praying, is praying, yet not really expecting anything: "Without faith it is impossible to please God, because anyone who comes to him must believe that...he rewards those who earnestly seek him" (Heb 11:6 NIV). You say, "So how do I get more faith?" By filling your mind with the Scriptures! "Faith cometh by hearing, and hearing by the word of God" (Ro 10:17). When you immerse yourself in God's Word an amazing thing happens: faith takes root and begins to grow. And faith is what makes your praying effective.

But what if your prayer lines up with God's Word, yet the answer is delayed? Keep praying and believing! "Do not throw away your confidence; it will be richly rewarded. You need to persevere so that when you have done the will of God, you will receive what he has promised" (Heb 10:35-36 NIV). So when you pray for rain, bring your "red umbrella!"

YOU ARE SOMEBODY'S HERO!

Who is it he is trying to teach?...children.
ISAIAH 28:9 NIV

A father writes: "Dear Coach, I just read your letter to my son telling us of your expectations for your athletes. Johnny's mother and I couldn't agree more. We've long recognized the value derived from high school sports. Judging from your records you must teach the game very well. But there's another phase of coaching that's even more important. Let me explain. We are giving you our most prized possession. Throughout the next four years our son will make you one of our prime household conversations. He'll tell us about how you could have made the team for the Green Bay Packers if only you hadn't hurt your knee back in '65. He'll tell us about your emotional half-time talk when you came from behind and beat Rivaltown. We'll hear about how you can still pass or kick the ball. When we're hearing all this talk our son's eyes will shine. You see, Coach, he'll idolize you. We don't have heroes anymore. Many professionals would sell their souls for a buck. Some college athletes made the news this year in a very negative manner. We know all athletes don't shoplift and do drugs, but that's what we hear about. So, *you* are our son's hero. We're relying on you. His muscles are nearly developed, but his mind is still fragile, and so impressionable. Your responsibilities are great. Impress him, Coach. Pour it on!"

Isaiah writes: "Who is it he is trying to teach?...children." You are somebody's hero. The world is full of gangs, drugs and violence because a kid picked the wrong hero. But you can change that, if only for one or two kids.

LET GOD NAME YOU

I will write on him the name of my God.

REVELATION 3:12 NIV

When Rachel the wife of Jacob was dying in childbirth, she named her son Benoni, meaning "Son of my sorrow." In the Bible, names were prophetic; they were given to forecast destiny. So after the funeral Jacob announced, "He shall not be called Benoni, son of my sorrow. He shall be called Benjamin, son of my right hand. He is my strength, not my sorrow!" And guess which name prevailed? Benjamin! *You are who your Heavenly Father says you are. Try to remember that!*

Maybe you're like Hananiah, Mishael and Azariah. If you don't know them perhaps you'll recognize them by the heathen names King Nebuchadnezzar gave them: Shadrach, "command of Aku;" Meshach, "pagan name;" and Abednego, "servant of Nego." These names expressed worship to heathen gods. The real names of the three Hebrew children, however, were Hananiah, "Jehovah is gracious;" Mishael, "Who is like God;" and Azariah, "Jehovah has helped." When the king threw them into the fiery furnace the names God called them prevailed. There's nothing like trouble to bring out your true identity! Aren't you glad you're not limited to public opinion? God's opinion will always prevail. The old king tried to change the name on the package, but he couldn't change the contents! Can you imagine these boys shouting when they came out of the fiery furnace? One would say, "Who is like God?" Another would lift his hands and shout, "Jehovah is gracious!" The other would smell his clothes, touch his hair and declare, "Jehovah has helped!" *So stand up, step out, go forward in the name that God has given you!*

BULLETS OR SEEDS

The Lord God has given me his words of wisdom
so that I may know what I should say.
ISAIAH 50:4 TLB

Richard Halverson writes: "You can offer your ideas to others as *bullets* or as *seeds*. You can shoot them or sow them. Ideas used as bullets will kill inspiration and motivation. Ideas used as seeds will take root, grow and bear fruit in the life in which they are planted. But there's a risk; once it becomes part of those in whom it's planted, you probably will get no credit for originating the idea. But if you're willing to do without the credit…you'll reap a rich harvest."

Consider these two things: (1) Good ideas are wasted when you use a 'ram-it-down-your-throat' approach. You've got to learn how to say the right thing, the right way. Solomon writes: "A man of knowledge uses words with restraint, and a man of understanding is even-tempered" (Pr 17:27 NIV). To get the job done, you must have the right answer—and the right attitude. (2) Your efforts at helping others to change will fail, or worse, alienate them, if you don't approach them in love and humility. Most folks already *know* what their problem is; they've been dealing with it long enough. And deep down they *want* to do better. But unless you want a "who-are-you-to-tell-me?" response, you've got to approach them the right way. "Pleasant words are a honeycomb, sweet to the soul and healing to the bones" (Pr 16:24 NIV). The truth will always set people free. But if they refuse to listen to the truth in the way you're sharing it, maybe the problem's not theirs—it's yours. Maybe you're firing bullets instead of planting seeds.

BEING HAPPY ON THE JOB

The Lord shall command [His] blessing upon...
all that thou settest thine hand unto.

DEUTERONOMY 28:8

Happiness involves feeling good about yourself. It's based on your relationships and achievements. When your gifts and abilities are fully developed and utilized through your life's work, you grow in confidence and strength. Here are seven keys to being happy on the job:

(1) See work as God's gift, not punishment. "When God gives any man wealth and possessions, and enables him to enjoy them, to accept his lot and be happy in his work—this is a gift of God" (Ecc 5:19 NIV). *(2) Recognize God as your true employer.* "Serve wholeheartedly, as if you were serving the Lord, not men, because you know that the Lord will reward everyone for whatever good he does" (Eph 6:7-8 NIV). *(3) Pursue work compatible with your gifts.* "If anyone serves, he should do it with the strength God provides, so that in all things God may be praised" (1Pe 4:11 NIV). *(4) Learn everything possible about your job.* "Let the wise listen and add to their learning, and let the discerning get guidance" (Pr 1:5 NIV). *(5) Use criticism to your advantage.* In fact, make it work for you; ask for suggestions and correction: "Poverty and shame shall be to him that refuseth instruction: but he that regardeth reproof shall be honoured" (Pr 13:18). *(6) Do more than is expected of you.* "And whosoever shall compel thee to go a mile, go with him [two]" (Mt 5:41). Be an extra-miler! *(7) Make Jesus your work partner.* Stay Christ-conscious throughout the day as you perform your duties faithfully: "Thou wilt keep him in perfect peace, whose mind is stayed on thee: because he trusteth in thee" (Isa 26:3).

SO FAR SO GOOD! (1)

As the Spirit...works within us, we become...like him.
2 CORINTHIANS 3:18 TLB

Are you striving to become more like Jesus, but some days it feels like two steps forward and three back? Growing up spiritually isn't easy; that's why Paul encourages us not to "grow weary while doing good, for in due season we shall reap if we do not lose heart" (Gal 6:9 NKJV). You don't notice yourself growing older *physically* till you look at an earlier photo, then it hits you. And it's the same with *spiritual* growth; it's hard to gauge how far you've come till you look back and see where you were before Jesus saved you and turned your life around. The Bible says: "As the Spirit...works within us, we become more...like him." But growing up involves growing pains!

One day a high-rise construction worker slipped and fell from a scaffold forty floors up. As he plummeted past the twentieth floor a woman in an office shouted, "How're you doing?" The man replied, "So far so good!" Never forget that you're on a spiritual journey, you're making progress, and that the Devil will always look for ways to remind you how far you still have to go. Don't listen to him! Jesus said: "There is nothing truthful about him...everything he says is a lie" (Jn 8:44 CEV). If you get discouraged and give up, Satan wins. Paul says, "Capture...rebellious thoughts...teach them to obey Christ" (2Co 10:5 NLT). Learn to live beyond your feelings, to dig down inside to where God's Spirit lives. And take heart! It may not always feel like it, but every day you're maturing and growing stronger in Christ. So don't even *think* about throwing in the towel!

SO FAR SO GOOD! (2)

Before I formed you...I...approved of you.

JEREMIAH 1:5 AMP

Spiritually speaking, you're probably not as far up the road as you'd like to be—but thank God you're still *on* the road! At one time you were a stranger to God's grace, now you belong to the "household of faith." Paul writes: "You received the word...not as the word of men, but...the word of God, which ...effectively works in you who believe" (1Th 2:13 NKJV). Did you get that? As long as you keep *believing* it, God's Word will keep *working* in you. Plus, you'll mature faster when you stop being so hard on yourself, learn to relax and start living by what God's Word says about you—not how you *feel!*

How you see yourself affects your spiritual progress. Until your self-concept lines up with God's concept of you as revealed in His Word, you'll keep seeing yourself as inferior and unworthy—and that will retard your spiritual growth. Nobody knows you like God does. And in spite of your struggles and stumblings, He loves and accepts you just as you are. God told Jeremiah, "Before I formed you...I knew...and approved of you." Stop worrying about being rejected when you don't "perform" perfectly. The world operates like that, but not God. Plus, if you were as perfect as you'd like to be you wouldn't need His grace, right? Like Jacob's limp, sometimes God leaves flaws in us to remind us how much we need Him each day. So enjoy where you are *now,* and don't compare yourself with other people. Don't worry if they're further along than you. They went through the *same* places to get to where they are today.

SO FAR SO GOOD! (3)

When we were children.

1 CORINTHIANS 13:11 CEV

A well-known Bible teacher says: "As a new Christian…I tried to become what I thought all Christians were…I thought they'd mastered a level of holiness that seemed to elude me. I admired those 'faith heroes' whose flowery testimonies hung around the ceiling like steam gathering in a shower. They seemed so changed, so sure, so stable…I thought God's love was doled out according to a merit system. If I did well today, God loved me…if I failed, He didn't. What a roller-coaster ride! …I didn't realize everything that's born has to grow and develop to maturity. I was expecting an immediate, powerful, all-inclusive metamorphosis that would transform me into… perfection." Do you feel that way? Like there's something wrong with you because you never seem to measure up?

Paul says: "When we were children, we…reasoned as children…But when we grew up, we quit our childish ways." Every "new man" starts out as a child needing time and training to grow up. Quick fix, do-it-yourself righteousness will make you try to impress others with a false sense of holiness. It'll stop you from being honest before God, and make you think you should be further along than you are for your "spiritual age." Remember when you were a child and you dressed up in your Mom's high heels or your Dad's work boots? No matter how much you wanted them to fit, they didn't look right. That didn't mean there was something wrong with you; it just meant you were exactly where you should have been for your age. And it's the same in your walk with God. It's important to give Him time to mature you.

DON'T LET IT HAPPEN TO YOU (1)

Have a sane estimate of your capabilities.

ROMANS 12:3 PHPS

Leadership consultant Sally Morgenthaler, whose husband "crashed and burned" in the ministry, writes: "Many pastors paint unrealistic pictures of themselves...[crafting] a leadership icon rather than presenting his God-given, multi-faceted self. Image building is dangerous...looking good at all costs. When a pastor gauges his [success] by the admiration he receives, he intimates, 'I'll overwork to emotional and physical exhaustion ...deplete myself and my family...be everything you expect if you give me status, appreciation and financial compensation.' This unwritten contract is the people-pleasers' demise...No pastor can fulfill all of a congregation's expectations. Congregations by their nature are filled with sinful, unrealistic, needy people who'll take whatever the pastor gives, and keep coming back for more. Very few are cut out for this kind of leadership. When a pastor gets tired of giving and not getting back, he'll find some way to make up the difference." Sadly, some of those ways prove destructive!

Paul counsels: "Have a sane [reasonable] estimate of your capabilities" (Ro 12:3 PHPS). "Stay within the boundaries of God's plan" (See 2Co 10:13 NLT). God works through different people in different ways, but it is the same God who achieves His purposes through them all. Rick Warren writes: "It's easier to work with the grain than against it. When you're forced to minister in a manner that's out of character for your temperament, it creates tension and discomfort...and produces less than the best results. This is why mimicking someone else's ministry never works. God made you to be *you!* When you minister in a manner consistent with the personality God gave you, you experience fulfillment and fruitfulness."

DON'T LET IT HAPPEN TO YOU (2)

Do your own work well...
don't compare yourself with others.

GALATIANS 6:4 CEV

Sally Morgenthaler continues: "Pastors are seen as givers, not takers...shepherds, counselors who visit the sick and weep with the bereaved...if someone dies while the pastor's on vacation, he comes home. But here's the reality; a well-meaning pastor can work 80-hour weeks...and *still* not be able to please his flock. When [he] works hard only to be rewarded with conflict and dissatisfaction, the unrelenting disappointment can push even the most idealistic well-balanced clergy to believe he deserves better. Entrepreneurial church wisdom says a pastor must be...a risk-taker...innovator...spiritual guide... top-of-the-heap speaker...and if [he] doesn't have the...sole-visionary style...he'll become someone else, invalidate and dismiss his own gifts...God-given leadership style...strengths and passions...to emulate the large church pastor he's admired from afar." Do you recognize *yourself* in any of this?

Pastor, try to realize this: the enemy wants you to: (1) conform to outside expectations; (2) compare yourself to others. In fact, if you've lost your joy it's probably due to one of those two things. The Psalmist says, "Don't bother with those who climb the ladder, who elbow their way to the top" (Ps 37:7 TM). And Paul adds: "Do your own work well...don't compare yourself with others." God knew exactly what He was doing when He made you who you are! Again Paul writes: "What right have you...to say...'Why did you shape me like this?'...a potter can do what he likes with the clay!" (See Ro 9:20-21 TM). Instead of struggling to be something you're *not,* ignore your critics and build on who you *are.*

THE CHOICE IS YOURS!

If anyone hears my voice and opens the door,
I will come in.
REVELATION 3:20 NIV

Max Lucado writes: "Ever wonder why there were two crosses next to Christ? Or why Jesus was in the center? Those two crosses symbolize one of God's greatest gifts—the gift of *choice*. The two criminals have much in common; convicted by the same system, condemned to the same death, surrounded by the same crowd, and equally close to the same Christ. In fact, they began with the same sarcasm; the two criminals each said cruel things to Jesus. But one changed. He said, 'Jesus, remember me when you come into your kingdom.' Jesus answered him, 'I tell you the truth, today you will be with me in paradise' (Lk 23:42-43 NIV). While we rejoice at the thief who changed, we dare not forget the one who didn't. There are times when God sends thunder to stir us. There are times when God sends blessings to lure us. But there are times when God sends nothing but silence, as He honors us with the freedom to choose where we spend eternity. We have never been given a greater privilege than that of choice. Think about the thief who repented. Though we know little about him, we know this: in the end, all his bad choices were redeemed by a solitary good choice. He chose Christ!"

No matter how many bad choices you may have made in your past, you can be redeemed by one good choice—the choice to give your life to Christ and follow Him. Will you make that choice now? If you do you'll never regret it.

NO PEACE? IT'S 'OUT!'

Let the peace of Christ rule in your hearts.
COLOSSIANS 3:15 NIV

When God speaks to us He gives us a deep sense of inner peace to confirm that the message is truly from Him. Beware of false peace! When we have a strong desire to do something it can produce a false sense of peace that actually comes only from our excitement. As time passes this false peace disappears and God's true will emerges for our lives. So we should never move too quickly on important decisions.

When the Devil speaks to us he cannot give us peace. And when we try to solve things with our own reasoning, we cannot get peace. "But if the Holy Spirit controls your mind, there is... peace" (See Ro 8:6 NLT). Lay your decision on the scales of peace. Don't proceed if your inner peace cannot hold its weight against what you think or hear. You don't have to explain to others why you don't have peace about it; sometimes you won't know why. Just say, "It's not wise for me to do this because I don't have peace about it." There's power in having peace! And once you know you've clearly heard from God, you must do all you can to "keep your peace" and not become anxious.

Peace is an inner "knowing" that your actions are approved by God. "Let the peace (soul harmony which comes) from Christ rule (act as umpire continually) in your hearts [deciding and settling with finality all questions that arise in your minds, in that peaceful state] to which...you were also called [to live] (Col 3:15 AMP). God leads us by peace. His peace is like a baseball umpire who decides what's "safe," or what's "out." No peace? It's "out."

GROWING STRONG ROOTS

*May your roots go down deep
into the soil of God's marvelous love.*

EPHESIANS 3:17 TLB

Philip Gulley writes: "Growing up I had an old neighbor named Dr. Gibbs. When he wasn't saving lives he was planting trees. The good doctor had some interesting theories on plant husbandry. He came from the 'no pain, no gain' school of horticulture. He never watered his new trees. He said watering plants spoiled them; if you water them, each successive generation will grow weaker. So you have to make things tough for them and weed out the weenie trees early on. He talked about how watering trees made for shallow roots, and how trees that weren't watered had to grow deep roots in search of moisture. He'd plant an oak, and instead of watering it, every morning he'd beat it with a rolled-up newspaper. Smack! Slap! Pow! He said it made the trees pay attention. Dr. Gibbs went to glory a couple of years after I left home. Every now and again I'd walk by his house and look at those trees he planted twenty-five years ago. They are granite strong, big and robust. They wake up every morning and beat their chests and drink their coffee black. I planted a couple of trees a few years back. Carried water to them for a solid summer, sprayed them, prayed over them. Three years of coddling has resulted in trees that expect to be waited on hand and foot. Whenever a cold wind blows in, they tremble. Sissy trees. Funny thing about those trees of Dr. Gibbs. Adversity seems to have benefited them in ways comfort and ease never could."

GOD'S STILL IN CHARGE!

Are You not ruler over all...of the nations?

2 CHRONICLES 20:6 NAS

This country we call "home" exists only by God's permission and power. "He made from one man every nation...having determined their appointed times and the boundaries of their habitation" (Ac 17:26 NAS). In the final analysis summit conferences don't shape the geography of countries, God does. Leaders don't determine the future of countries, God determines the hearts of leaders. "The king's heart is like a stream of water directed by the Lord; he guides it wherever he pleases" (Pr 21:1 NLT). The stubborn will of the most powerful politician can be directed by God as easily as a farmer reroutes a shallow canal on his farm.

Remember the account of Cyrus, king of Persia? When God wanted the Jews to return to Jerusalem He simply prodded him to make an "official announcement" (Ezr 1:1 TM). God not only set the Israelites free from four hundred years of slavery in Egypt, He caused their captors to equip them with supplies. "[They will] load you down with gifts...so...you will [not leave] empty-handed" (Ex 3:21 TLB). That would be like post-civil war plantation owners signing their cotton fields over to the slaves.

If we enjoy a great economy, personal freedom and a high tide of justice, we don't limit our thanks to politicians. No, we thank God: "He makes nations great, and destroys them; he enlarges nations, and disperses them" (Job 12:23 NIV). Tally this up. God sets national boundaries. He determines leaders. He dispenses blessings. And we are the privileged recipients of each and every one of His blessings. Can we afford to forget this? Only at a terrible risk!

HE DID IT FOR YOU

By his wounds we are healed.

ISAIAH 53:5 NIV

Max Lucado writes: "I received a call from a friend named Kenny. He'd just returned from Disneyworld. 'I saw a sight I'll never forget,' he said. He and his family were in Cinderella's castle. Suddenly all the children rushed to one side... Cinderella had entered. She stood waist-deep in kids, each wanting to be touched. Kenny turned toward the other side of the castle. It was now vacant, except for a boy; his age was hard to determine because of the disfigurement of his body... he stood watching...longing to be in the middle of the kids reaching for Cinderella. But can't you feel his fear; fear of yet another rejection? Fear of being...mocked again? Don't you wish Cinderella would go to him? Guess what? She did! She walked across the floor, knelt at eye level with the stunned little boy and placed a kiss on his cheek. 'I thought you would appreciate the story,' Kenny told me.

"I did. It reminded me of another one. The names are different, but isn't the story the same? Rather than a princess of Disney, it's the Prince of Peace. Rather than a boy in a castle, it's a thief on a cross. In both cases a gift was given. In both cases love was shared. In both cases the lovely one performed a gesture beyond words. But Jesus did more than Cinderella. Cinderella gave only a kiss. When she stood to leave she took her beauty with her. The boy was still deformed. What if Cinderella had done what Jesus did? What if she assumed His state? What if she had somehow given her beauty and taken on his disfigurement?" *That's what Jesus did—for you!*

SHARE YOUR FAITH—SOMEBODY NEEDS IT!

Then I will teach transgressors your ways.

PSALM 51:13 NIV

Roger Simms was hitchhiking home when he was picked up by Mr. Hanover. As they drove toward Chicago, Roger felt God urging him to share his faith. When he overcame his fear and asked the man if he would like to receive Christ, Mr. Hanover stopped, bowed his head on the steering wheel, began to cry, and accepted Christ. "This is the greatest thing that has ever happened to me," he said. Shortly afterwards he dropped Roger at his house and went on to Chicago, which was about an hour down the road. Years later, while preparing for a business trip to Chicago, Roger came across the gold-embossed business card Mr. Hanover had given him years earlier. When he arrived in Chicago he decided to look up Hanover Enterprises and found it located in a skyscraper downtown. When he asked the receptionist if he could see Mr. Hanover, she said, "No, but his wife is here." "You knew my husband?" the woman in her fifties asked. Roger explained that her husband had given him a ride and how he'd led him to Christ. "When was that?" she asked. "May seventh, five years ago, the day I was discharged from the army." She began to sob. After several minutes she regained control and said, "I prayed for my husband's salvation for years, believing God would save him. But right after he let you out of his car, on May seventh, he was killed in a head-on collision. I thought God had not answered my prayer, and I stopped living for Him five years ago." That day she recommitted her life to Christ. *Share your faith—somebody needs it!*

AGING WELL (1)

I've run hard right to the finish, believed all the way.
All that's left now is…God's applause!

2 TIMOTHY 4:7 TM

Writer Brenda Smith learned the following lessons from observing her aging parents: *(1) Aging isn't optional; being "old" is.* Keep making plans or you're subconsciously giving yourself permission to die. Dad believed he owed rent on his earthly space and he paid it by giving back to others. *(2) God is real.* Mom struggled with depression as her Parkinson's disease progressed. However, she looked for God's hand in everything, and a lifetime of believing helped her to see His sufficiency even more in her final years. *(3) Time is a gift.* David said, "Teach us to use wisely all the time we have" (Ps 90:12 CEV). Dad told a friend of his, "When you've so little time left, you can't spend it doing stupid things. You learn to invest in things that count." *(4) Sickness doesn't create sainthood.* It's a test of patience, emotional restraint and maturity. When Dad was incapacitated he discovered that old age and sickness don't automatically draw you closer to God. He still had to discipline his mind to delight in the Lord and to find true joy in Christ. *(5) Laughter revives the soul.* After her father became ill, Smith writes about how this revered writer, speaker and consultant, "ended up smiling as he stared down at his size 46 waistline that took a dive each time he stood up from his wheelchair!" When Mother Nature and Father Time get through with all of us, we'll gaze into the mirror and either laugh or cry. Since "[Laughter] doeth good like a medicine" (Pr 17:22), and since God's prepared a wonderful new body for us in heaven, make up your mind to go out with joy!

AGING WELL (2)

When he comes we will be like him.

1 JOHN 3:2 TLB

If you're "feeling your age" these days, don't despair, there are still some perks left. For instance, you don't have to suck in your stomach, no matter who walks by...you actually enjoy hearing about *other* people's surgery...you no longer see the speed limit as a challenge...your joints are more accurate than the National Weather Service...your secrets are safe because your friends can't remember them...and all the money you spent on health insurance is finally paying off!

Seriously, the Bible says: "We are already God's children, and we can't...imagine what it is going to be like [when Christ returns]. But we...know...we will be like him." Henri Nouwen writes: "Speculations about our final days...are useless, but making each one into a celebration allows us to live [them] as... birthing days. The pains of dying are labor pains. Through them we leave the womb of this world and are born to the fullness of children of God...There's nothing morbid about it... it's a joyful vision of life and death. As long as we're in this body let's care well for [it]...But when the time has come...let us rejoice that we can go home and be united with the One who calls us the beloved." The Bible says: "He will wipe every tear... and there will be no more death or sorrow or crying or pain. All these things are gone forever" (Rev 21:4 NLT). Your future has never looked better!

An elderly Christian man lay dying. His family sat by his bedside. All his life he'd faithfully served the Lord. "Are you afraid?" one of them asked. "No," he replied, "my Father owns the land on both sides of the river." What a way to go!

BE A PEACEMAKER

Blessed are the peacemakers.

MATTHEW 5:9 NIV

When you walk into a scene of conflict you have two options: you can be a troublemaker or a peacemaker; you can add to the stress or bring a solution. Zig Ziglar tells of a little guy who was confronted by three bullies, any one of whom could have flattened him. And clearly, that's what they had in mind. But the little guy was very bright. He backed away, drew a line in the dirt, backed up a few more steps, looked into the eyes of the biggest of the three and said, "Now, you just step across that line!" The big bully did. At that moment the little guy grinned and said, "Good, now we're both on the same side!"

Peacemakers look for common ground, and try to get everyone onto it. Their goal is to find a win-win situation. Barnabas, whose name means "Son of consolation" (Ac 4:36), stood up for the newly converted Saul of Tarsus when he was "persona-non-grata" to the leaders of the church in Jerusalem. And given Saul's track record, who could blame them? But Barnabas wasn't looking at Saul's troubled past, he was thinking about his potential. In essence he told the apostles, "If you can harness and direct this horse, you'll win the race." And he proved right. Saul the persecutor became Paul the apostle! But Barnabas had to put his credibility on the line. Peacemaking means taking a risk on people, judging them by their best moments and qualities rather than their worst. Here's the bottom line: peacemakers are big picture thinkers; they're governed by grace, not petty opinion or temporary conditions. So, are you ready to be a peacemaker?

DEALING WITH PANIC

Do not be afraid of sudden fear.

PROVERBS 3:25 NAS

The words "sudden fear" describe a form of panic; you can't breathe, your palms sweat, your chest gets tight and you feel weak. If you've ever dealt with panic and you recognize these symptoms, you're not alone. Jesus said in the last days, "Men will faint from terror" (Lk 21:26 NIV). Every year one-third of us experience at least one panic attack. What's the answer? The Bible says, "[Do] not...panic...the Lord shall be your confidence" (Pr 3:25-26 AMP). Here are some practical tools you can use to help yourself:

(1) Breathe: Panic makes you breathe in short, shallow bursts, whereas breathing deeply helps to calm and relax you. Remember, "He himself gives all men life and breath" (Ac 17:25 NIV). So when you start to feel overwhelmed, just breathe the name of Jesus. Try it, it works! *(2) Don't respond with more panic:* If you do, you'll end up in double-trouble. Franklin D. Roosevelt said, "We have nothing to fear but fear itself." Now, while allowing yourself to feel fear without reacting to it may sound difficult at first, it's what helps to break the cycle. *(3) Do something calming:* This is the last thing you'll feel like doing because panic makes you instinctively think thoughts that feed and fatten your fear. So take a minute to whisper a prayer, quote a Scripture, listen to inspirational music, or talk to a friend. And if your panic continues to be an ongoing issue, there's no shame in getting professional help. After all, it's God who gives doctors the skills and abilities to intervene. Either way, take action today and don't let panic control your life!

REFLECTING, AND BEING GRATEFUL!

I was eyes to the blind and feet to the lame.

JOB 29:15 NIV

Chuck Swindoll tells of *The Giving Tree:* "When the boy was young he swung from the tree's branches, ate her apples and slept in her shade. The tree loved those years. But as the boy grew he spent less and less time with the tree. 'Come on, let's play,' said the tree, but the young man was only interested in money. 'Then take all my apples and sell them,' said the tree. He did, and the tree was happy. He didn't return for a long time, but the tree smiled when he passed one day. 'Come on, let's play!' But the man was older and tired of the world. He wanted to get away from it all. 'Cut me down. Take my trunk, make yourself a boat, then you can sail away,' said the tree. The man did, and the tree was happy. Many seasons passed—and the tree waited. Finally, the old man returned, too old to play, or pursue riches, or sail the seas. 'I have a pretty good stump left. Just sit down here and rest,' said the tree. He did, and the tree was happy."

Swindoll continues: "I stared into the fire, reviewing my life as I grew older with the tree and the boy. I identified with both—and it hurt. How many giving trees have there been? How many people have given of themselves so that I might grow, accomplish my goals, and find wholeness and satisfaction? Thank you Lord for each one. That night I crawled into bed. I had wept, now I was smiling. 'Goodnight, Lord.' I was a thankful man. Thankful I'd taken time to reflect."

FAITH (1)

With God on our side...how can we lose?

ROMANS 8:31 TM

Faith is like a muscle; opposition may strain it, but in the end it grows stronger. The Psalmist David understood this principle. He was continually hounded by his enemies. Even when he was being anointed to sit on the throne, Saul the old king was still occupying it. But instead of losing faith in God's promise, David understood that "the Lord has set apart [earmarked] the godly man for Himself" (Ps 4:3 NAS). So he declared, "In peace I will...lie down...For You...Lord, make me to dwell in safety" (Ps 4:8 NAS). When the Philistines captured him he prayed, "When I am afraid, I will...trust in You" (Ps 56:3 NAS). And when he ended up in a cave while fleeing from Saul's jealous rage he said, "I will hide beneath the shadow of your wings until this...is past" (Ps 57:1 TLB).

During the third century, when St. Felix of Nola was running from his enemies, he took refuge in an abandoned building. Eventually a spider began to weave a web across the door, sealing it off and making it look like nobody had been inside for months. As a result his pursuers passed by and didn't bother looking there. Later, stepping out into the sunshine, Felix declared, "Where God is, a spider's web is a wall. And where He isn't, a wall is but a spider's web." Jesus said you'd have problems on earth; people will disappoint you, and you'll disappoint yourself. Sometimes you'll end up in trouble because of something you did, and other times because of circumstances you have no control over. But God is with you either way. And like Paul said, "With God on our side...how can we lose?"

FAITH (2)

Job...fell to the ground and worshiped.

JOB 1:20 NIV

Every day God sends us opportunities for spiritual growth—disguised as problems. Nowhere is this more evident than in the life of Job the patriarch. After losing his house, his children, his livestock, and his health, the Bible says, "Job...fell to the ground and worshiped." That's not the normal human response to tragedy, is it? Job didn't react that way because he understood everything that was happening to him. No, he bowed in worship *in spite* of his circumstances! He was able to respond that way because: *(a) He looked up!* In the midst of his troubles, Job saw the God who promised to direct each step we take. More importantly, he trusted God's heart of love and recognized His sovereign right to decide all things. *(b) He looked forward!* He reminded himself that in the final analysis God will make everything right for us. *(c) He looked inside!* He knew that God was teaching him something valuable through this experience: "When He has tried me, I shall come forth as gold" (Job 23:10 NAS). Like clay in the hands of the potter, Job decided to trust God.

That kind of thinking was no easier for *him* than it is for *you.* Our human nature always wants to cling to the familiar and return to the safety of yesterday, even though we know it's not where God wants us. The fears, surprises and adversity that lie around the bend make us want to cut and run. But if you do you'll short-circuit God's plan for your life. So what should you do? "Stand...still, and see the salvation [deliverance] of the Lord" (2Ch 20:17), because *trust* always leads to *deliverance.*

FAITH (3)

When we trust...him, we're free...
to go wherever we need.

EPHESIANS 3:12 TM

When you walk by faith God will test you—like He tested Elijah! The prophet was sitting alone beside a dried-up stream when God sent him on a 100-mile hike through the desert to Zarephath. And at the time Elijah was a wanted man, so coming out of hiding meant *really* trusting God for his safety. Next, God told him that when he got there an impoverished widow would provide for him—a humbling prospect for a leader who's used to ministering to others. Elijah found the widow in the middle of a famine, cooking her last meal. Her circumstances looked grim. But he challenged her to obey God, promising: "There will always be flour and olive oil...in your containers until...the Lord sends rain and the crops grow" (1Ki 17:14 NLT). What gave Elijah the faith to say that? Because he'd personally proven God's faithfulness throughout his own life! You can *talk* that way when you *walk* that way!

Rubbing shoulders with people who trust God is contagious; it builds your faith. And this woman was no exception. She and her son may not have eaten gourmet meals every night, but God made sure that as long as the famine lasted they had all they needed. So if you don't have everything you want right now, honor God with what you've got, and trust Him that when the time is right He'll send an increase. Paul says: "When we trust...him, we're free...to go wherever we need." If God is directing you to your own personal "Zarephath," or anywhere else that doesn't make sense to you right now, don't argue. Go, because *His* promises hinge on *your* obedience.

FAITH (4)

Faith is the reason we remember great people.

HEBREWS 11:2 NCV

When the Bible says, "Faith is the reason we remember great people," maybe you think *you* would never qualify to march in that parade. You might be surprised; listen to some of the people God singles out in Hebrews chapter eleven.

Noah was a farmer-turned-boat-builder who got his name in lights because the boat he built survived a universal flood. What we sometimes overlook is that afterwards he got blind drunk and disgraced his family. *Abraham* wasn't a prophet or a teacher; he was a businessman with a character flaw who tried to save his neck by lying and compromising his wife's safety. *Sarah,* a homemaker, laughed when God told her she'd give birth to a child at ninety years old (and you'd probably have done the same!). There's *Joseph,* a slave with a prison record, who ended up becoming Prime Minister. Then there's *Rahab* the harlot; how did somebody with her background ever become a woman of faith? You'll have to ask God; He included her on the list. And how about *Jacob* the con artist: would you like to do business with him? Of course there was *David,* whose womanizing led to murder. And what about *Gideon* and *Samuel,* two spiritual leaders whose children went astray?

The bottom line is, all these "greats" were human just like us. In fact some of them would make us look like saints! You won't find any stained-glass material in this chapter. They faltered, fumbled the ball, and went through hard times. Their *only* distinction is—they believed God and He honored their faith!

ARE YOU READY FOR BIGGER THINGS?

You...enlarged me when I was in distress.
PSALM 4:1 AMP

Did you know that the hermit crab looks for a shell that fits him, then lives in it till he outgrows it? At that point he has to scurry along the ocean floor and find a bigger one; it's a process that repeats itself throughout his entire life. Are you clinging to something that no longer fits you, just because it's easy and familiar? David said, "You...freed me when I was hemmed in and enlarged me when I was in distress." To develop and grow spiritually you must be willing to move out of your comfort zone and deal with a little "distress." What worked for you yesterday may not work today. Maybe it's a job you've outgrown, a relationship you need to reexamine or a behavior you need to change. Regardless of what it is, never become so "settled" that you can't let go and move on when you need to.

Patience and persistence are admirable, but they won't work in situations you've outgrown. Instead of hanging in and trying harder, at certain points you have to stop and ask yourself, "Is this situation good for me?" If you're not sure, ask God for "an understanding mind [to]...know the difference between ...right and...wrong" (1Ki 3:9 TLB). His Word says, "If you need wisdom...ask [him], and he will [gladly] give it to you" (Jas 1:5 NLT). When God says it's time to move on, it's because there's another shell out there that will fit you even better. But you can't take occupancy till you vacate the old one. So how about it—are you ready for bigger things?

GOD'S GRACE/FAVOR

A good man [or woman] will obtain favor from the Lord.
PROVERBS 12:2 NAS

Because God's blessings aren't all packaged the same way, we get the idea that He somehow gives preferential treatment to certain people, especially since the Bible says He "does not show favoritism" (Ac 10:34 NIV). But in the English New Testament the words *grace* and *favor* are used interchangeably because both come from the Greek word *charis* [gift]. Think about it: when you ask somebody for a favor you're asking them for something you don't deserve. You're counting on their kindness and generosity when there's no obvious reason for them to do it, right?

Throughout Scripture God's grace/favor is what made it possible for people who otherwise wouldn't have amounted to much, to do great things. For example, when God chose a teenager called Esther to deliver her people and she stepped out in faith to approach the king, "she obtained grace and favor in his sight" (Est 2:17 AMP). God made a way for her to do the job He'd given her. And without divine grace/favor it's certain that Ruth, a Moabitess, wouldn't have been accepted by the Israelites. But because God had plans for her life, and her heart was pure before Him, she ended up marrying Boaz, "a man of great wealth" (Ru 2:1 NKJV). And from their ancestral line came King David, from whom descended our Lord. Pretty impressive—eh?

David said, "You bless the righteous; you surround them with your favor" (Ps 5:12 NIV). When God approves of you, people start favoring you too—often for reasons even *they* can't explain! Solomon said, "A good man [or woman] will obtain favor from the Lord." So ask for God's favor, expect it, and walk in it!

CAN OTHERS SEE JESUS IN YOU?

Let us go with you, for we have heard...God is with you.
ZECHARIAH 8:23 NRS

God told His people through the prophet Zechariah: "Many...shall...seek the Lord...saying, 'Let us go with you, for we have heard that God is with you'" (vv. 22-23 NRS). God's presence changes everything! When it shines through your life others are drawn to what they can see and sense. It happened to a short-order cook named Nicholas Herman. Dissatisfied with his life, he worried constantly about whether or not he was even saved. Then one day as he studied a tree, he was struck by the same truth that David talks about in Psalm 1:3, that the secret to growing spiritually lies in being rooted and grounded in something (and Someone) deeper than yourself. So Nick decided to make his life an experiment in what he termed "the habitual, silent, secret conversation of the soul with God." These days he's better known as Brother Lawrence, the name his friends gave him. Chances are you've heard of him and his writings. Although he spent his life in obscurity working in a kitchen, *how* he interacted with God has made people around the world long to know God like he did. His friends said he "found God everywhere... as much while repairing shoes as...praying with the community." And after he died they compiled a book of his letters and conversations called *Practicing the Presence of God*. It's one of the most widely read books of the last four centuries. Jesus said, "If I am lifted up...I will make everyone want to come to me" (Jn 12:32 CEV). So the more you allow Him to express Himself through your life, the more others will be attracted to Him.

TAKE CHARGE OF YOUR FINANCES (1)

One who plants generously will get a generous crop.
2 CORINTHIANS 9:6 NLT

The surest way to keep track of your finances is with a budget. Try it! You'll be surprised where your money goes every month. And since your spending habits reflect your *real* priorities, buckle up and get ready for a few eye-openers!

First: The top 10 percent of your income belongs to God—end of discussion! "Bring...the tithes into the storehouse... and...I will...open...the windows of heaven, and pour you out a blessing...there shall not be room enough to receive" (Mal 3:10). And God wants you to pay what you owe Him happily, not grudgingly or like you're cutting a deal. Paul says when you plant generously you'll "get [back] a generous crop... don't give reluctantly...God loves a person who gives cheerfully...you will always have everything you need and plenty left over to share" (2Co 9:6-8 NLT). Giving to God puts you in partnership with Him. *Second:* If you want the guarantee of a secure future—with options—discipline yourself to invest a percentage of your income into savings. Don't worry that it's a modest amount; just make it a priority! If you don't you'll spend it on other things and never achieve your long-term goals for college, retirement, or helping with the work of the Lord. *Third:* After tithing to God and saving for the future, strive to pay off all your other financial obligations. Lose this mentality of "paying only the minimum" on credit cards. By not repaying in full every month you end up paying much more than you should. Put as much as you can toward retiring your outstanding debts, even if you have to stretch yourself and do without a few things for a while. In the long run you'll be way ahead.

TAKE CHARGE OF YOUR FINANCES (2)

Blessed are those who are generous.

PROVERBS 22:9 NLT

We're wasting too much time arguing about both poverty *and* wealth, coming up with litmus tests for judging somebody else's level of spirituality based on their lifestyle, or how well they conform to our interpretation of "biblical standards!" In the New Testament Jesus honored a little widow for giving her last two cents. He said, "Others gave what they'll never miss…she gave her all" (Mk 12:44 TM). On the other hand, businessman Barnabas "sold a field he owned and brought the money and put it at the apostles' feet" (Ac 4:37 NIV). "Great gifts mean great responsibilities" (Lk 12:48 TM). The more God blesses you with, the more accountable He'll hold you for how you handle His blessings. During the offering a pastor told his congregation to reach out and grab the wallet or purse of the person sitting in front of them. "Now," he said, "Open it and give as much as you always wanted to, but felt you couldn't afford!" Hello! Solomon said, "The godly love to give!" (Pr 21:26 NLT), and while you may have less to give than the next guy, we've *all* been called to equal generosity and loyal sacrifice.

Isn't it interesting how you sometimes go to dinner at the home of somebody who doesn't have a lot, yet come away feeling like royalty because of the hospitality you experienced? That's because the essence of generosity is self-sacrifice. God entrusts financial increase to people who aren't controlled by the love of money! His Word says: "Blessed are those who are generous." "[They] prosper and are satisfied" (See Pr 11:25 NLT). You'll be amazed what God will do in your life when you're open-handed with your finances.

GET ON THE BUS!

Therefore, my dear brothers, stand firm.
Let nothing move you.
1 CORINTHIANS 15:58 NIV

Patsy Clairmont writes: "Jason, our youngest, has two goals in life. One is to have fun; the other is to rest. And he does both quite well. So I shouldn't have been surprised about what happened when I sent him to school one fall day. As Jason headed off for the bus I busied myself, preparing for a full day. The knock on the door was a surprise, and disruptive to my morning rhythm, which is not something I have a lot of. I flew to the door, jerked it open, only to find myself looking at Jason. 'What are you doing here?' I demanded. 'I've quit school,' he announced. 'Quit school?' I repeated in disbelief and at a decibel too high for human ears, swallowing once, and trying to remember some motherly psychology. But all that came to my mind was 'a stitch in time saves nine' and 'starve a fever, feed a cold,' or something like that. Somehow they didn't seem to apply to a six-year-old dropout dilemma. So I questioned 'Why have you quit school?' Without hesitation he proclaimed, 'It's too long, it's too hard, and it's too boring!' 'Jason,' I instantly retorted, 'You have just described life. Get on the bus!'"

When it comes to the Christian life, God promises no bed of roses on the battlefield and no carpet on the racetrack, just a checkerboard of adversity and advancement! His Word says: "Stand firm. Let nothing move you. Always give yourselves fully to the work of the Lord, because you know that your labor in the Lord is not in vain." So the word for you today is —get on the bus!

KEEPING THE LINES OPEN (1)

Love...Never looks back.

1 CORINTHIANS 13:4&7 TM

A woman quipped to her counselor, "We got married twenty years ago for better or worse. And looking back, *he* couldn't have done any better and *I* couldn't have done any worse!" Seriously, any good counselor will tell you that marriage is a process of adjusting to things you couldn't have anticipated. And good communication is crucial. It's important to:

(1) Talk to yourself before talking to your mate. Before you charge in with guns blazing, ask yourself whether fear, stress or worry could have provoked your mate's response. Is he/she deliberately trying to hurt you? Is it bothering you more right now because you're feeling insecure or unappreciated? Could you be misreading or exaggerating the problem? Identifying what you're feeling will help you communicate more calmly and clearly. *(2) Adjust your expectations.* We have a right to expect our mates to love and respect us, and to be faithful. But some other expectations are unrealistic; for example, keeping track of certain things your "ex" never did, expecting your spouse to do them. Paul says, "Love...Never looks back." *(3) Be honest concerning trust issues.* It's better to be truthful than to let things build up. It's okay to admit that some days you are more needy than others. For example, Dr. Gary Oliver says: "When a woman feels panicked every time her husband comes home late, because her previous husband had an affair ...it's okay to say...'I know it's irrational, but I'm having a panicky day!'" That kind of honesty will strengthen your relationship.

KEEPING THE LINES OPEN (2)

Love...Always looks for the best.
1 CORINTHIANS 13:4&7 TM

The last couple to "live happily ever after" may have been Snow White and Prince Charming! Chuck Swindoll writes: "Even though you're committed to your mate there will still be times of tension, tears, struggle, disagreement and impatience... but the good news is...with Christ living in you, and the Bible to call on for counsel...no conflict is beyond resolution." Married couples face unique challenges that sometimes involve sorting through what doesn't work to find out what does. Here are three good marriage-building pointers:

(1) Never resort to threats. The "D" word (Divorce) can surface quickly, so don't use it. In fact, don't even *think* it! Threats just make your mate defensive and insecure. As a result they can't hear what you're saying and nothing gets resolved. Jesus said we'll "have to give account...for every careless word" (Mt 12:36 NIV). So before you "sound off" consider the consequences. Take time out to calm down and think rationally. *(2) Drop the baggage from previous relationships.* Paul says: "Love...Always looks for the best...Never looks back" (1Co 13:4&7 TM). It's wrong to make your mate keep "proving" themselves over and over. Leave the bodies buried. Don't assume that your old relationship problems are destined to keep repeating themselves. They won't if you're communicating and growing! *(3) Keep your words soft and sweet; you may have to eat them.* Any time you think something nice about your mate—tell them. And when they reciprocate, accept what they're saying graciously. Remember, sharp words create more wounds than the best surgeon in the world can heal, but "A gentle response defuses anger" (Pr 15:1 TM).

THE WAR BETWEEN YOUR TWO NATURES!

The war...lasted a long time.

2 SAMUEL 3:1 NIV

When you decide to follow Jesus your old nature becomes Spirit *controlled*, not Spirit *destroyed*. Paul said: "While we are in this [body], we...are burdened, because we...wish to be...clothed with our heavenly dwelling, so...what is mortal may be swallowed up" (2Co 5:4 NIV). Note the words, "we are burdened." Struggle all you want (and most of us do!) to bring about a sudden transformation, but lasting change happens on God's timetable, not ours. We grow up spiritually *while* we're grappling with the burden of our lower nature. That's because our weakness is the perfect showcase for His power. Paul says: "Even though I received wonderful revelations from God...to keep me from getting puffed up, I was given...a messenger from Satan to torment me...I pleaded with the Lord... that it might depart...And He said...'My grace is sufficient for you. My strength is made perfect in [your] weakness'" (See 2Co 12:7-8 NKJV). Dealing with your old nature is a time-consuming, grace-developing, ego-destroying, character-building process that happens day-by-day, and sometimes moment-by-moment. When God's grace rubs against our stubborn wills and self-serving ways, a refining process happens that can't be rushed or accomplished any other way.

The Bible says: "The war between the house of Saul (which represents your old nature) and the house of David (which represents your new nature) lasted a long time. David grew stronger and stronger, while...Saul grew weaker and weaker." Only as you're willing to strip away the façade, get down on your knees day by day and ask God to work in you, will you experience His life-changing power.

CHOOSE YOUR HEROES CAREFULLY!

I'm...only a man, no different from you.

ACTS 10:26 TM

Role models inspire and motivate us, especially when they've walked the same path we have. And it's good to respect and appreciate them. But the moment you set them on a pedestal you lose sight of what's important. When you devote your life to emulating somebody else you risk becoming just another carbon copy. Remember, our heroes wrestle with blind spots and character flaws too. And none more than Paul, who describes himself as "not...good enough to be called an apostle," then adds, "God's grace has made me what I am" (1Co 15:9-10 NCV). Same thing with Peter; when Cornelius sent for him, "The minute Peter came through the door, Cornelius was... down on his face worshiping him! Peter pulled him up and said, 'None of that—I'm...only a man, no different from you'" (Ac 10:25-26 TM). Unfortunately some of the people we look up to aren't that humble!

The danger in hero-worship comes from forfeiting your individuality and missing the path God mapped out for you. Some of the lessons God teaches us may be similar, but another person's *purpose, journey,* and *time frame,* will be completely different from yours. For example, a friend starts a business and makes money, but when you quit your job to follow in their footsteps you go broke. Or a co-worker wears something that looks great on her, but on you the same outfit looks like a sack tied in the middle! "God is...a jealous God" (Dt 4:24 NKJV), not because He's petty or punitive, but because He wants to protect us from anything that robs us of our uniqueness, or threatens our relationship with Him. That's why when you make *Jesus* your reference point and hero, you're on safe ground!

OPPORTUNITIES TO GROW IN GRACE

Wear love. It's your basic, all-purpose garment.
COLOSSIANS 3:14 TM

A grandmother celebrating her golden wedding anniversary shared the secret of her long, happy marriage: "On my wedding day I decided to make a list of ten of my husband's faults, which for the sake of our marriage I would overlook. I never did get around to listing any. Each time my husband did something I didn't like I would say to myself, 'Lucky for him that's one of the ten!'" She was a wise lady!

Physical intimacy may *bring* you together, but growing in grace will *keep* you together! Here's an idea that will help your marriage go the distance. When your mate upsets you, instead of responding with angry words (or angry silence), stop and remind yourself that this is an opportunity to "grow in grace." And don't worry if you didn't do too well last time, you'll get another opportunity—probably before today is over. And you'll *keep* getting them. Opportunities to be nice, opportunities to be forgiving, opportunities to put your mate first.

Frame these words and put them on your wall: "Dress in the wardrobe God picked out for you: compassion, kindness, humility, quiet strength, discipline. Be even-tempered, content with second place, quick to forgive an offence. Forgive as quickly and completely as the Master forgave you. And regardless of what else you put on, wear love. It's your basic, all-purpose garment. Never be without it. Let the peace of Christ keep you in tune with each other, in step with each other. None of this going off and doing your own thing" (vv. 12-15 TM).

PRACTICE SELF-DISCIPLINE!

[For a servant]...discipline is needed.
PROVERBS 29:19 TLB

Solomon said: "[It is] better to have self-control than to con-quer a city" (Pr 16:32 NLT). So, how are you doing when it comes to self-control? Here are some nuts-and-bolts things you can start doing to make it more of a reality in your life: *(a) Begin your day by doing the hard things first.* If you get sidetracked, make yourself go back and complete them. For example, make your bed, pick up your clothes and wash the dishes; don't make extra work for others: "Work hard at whatever you do" (Ecc 9:10 CEV). And don't start several projects at once; do one thing at a time. *(b) Discipline yourself to be punctual.* Tardiness is a hard habit to break. To conquer it you must be willing to call it what it is—inconsiderate, selfish behavior. *(c) Plan ahead.* Everything takes longer than you think, so don't wait till the last minute then rush around like a chicken with its head cut off. Living under the gun can give you ulcers, whereas allowing yourself extra time is good for your health and brings peace. *(d) Accept correction from those who care about you without sulking or retaliating.* The Bible says, "Wisdom is found in those who take advice" (Pr 13:10 NIV). If you're wise you'll welcome feedback and seek counsel.

Gandhi once said, "There's always a limit to self-indulgence, but none to self-restraint." So ask God to help you control your unruly thoughts, feelings, desires and behavior. Identify unmanageable areas in your life, ditch the excuses, face the truth even when it hurts, refuse to feel sorry for yourself, and set a few attainable goals. In other words, "Learn to sense what is vital...and of real value" (Php 1:10 AMP).

GOD DELIGHTS IN YOUR OBEDIENCE

I delight to do thy will, O my God.

PSALM 40:8

Ruth Graham writes: "Tonight I sit on the porch, our old German Shepherd dog lying at my feet. Thunder rumbles in the distance. As the storm nears, he tears into the front yard to meet it…furiously doing battle. As it passes he returns to the porch, convinced he has driven it away. He's a German guard dog carefully trained in search and rescue, attack and obedience. Search and rescue in these mountains can come in handy. I cannot imagine an occasion on which I would give the order to attack. But a well-trained dog can sense hostility or spot a weapon (even what resembles a weapon), in which case it's a wise person who freezes in his tracks. But it's the obedience training that gives real joy. To stop, to sit, to lie down, to go away, to search, to stay, to heel. A disobedient dog is not only a headache; he can be a liability. Obedience makes a dog a joy. Is it less so with God and His children? There are some I knew who have been trained in attack. We will not mention their names. You may know a few, but they are skilled at it. Then there are those trained in search and rescue. (I'd put the Salvation Army in this group.) And there are those who have been trained in obedience. I think this, more than anything else, must give the Lord pleasure. Simple obedience. Joyful, eager, unquestioning obedience; to be able to say with the Psalmist, 'I delight to do thy will, O my God,' would be the height of training for the Christian. For this is what gives God the greatest pleasure."

UNREALISTIC EXPECTATIONS

Don't do...good deeds...to be admired.
MATTHEW 6:1 NLT

When you do something nice for somebody expecting the favor to be returned, you're setting yourself up for disappointment. Jesus said, "When you help someone...do it—quietly and unobtrusively" (Mt 6:3-4 TM); "Your Father knows what is done in secret, and he will reward you" (Mt. 6:4 CEV). There are certain things everybody has a right to expect, like common courtesy and respect. But too often we place expectations on other people that aren't their responsibility to fulfill. Then when they don't meet our demands we act hurt and disillusioned, when in reality it was our own misguided assumptions that caused the problem.

A well-known counselor says: "Many of us have unmet needs from the past...we want others to fulfill our desire to be loved unconditionally...some of us are so needy we drive people away." Husbands and wives are famous for holding each other accountable for things *they* need to work on personally. It's not fair to expect another person to "fix" you, or change your life, or suddenly become who you want them to be in order to make you happy. That kind of behavior just causes stress, resentment, hostility, and an unhealthy dependency you'll end up dealing with later. Another problem is expecting others to read your mind when you haven't taken the time to spell out your expectations. How can you blame somebody for not doing something they didn't know you wanted? Understand this: *people* aren't your answer, *God* is. If He chooses to use a certain person to bless you He'll do it; if not He'll use somebody else. So examine your thinking today and ask God to reveal and remove any unrealistic expectations you're living with.

PEACE "IN SPITE OF"

*You will experience God's peace, which is far
more wonderful than the human mind can understand.*
PHILIPPIANS 4:7 TLB

Catherine Marshall writes: "A king once offered a prize to the artist who could paint the best picture of peace. Many tried, but there were only two the king really liked. One was of a calm lake. It was a perfect mirror for the peaceful towering mountains all around it. Overhead was a blue sky with fluffy white clouds. The other picture had mountains too. But they were rugged and bare. Above them was an angry sky from which fell rain, and in which lightning played. Down the side of the mountains tumbled a waterfall. This did not look peaceful at all. But when the king looked closely he saw behind the waterfall a tiny bush growing in a crack in the rock. In the bush a mother bird had built her nest. There, in spite of the rush of angry water, she sat on her nest—in perfect peace. Which picture do you think won the prize? The king chose the second picture. Why? 'Because,' explained the king, 'Peace does not mean to be in a place where there is no noise, trouble or hard work. Peace means to be in the middle of all these things and *still* be calm in your heart.'"

At some point we all discover that there's no safe harbor free from storms; that peace is not the absence of storms, but: (a) the assurance of God's presence and protection in the midst of them; (b) the growth of our faith and character because of them; (c) His rock-solid promise to bring us through them stronger and wiser.

DON'T OFFER GOD YOUR LEFTOVERS!

Nor will I offer...the Lord...that which costs me nothing.
2 SAMUEL 24:24 NKJV

Hard work makes you sweat. Notice, when Adam and Eve were banished from the Garden of Eden they had to "sweat to earn a living" (Ge 3:19 CEV). Farmers sweat to turn their crops into cash, the same as bricklayers on a construction site or an executive writing a report in a high-rise office suite. You tend to value what you have to work for—and God values your efforts as well. That's why when David had the chance to offer God a sacrifice he said, "Nor will I offer...the Lord...that which costs me nothing."

Whether you do it figuratively or literally, you sweat to earn a living. And you'll also do the same when you're committed to worshipping God. This doesn't necessarily mean praising Him loudly and raising your hands in church; those things are good at the proper time. But in-depth worship goes far beyond that. The word *worship* comes from the Anglo-Saxon word "worth-ship," which is "the act of ascribing worth or value to a person or object." In the New Testament worship encompasses service, adoration, reverence, humility, love, and giving. For example, tithes and offerings are the part of worship where you give God the first portion of your earnings (See Pr 3:9). It's another way of honoring Him with the fruits of your time and energy. When you sacrifice sleep to get up early and spend time with God, you're also doing something that costs you. And when you inconvenience yourself to help somebody in need, you're offering God something of real worth (See 1Jn 3:17-18). So examine your heart today and make sure you're offering Him something of value, and not just your leftovers.

YOUR QUIET TIME WITH GOD (1)

O God, you are my God, earnestly I seek you.
PSALM 63:1 NIV

When you come to meet with God you should have an attitude of: *(1) Expectancy.* Expect to "give and get" from your time together. And make it a time of intimacy. It's impossible to have a love affair in a crowd or a public place; intimacy calls for being alone with the one you love. The Bible speaks about Christ as the groom and believers as His bride. Think of the anticipation and excitement shared in such moments. *(2) Reverence.* Don't rush into God's presence. Prepare your heart by being still before Him and letting the quietness clear away the thoughts of the world. Remind yourself Who it is you're meeting with—God! "You are worthy...to receive glory and honor" (Rev 4:11 NIV). *(3) Alertness.* Get to bed early so you'll be in good shape to meet God in the morning. He deserves your full attention. Give God the best part of your day—when you are the freshest. Follow the example of Christ: "Very early in the morning...Jesus...went off to a solitary place, where he prayed" (Mk 1:35 NIV). Hudson Taylor said, "You don't tune up the instruments after the concert is over...you tune them up before you start." *(4) Willingness.* This attitude is crucial: you don't come to your quiet time to choose what you will or won't do, but with the purpose of doing anything and everything God wants you to do. Jesus said: "If anyone chooses to do God's will, he will find out whether my teaching comes from God" (Jn 7:17 NIV). So come to meet with the Lord, having already chosen to do His will—no matter what!

YOUR QUIET TIME WITH GOD (2)

O God, you are my God, earnestly I seek you.
PSALM 63:1 NIV

Stephen Olford said, "I want to hear God's voice before anyone else's in the morning. And His is the last voice I want to hear at night." David and Daniel met with the Lord three times daily (See Ps 55:17; Da 6:10). Whatever time you set, be consistent. Put it on your calendar; make an appointment with God as you would with anyone else. And keep it. Don't stand Him up! The question is often asked, "How much time should I spend?" Here are some guidelines:

(1) Don't start with a two-hour quiet time. You'll get discouraged. You'll create memories of failure rather than memories of success. You must grow in this relationship as you do in any other. So begin with a few minutes and let it grow. *(2) Don't clock-watch.* That'll ruin your quiet time faster than anything else. Decide what you can do in God's Word and prayer during the time you've selected; then do it! Sometimes it'll take more time than you have set aside, sometimes less. But don't keep looking at your watch. *(3) Emphasize quality, not quantity.* It's what you do during your quiet time—whether fifteen minutes or two hours—that's important. *(4) Choose a special place.* "Next morning Abraham got up and returned to the place where he had stood before the Lord" (Ge 19:27 NIV). Your special place ought to be a place where: (a) you can pray aloud without embarrassment; (b) you're comfortable. (Don't have your quiet time in bed—that's *too* comfortable!) As the days go by, your special place will come to mean everything to you because of the wonderful times you have there with the Lord.

YOUR QUIET TIME WITH GOD (3)

O God, you are my God, earnestly I seek you.
PSALM 63:1 NIV

For the next few days let's deal with some "quiet time problems."

The problem of discipline! This is known as "the battle of the blankets." It faces you the moment you wake up. The Devil will exaggerate how tired you are. And when he and your flesh team up, it's a battle to get out of bed. So here are some tips on overcoming this problem: *(a) Go to bed on time.* Too many of us stay up late watching TV, therefore we have a hard time getting up in the morning. Dawson Trotman lived by the Scripture, "Early will I seek thee" (v. 1 NKJV). Even if he had company the night before, he would excuse himself and go to bed because his top priority was meeting with Christ each morning. *(b) Get up immediately upon waking.* If you wait to think about it, you've already lost the battle. Furthermore, when you wake up in the morning it's not the time to pray about deciding to get up. If you have to pray about it, do so the night before, and pray that you'll have the willpower to do it. Plan it. Be intentional! Resolve like the Psalmist, "In the morning, O Lord, you hear my voice" (Ps 5:3 NIV). *(c) Go to bed with thoughts of Scripture.* Fall asleep with the attitude of "See You in the morning, Lord." Ask Him to wake you up with thoughts of Him. One of the best ways to do that is to go to sleep with a Scripture verse on your mind. "Do not let this Book...depart from your mouth; meditate on it day and night" (Jos 1:8 NIV).

YOUR QUIET TIME WITH GOD (4)

O God, you are my God, earnestly I seek you.
PSALM 63:1 NIV

You say you're not getting much out of your quiet time? Rick Warren refers to this as "the battle of the blahs." He writes: "You can never judge your quiet time by your emotions. Emotions may lie; feelings may come and go. If you only have a quiet time when you 'feel' like it, the Devil will make sure you never feel like it. Some days will seem bland. On other days you'll think heaven has opened up to you. So don't expect a glorious 'experience' every morning. Not having goose-bumps doesn't mean God is not present." Dry spells can be caused by: *(a) Disobedience.* God won't bless you beyond your last act of disobedience. And He won't reveal step two until you've taken step one. *(b) Being in a hurry.* Samuel Chadwick said, "Hurry is the death of prayer." So go for quality and content, not mileage! *(c) Being in a rut.* When your quiet time becomes a ritual instead of a relationship, it dies. So be flexible; change your routine, keep it interesting—for you and the Lord. *(d) Not sharing your insights with others.* When we give out, we get back more in return. Share your quiet-time thoughts with others and see what happens.

If you're still not getting anything out of it, tell God about it. It takes time to develop a relationship. You must learn to see God in all kinds of circumstances in order to get to know Him well. So don't give up: "Let us not become weary in doing good, for at the proper time we will reap a harvest if we do not give up" (Gal 6:9 NIV).

YOUR QUIET TIME WITH GOD (5)

O God, you are my God, earnestly I seek you.
PSALM 63:1 NIV

Once you have won "the battle of the blankets" and "the battle of the blahs," you'll have to fight "the battle of the brain." Your mind will wander off in 101 directions during your quiet time. The Devil will make sure it does. You'll find yourself distracted by noises, lack of sleep, tensions with others, work, and things you "just can't forget." So here are some helpful suggestions: *(1) Be sure you're thoroughly awake.* Take a shower, splash cold water on your face, or do some exercise. Get the adrenalin flowing! The Psalmist writes: "As the deer pants for streams of water, so my soul pants for you, O God" (Ps 42:1 NIV). A deer being pursued by a hunter has only one thing in mind: getting to the stream where its wounds can be healed, its thirst quenched, and its strength renewed. *(2) Use a memo pad.* When you decide to spend time with God you'll suddenly "remember" everything you have to do, or have left undone. So write things down as they come to you, then tell yourself, "I'll get to that later," and go back to prayer. *(3) Walk while you're praying.* You won't fall asleep while standing up, so move around. *(4) Personalize the Scriptures.* Pray them back to God. Since God's Word is always in line with God's will, your prayers will get answered. For example, use Psalm 23: "Lord, You are my Shepherd, therefore I shall not want for anything. Thank You for leading me in paths that are right when I don't know which way to go." This simple technique can transform your quiet time.

YOUR QUIET TIME WITH GOD (6)

O God, you are my God, earnestly I seek you.
PSALM 63:1 NIV

Nothing is more difficult to maintain than your quiet time with God. When pressures mount, what's the first thing you're tempted to drop? Satan knows if he can keep you from it he's won the battle, because he'll have no opposition from you. Backslidden Christians will tell you, "It started when I began to neglect my quiet time with God."

"So how can I overcome this problem?" you ask. *(1) Make a covenant with God.* And be serious about it: "When you make a vow to God, do not delay in fulfilling it...It is better not to vow than to make a vow and not fulfill it" (Ecc 5:4-5 NIV). *(2) Put it on your schedule.* Block out time to meet with God each day, just like you plan a doctor's appointment or a business luncheon. Can you imagine keeping an appointment that's more important? *(3) Be ready for the Devil's excuses and attacks.* To be forewarned is to be forearmed. So follow the Boy Scout motto, "Be prepared!" Dr. Robert G. Lee used to say, "If you wake up in the morning and don't meet the Devil face on, it means you're headed in the same direction!" *(4) Leave your Bible open the night before at the passage you intend to read in the morning.* When you wake up it will serve as a reminder to have your quiet time.

"But what if I miss a day?" Don't worry, and don't go on a guilt trip. If you miss a meal it doesn't mean you gave up eating. You simply eat a little more at the next meal, and go on from there.

YOUR QUIET TIME WITH GOD (7)

O God, you are my God, earnestly I seek you.
PSALM 63:1 NIV

Psychologists say it takes up to three weeks to get familiar with a new habit, then another three weeks before it takes root. You've got to get beyond that six-week barrier!

Here's a simple formula for developing a habit: *(1) Make a strong resolution!* If you begin half-heartedly you'll never succeed. The Bible says: "Encourage one another daily" (Heb 3:13 NIV). So become accountable to someone. Ask them to encourage you, and to remind you of the promise you made to God. *(2) Never allow an exception.* A habit is like a ball of twine: every time you drop it some of the strands unwind. So never allow "just this once" to occur. Each act of yielding weakens your will and causes you to lose ground. *(3) Seize every opportunity to practice your new habit.* Whenever you get the slightest urge to practice it, do it right then. Don't wait; use that moment to reinforce it. It doesn't hurt to overdo a new habit when you are first starting. *(4) Rely on the power of God.* When all is said and done, you must realize you're in a spiritual battle and that you can only succeed by the indwelling power of the Holy Spirit. So pray that God will strengthen you. Depend on Him to help you develop the habit for His glory. Write down the following words and sign your name to the bottom of them. Then keep them before you constantly: "Lord, I commit myself to spending a definite time with You every day, no matter what the cost. And I'm depending on You to help me to be consistent. Amen."

KEEP STROKIN'!

Let us go over to the other side.

MARK 4:35 NIV

Sometimes you only learn to swim by getting thrown into the deep end. When that happens you discover that: (a) if you let it, your fear will take you under; (b) you can only tread water for so long; (c) when you get to a certain point there's no turning back, you have to keep going. It's fatal to stop or give up in the middle of the process; (d) what God has put within you (the air in your lungs) will sustain you and keep you afloat if only you learn to relax, trust God, and keep strokin'!

If you're really serious about getting to the other side—you've got to take what's in front of you and keep pushing it behind you. In other words, keep strokin'! You might be crying while you're swimming, but keep strokin'. Your heart may be about to come out of your chest, but keep strokin'. It's when you feel backed into a corner with nowhere to go, that you've got to reach down, take hold of what God put within you, and keep strokin'. "The kingdom of heaven suffereth violence, and the violent take it by force" (Mt 11:12). Notice the word "violence"—sometimes you have to rise up in faith and fight your way through, confident that God is on your side. The waters you're in don't determine your destiny; they can either carry you over or take you under. Your *faith* has got to rise up and fight your *fear.* If you quit, God can do nothing more for you. So whether you're doing the breaststroke, the backstroke, or some other kind of stroke nobody's even heard of—keep strokin'!

DON'T NULLIFY GOD'S GRACE!

If a...relationship with God could come by
rule-keeping...Christ died unnecessarily.
GALATIANS 2:21 TM

Grace doesn't give anyone a license to live as they please. But the judgmentalism that comes from insisting that others live by *our* standards has caused untold damage. A well-known preacher writes: "Legalism spreads a paralyzing venom...blinds our eyes, dulls our edge and arouses pride in our heart...Love is overshadowed by a mental clipboard with a long check-list... requiring others to measure up...Soon friendship is fractured by a judgmental attitude and a critical look." Think you're not guilty? Observe your initial reaction when you meet another believer who doesn't think, act, or dress the way *you* do. Even when you think you're sophisticated enough to disguise your real feelings, they come out in the stony stare and the holier-than-thou attitude. Jesus said: "Never criticize...or it will all come back on you" (Lk 6:37 TLB). When you throw mud you don't just get your hands dirty, you lose ground! "Let the one who has never sinned throw the first stone!" (Jn 8:7 NLT). Blowing another person's light out won't make *yours* shine brighter.

Paul writes: "If a...relationship with God could come by rule-keeping...Christ died unnecessarily." You say, "But what if someone is getting off track or deliberately sinning?" Paul answers: "If another believer is overcome by some sin...humbly help that person back onto the right path...be careful not to fall into the same temptation yourself" (Gal 6:1 NLT). When you judge others you're in danger of nullifying the grace you may need *yourself* before the day is through!

ASK GOD FOR WHAT YOU WANT!

The reason you don't have what you want is...
you don't ask God.
JAMES 4:2 TLB

Imagine walking into a restaurant on a whim and asking if your order is ready. "When did you call it in?" the server asks. "Oh I didn't," you reply, "I just thought perhaps you'd have something with my name on it." Sound ridiculous? No more so than expecting God to answer requests you haven't made—or have made without faith. James says: "The reason you don't have what you want is...you don't ask God." Does that mean He'll automatically give you everything you ask for? No. James adds: "Even when you do ask you don't get it because...you want only what will give you pleasure" (v. 3 TLB). Your motives need to be in tune with what God knows is best for you. John says, "This is the confidence...we have in Him...if we ask anything...*according to His will*...He...hears" (1Jn 5:14 AMP).

Lamentations 3:25 says: "The Lord is good to those who wait...expectantly for Him" (AMP). Expectant prayer demonstrates confidence in God's goodness. Instead of fretting and taking matters into your own hands, when you say, "Lord, I'm going to trust You with this, regardless of the outcome," He'll honor your faith. Paul says: "Pray and ask God for everything you need, always giving thanks" (Php 4:6 NCV). Do you need a job? Help overcoming a problem? Salvation for your loved ones? A deeper walk with God? Physical or emotional healing? Jesus said: "It gives your Father great happiness to give you the [benefits of his] Kingdom" (Lk 12:32 NLT). God *wants* to be good to you, so tell Him the "desires of your heart" (Ps 37:4 NKJV). And thank Him that the answer will come—in *His* time!

LIFE IS WHAT YOU MAKE IT

Always full of the joy of the Lord, and always thankful.
COLOSSIANS 1:11-12 TLB

Once there was an old and very wise man. Every day he and his granddaughter would sit outside a gas station in his rocking chair, waiting to greet tourists as they passed through his small town. One day a tall man who surely had to be a tourist, began looking around as if he were checking out the area for a place to live. "So what kind of town is this?" he asked. The old man replied, "Well, what kind of town are you from?" The tourist said, "One where everyone is very critical of each other. It's a real negative place to live." The old man said "You know, that's just how this town is." Later, a family passing through also stopped for gas. The father stepped out and asked the old man, "Is this town a good place to live?" "Well, what about the town you're from?" The father said, "In the town I'm from everyone is very close and always willing to lend a helping hand. I really hate to leave it." The old man smiled and said, "You know, that's a lot like this small town." After the family had left the granddaughter looked up and asked, "Grandpa, how come when the first man came you told him this was a terrible place to live, yet when that family came you told them it was a wonderful place to live?" The old man looked down into his granddaughter's wondering blue eyes and said, "No matter where you go, you take your attitude with you. And that's what makes it terrible or wonderful." Yes, life is what you make it!

HE'S ALWAYS LOOKING OUT FOR YOU

The Lord is in this place, and I was not aware of it.

GENESIS 28:16 NIV

Author Frederick Buechner said: "There's no event so commonplace, but that God is present…leaving you room to recognize Him, or not." Aren't you glad God's presence isn't reserved for people who "deserve it." He visits whiners and complainers, the impatient and disgruntled, the doubtful and indecisive; flawed people like you, who've been saved by His grace. For example, Jacob was no spiritual giant. Running away after swindling his brother and deceiving his father, he didn't deserve what God did for him. After stopping for the night, he dreamed he saw a ladder to heaven with angels on it, ascending and descending. Then God gave him this promise: "I am with you and will watch over you wherever you go" (v. 15 NIV). When Jacob awoke the next morning he said, "The Lord is in this place, and I was not aware of it." Pearl Buck said, "We see God every day; we just don't recognize Him." Some of us are "tuned in" when it comes to sensing His presence; others like Jacob "miss it" every time.

William Barry says: "Whether we're aware of it or not… every moment…we're encountering God…who is trying to catch our attention…to draw us into a reciprocal conscious relationship." You never know where He'll appear or who He'll speak through. After the resurrection Mary Magdalene thought Jesus was just the gardener! Paul writes: "Wake up…sleeper" (Eph 5:14 NIV). You can be awakened by a miraculous healing, a restored relationship, or even a severe trial. Later God revealed Himself to Jacob by wrestling with him and dislocating his hip. What will it take to get *your* attention?

FAITH VS. CONTROL

If you give up your life for me, you will save it.
LUKE 9:24 CEV

When you obsess over problems instead of looking to God for solutions, the Enemy will magnify your fears. If he can't get you to worry about the present he'll remind you of everything that could go wrong in the future! Ralph Waldo Emerson said, "All I have seen, has taught me to trust God for all I haven't seen." The last time you checked, wasn't God still bigger than any terrorist attack, financial disaster, illness, accusation, or mess you found yourself in? Well, He hasn't changed! The Psalmist said, "He won't go to sleep...The Lord is...at your right side...[He] will...keep you safe...wherever you go" (Ps 121:3-8 CEV); plus His angels are watching over you 24/7.

It all comes down to faith vs. control. You can struggle to handle things on your own—or trust your heavenly Father. That's the choice! It's not about "blind faith," it's about believing that God is who He says He is. And it's an issue you need to settle in your mind once and for all, because if you don't believe He wants only the best for you, you'll keep trying to run the show. Control isn't responsibility. *Responsibility* is doing your part by praying, obeying, and trusting God. *Control* is manipulating the circumstances to engineer the outcome you want. Jesus knows how we like holding on to things we're not wise enough to control, so He said: "If you want to save your life, you will destroy it. But if you give up your life for me, you will save it." Bottom line—you either trust God or you don't!

FOCUS ON YOUR STRENGTHS

God has given each of us the ability
to do certain things well.

ROMANS 12:6 TLB

Work where you're *strongest* 80 percent of the time. Work where you're *learning* 15 percent of the time. Work where you're *weakest* 5 percent of the time. Is that wise? Absolutely! "God has given each of us the ability to do certain things well." What happens to a team when its members play "out of position?" First, morale weakens because the team isn't playing up to its capacity. Those working in an area of weakness resent that their skills are untapped. Soon they become unwilling to work as a team, everyone's confidence erodes and the situation gets worse. Then the competition takes advantage of their weaknesses, and they never win. When people aren't doing what they're supposed to do, things don't run well.

Do you know what your greatest strengths are? If not, follow these guidelines: *(1) Be secure*: If you allow your insecurities to get the better of you, you'll become inflexible and resistant to change. And if you don't change you won't grow! *(2) Get to know yourself*: Spend time exploring your gifts. Ask for feedback. Acknowledge your blind spots. *(3) Trust your leader:* If you can't, look for one you can trust, or get on another team. *(4) See the big picture:* Your place on any team only makes sense in the context of the big picture. If your only reason for finding your niche is personal gain, your wrong motives will rob you of the very joy, fulfillment and success you desire. *(5) Rely on your experience:* There's only one way to know you've discovered your niche. Try things. Take risks. Learn from your failures and your successes. Discover what God made you for!

PUTTING THE OTHER GUY FIRST

Be humble...
consider others more important than yourselves.
PHILIPPIANS 2:3 CEV

A man bought a new TV and some of his neighbors were helping him install the antenna on the roof. They weren't making much headway until a new guy showed up with a big fancy toolbox and finished the job lickety-split. As they stood around congratulating themselves, they asked the new neighbor what he made with such elaborate tools. Grinning, he replied, "Friends, mostly!" Unfortunately that kind of helpful behavior has ceased to be the norm in our world today: selfishness has become standard procedure. The Bible says: "As the end approaches, people are going to be self-absorbed...self-promoting...dog-eat-dog...the kind...who smooth-talk...and take advantage" (2Ti 3:1-6 TM). Have you noticed any of that lately? Try sliding into a parking space another motorist wants, or watching shoppers in the checkout line elbowing one another to save thirty seconds! And while we're on the subject, how about "your seat" in church—the one you've been warming for thirty years?

The principle of putting others first didn't originate as a public relations strategy, it came directly from the God who inspired Paul to write: "Be humble and consider others more important than yourselves. Care about them as much as you care about yourselves" (Php 2:3-4 CEV). Jesus Himself said: "Here is a simple, rule-of-thumb...Ask yourself what you want people to do for you, then grab the initiative and do it for them" (Mt 7:12 TM). So the next time somebody cuts you off in traffic or treats you with less courtesy and consideration than you expect, instead of getting ticked off and retaliating, use it as an opportunity to practice putting the other guy first.

PRESIDENT KENNEDY'S QUESTION

We...will be caught up...to meet the Lord.
1 THESSALONIANS 4:17 NIV

Billy Graham writes: "A few days before President-elect John F. Kennedy was to be inaugurated I was invited to join him in Florida for a golf game. As we were driving back from the golf course President Kennedy turned to me and asked, 'Do you really believe Jesus Christ is coming back to earth again?' I was dumbfounded: 'Yes sir, I do,' I replied. For the next several minutes I had the opportunity to talk to him about the second coming of Jesus Christ. I've often wondered why he asked that question. I think part of the answer came a thousand days later when he was assassinated. At his funeral Cardinal Cushing read, and millions of people around the world watched and heard by television, these words: 'For the Lord himself shall descend from heaven with a shout, with the voice of the archangel, and with the trump of God: and the dead in Christ shall rise first: Then we which are alive and remain shall be caught up together with them in the clouds, to meet the Lord in the air: and so shall we ever be with the Lord' (1Th 4:16-17). That phrase 'caught up,' means to snatch away. The day is fast approaching when Jesus Christ will come back to 'snatch away' His followers from all the graveyards of the world. And those of us who are alive when it happens will join them in the great escape! That is the hope of the future for the Christian." And it brings up two all-important questions: (1) Are you living your life each day in the light of Christ's soon return? (2) Will you be ready when He comes?

'GO!'

I'll take the hand of those who don't know the way...
to show them what roads to take.

ISAIAH 42:16 TM

Are you facing a situation that feels overwhelming and you're afraid to make a wrong move? Or maybe you're saying *no* to something in your life that you'd really like to say *yes* to. A well-known counselor says: "For years I heard about hiking. It sounded elusive, difficult...and mysterious. When a friend asked me to go hiking...I began thinking...what if I couldn't do it well enough? Or I didn't know how to do it at all? 'Don't be ridiculous,' I scolded myself. 'You're making this more complicated than it is...it's just walking, and you've been doing that since you were a baby!' We left...and I followed...as he started up a steep incline. 'Just walk,' I told myself...'Put one foot in front of another...like you've done all your life.' I didn't make it to the top of the mountain that day, but I made it halfway... Start where you are. Start poorly. Just start...if you already knew how to do it well, it wouldn't be a lesson...and you'd never have the thrill of victory, years from now looking back."

God has promised to "take the hand of those who don't know the way...to show them what roads to take." You say, "But what if I get into difficulty?" You probably will! But God says: "When you're in over your head, I'll be there with you" (Isa 43:2 TM). But you've got to be willing to "go" in order for God to bring you "through!" In other words—you have to be willing to get your feet wet. The thing to keep in mind is: "God...goes ahead of you" (Dt 1:30 TM).

BALLOONS

Take this child...and nurse it for me.

EXODUS 2:9

Dr. James Dobson writes: "I attended a wedding in a beautiful garden setting in which 150 colorful helium balloons were released into the California sky. Within seconds they were scattered across the heavens—some rising hundreds of feet, others cruising toward the horizon. They all began from the same launching pad, were filled with the same helium, and ascended into the same conditions. Yet within minutes they were separated by a mile or more. A few balloons struggled to clear the upper branches of trees, while the show-offs became mere pinpoints of color on their journey to the sky. How interesting, I thought—and how symbolic of children."

Parent, you help determine how high your child will rise. So: *(a) Create the right climate in your home.* The words you speak, the order you establish, the music and television programs you allow, are molding their character and their future. If you're too busy to notice these things—you're too busy! *(b) Give them the right mentors.* Ruth followed Naomi. Timothy followed Paul. Your children are going to follow someone. The question is, who? Your best defense against destructive influences is offensive teaching, and a Christ-like example. Read God's Word to them each day. Pray over them—and with them. Do it! Don't be shy. The molester and drug dealer are not shy. Speak up! You can't improve on the words of Pharaoh's daughter, given to Moses' mother as she saved her son from the waters of the Nile that would have consumed him. "Take this child... and nurse it for me, and I will give thee thy wages." Parent, you have no greater responsibility! And if you do it right, you'll have no greater reward!

LEARN TO REALLY LISTEN

The wise listen to others.

PROVERBS 12:15 NLT

We live in the era of the "talking head," with reality TV, 24-hour news programs and talk radio. And while that's not all bad, we've learned to "broadcast" when we should be "tuning in." Solomon says, "Don't talk so much…Be sensible and turn off the flow" (Pr 10:19 TLB). In other words, when you've nothing to say—say nothing! Why? Because the more you talk at that point, the less people remember (or respect you). It's been said that God designed your ears to stay open and your mouth to close because listening rarely gets you into trouble! Solomon writes: "The man of few words…is wise…even a fool is thought…wise when he is silent" (Pr 17:27-28 TLB). So when you can't improve on silence—be quiet!

Proverbs 1:22-23 mentions people who are *foolish* and *simple*. The original term means, "thick…dull…sluggish." It describes those who are insensitive to the thoughts and feelings of others. We've all been at the mercy of the doctor who treated us with cold detachment, the teacher who put us to sleep with his lecture, and the salesperson that focused only on his commission. William C. Tacey writes: "Poor listeners range all the way from the impatient type (That's nothing! Wait'll you hear what I've done), to the person who's so absorbed in his own thoughts that he is not aware that someone has spoken. Learning to listen actively, and constructively, is as important as learning to speak, if your communication is to be effective." Remember, a gossip talks about others, a bore talks about himself, but a wise man talks *to* you, *about* you—then *listens* to what you have to say! When you're a good listener not only will people seek you out, you'll grow wiser—and win friends too!

WALKING THE PLANK!

Don't be afraid...I am with you.
ISAIAH 41:10 NLT

It's easy to walk across a plank that's on the ground, but raise it a little and it becomes harder. Now, imagine that same plank 100 feet up, without a safety net under it; looks scary, doesn't it? The Bible says, "Fear is crippling" (1Jn 4:18 TM). And the more that's at stake the harder it is; white-knuckle syndrome kicks in and you develop a case of the "what ifs." Fear is living in the future before you get there. And among the trolls lurking under the bridge to your future, inspirational speaker Dr. Joan Borysenko cites two things: *(1) Fear of failure.* She writes: "When I was admitted to Harvard, I was sure there'd been a computer error and that I'd be exposed as a fraud. A lawyer friend of mine stops short of terror every time she has to give a final argument before a jury. Even when you're an expert fear doesn't necessarily go away. Accepting fear as part of the journey instead of running from it helps you conquer it! *(2) Fear of imperfection.* This one makes it hard to do anything, because perfectionists set unattainable goals and berate themselves when they can't reach them. It's impossible to learn without making mistakes; so learn, and move on."

God says: "Don't be afraid...I am with you," so ask yourself what *He* wants and stop worrying about people pleasing. Solomon said, "Fear of human opinion disables [you]" (Pr 29:25 TM). When you look back at what you've already overcome, you begin to realize that most times failure doesn't do permanent damage—you actually grow through it! So stay focused; with God, you can walk *any* plank. Who knows, you might even begin to enjoy the challenge!

GET GOD INVOLVED IN YOUR FINANCES

You will be made rich...so that you can be generous.
2 CORINTHIANS 9:11 NIV

You need to *get* God involved in your finances, and *keep* Him involved. Your finances are an area in which you can experience an interactive relationship with Him. But you need to invite Him in. You've never heard anyone pray, "Lord, I've withheld from You all these years while I followed my own plan. As a result I've gotten into this financial mess. But I still think my plan can work. So I'll figure things out on my own, and You can go help somebody else." No, when the bottom drops out we all want God to get involved in our finances, so we start focusing on how to persuade Him to come to our rescue. At this point our prayers become an S.O.S.! "Help, Lord! Send some money! Please do something! Anything!" There comes a point when we're willing to acknowledge that God controls *everything*. Suddenly we're no longer bashful about asking Him to do what we've known all along He's capable of doing: to move some money here, or take away some financial pressure there.

So what's keeping you from asking God to get involved now—*before* the bottom drops out? Doesn't it make sense to position yourself to receive His direct intervention as *soon* and as *often* as possible? Paul writes: "Now he who supplies seed to the sower [not the hoarder]...will...increase your store of seed [so that you can sow more]...You will be made rich in every way so that you can be generous on every occasion" (vv. 10-11 NIV). Something happens when you open your hand to God— He opens His hand to you!

SCRIPTURAL KEYS TO SUCCESS IN LIFE (1)

A man's gift makes room for him.
PROVERBS 18:16 NAS

Your giftedness will get you noticed, separate you from the rest of the pack and give you a head start on others. But your advantage will only last so long. Songwriter Irving Berlin understood this truth when he said: "The toughest thing about success is, you've got to keep on being a success. Talent is only a starting point in business. You've got to keep working that talent." You can't coast on your abilities. If you try to wing it, others will soon fly past you. Mega-best-selling author Stephen King asserts that, "Talent is cheaper than table salt. What separates the talented individual from the successful one, is a lot of hard work."

And much of that work takes place in your character and your private world. Haven't you known people who should have risen to the top but didn't? They had all the talent they'd ever need, but they didn't succeed. Their talent made them stand out but their lack of integrity made them sit down. Their friends, families, coaches and bosses see their giftedness but wonder why they keep falling short of expectations. Their talent opens the door, but their wrong choices shut it.

Consider Nehemiah's *talent*. He rebuilt Jerusalem's walls in under two months—an astounding feat! Now consider Nehemiah's *character*. While some of his peers lined their pockets by lending money at such exorbitant rates people couldn't repay it, he said, "What you are doing is not right" (Ne 5:9 NLT). Then he announced, "I did not act that way. I also devoted myself to working on the wall" (vv. 15-16 NLT). Want to develop your character? Follow in his footsteps!

SCRIPTURAL KEYS TO SUCCESS IN LIFE (2)

I will never leave you nor forsake you.

JOSHUA 1:5 NIV

Imagine trying to fill the shoes Moses walked in. Joshua wondered, "Do I have what it takes?" Then God told him: (a) "I will give you every place where you set your foot" (v. 3 NIV). God promises success to those who have the faith to take the first step, and keep walking with Him regardless of what they encounter. That means showing up earlier, staying later, and working harder. (b) "No one will be able to stand up against you all the days of your life" (v. 5 NIV). Expect opposition; certain people will always "stand up against you." In his book *High Maintenance Relationships,* Les Parrott identifies the types of people who will do this: *Critics* who constantly complain or give unwanted advice. *Martyrs* who are forever the victim and wracked with self-pity. *Wet blankets* who are pessimistic and habitually negative. *Steamrollers* who are blindly insensitive to others. *Gossips* who spread rumors and leak secrets. *Control freaks* who are unable to let go and let things be. *Back-stabbers* who are two-faced. *Green-eyed monsters* who seethe with envy. *Volcanoes* who build steam and are always ready to erupt. *Sponges* who are always needy and never give anything back. *Competitors* who always keep track of tit-for-tat. (c) "Be strong ...because you will lead these people to inherit the land" (v. 6 NIV). Successful people are not necessarily more gifted, they're just more passionate. What do you pray about? Cry about? Dream about? What are you willing to risk everything for? *That's* the well from which you'll draw your strength and your strategies when you experience setbacks, when others disappoint you, when the job feels too big and you feel too small.

SPIRITUAL KEYS TO SUCCESS IN LIFE (3)

Be careful to obey all the law.

JOSHUA 1:7 NIV

Notice three things God said to Joshua: *(1) "Get ready to cross...into the land"* (v. 2 NIV). Henry Ford observed, "Before everything else, getting ready is the secret of success." The frustrating thing about preparation is, sometimes it takes more time than the actual event you're preparing for. There's an old saying: "You can claim to be surprised once; after that, you're unprepared." *(2) "Your territory will extend from..."* (v. 4 NIV). You have to know where you're going! You cannot be like Alice in *Through the Looking Glass* who asks the Cheshire cat, "Would you please tell me which way I ought to go from here?" "That depends on where you want to get," the cat replies. "I don't care much where," she answers. "Then it doesn't matter which way you go," the cat responds. People who are undecided cannot draw on their faith—or their gifting. As a result they merely drift along. Author Bill Copeland advises: "You've removed most of the road blocks to success when you know the difference between motion and direction." To be successful in life you must do the right things, moment by moment, day by day, following through with them in a consistent way. *(3) "Be careful to obey all the law...that you may be successful."* Identify your spiritual values! Henri Frederic Amiel stated, "The man who has no inner life is a slave to his surroundings." Our spiritual values are the principles we live by every day. They are the light that guides us. They give stability and structure to our inner world. And when that world is in order, we can navigate our way through anything.

SCRIPTURAL KEYS TO SUCCESS IN LIFE (4)

*Do everything written in it.
Then you will be...successful.*

JOSHUA 1:8 NIV

Have you ever wondered why God refers to His Word as "laws"? Because laws are meant to govern, guide, and guard us. Without order, all you have is chaos and confusion. Imagine living in a world where twelve inches no longer make one foot and 2 + 2 doesn't make 4. God established His laws for your good. When you disobey them you suffer; when you honor them you succeed. Furthermore, His laws are not an à la carte menu; you can't pick what you like and leave the rest. At the beginning of Joshua's career God gave him some foundational advice about His law: "Do everything written in it. Then you will be...successful." If you want to be successful in life, *talk* about, *think* regularly about, and *live* your life according to God's laws. Why? Because ultimately your character is more important than your career. Your career is what you do, your character is what you are!

Many people with talent make it into the limelight, but the ones who have neglected to develop strong character rarely stay there long. Absence of strong character eventually topples them. Why? Because you cannot climb beyond the limitations of your character! John Maxwell writes: "Talented people are sometimes tempted to take shortcuts. Character prevents that. Talented people may feel superior and expect special privileges. Character helps them to know better. Talented people are praised for what others see them build. Character builds what's inside them. Talented people have the potential to be difference makers. Character makes the difference in them. Talented people are a gift to the world. Character protects that gift."

DIVINE PROTECTION!

I will protect those who trust in my name.
PSALM 91:14 NLT

On a chilly March afternoon before going home for dinner, Pastor Walter Klempel fired up the church furnace in preparation for choir practice. When it was time to return to church with his family they were delayed because his daughter changed clothes. At the same time student Ladona Vadergrift was struggling with a geometry problem and stayed home to work on it. Sisters Royena and Sadie Estes' car wouldn't start. Herbert Kipf lingered over a letter he'd put off writing. Joyce Black was feeling "plain lazy" and stayed home till the last minute. Pianist Marilyn Paul fell asleep after dinner and her mom, the choir director, had trouble waking her. Pals Lucille Jones and Dorothy Wood were late because of a radio broadcast. Every single choir member was late; something that's never happened before nor since. Was it just a fluke? No! At 7:30 that night the West Side Church was flattened by an explosion from a gas leak ignited by the furnace...directly below the *empty* choir loft!

God's looking out for you when you don't even know you're in danger! As His child you: "Live within the shadow of the Almighty, sheltered by...God...He rescues you from every trap...He will shield you with his wings...His...promises are your armor...He orders His angels to protect you wherever you go" (vv. 1-11 TLB). The Bible says, "The Angel of the Lord guards and rescues all who reverence Him" (Ps 34:7 TLB); "To trust in God means safety" (Pr 29:25 TLB). You can call it coincidence, chance, fate, or you can call it what it really is—*divine protection!*

SINCERITY

Be sincere…until the day of Christ.
PHILIPPIANS 1:10 NAS

The word "sincere" comes from a Latin word meaning "without wax." In the original Greek it means "sun-tested." In Bible times merchants sold very fine porcelain that was greatly valued and therefore expensive. Sometimes when it was fired in the kiln tiny cracks would appear. Dishonest merchants would smear pearly-white wax over these cracks, which would pass for unblemished porcelain—unless it was held up to the light of the sun. Honest merchants marked their wares *sine cera*—"without wax." That's a picture of genuine sincerity. No sham, no hypocrisy, no hidden cracks to be covered over.

You say, "How can I live this way?" By keeping your eyes on Christ, not Christians! Paul writes: "As a prisoner for the Lord, then, I urge you to live a life worthy of the calling you have received" (Eph 4:1 NIV). When Paul wrote this he was under house arrest in Rome, yet he didn't regard himself as a prisoner of the Romans. No, he was a prisoner of Jesus, a voluntary slave, totally in subjection to the Lord. There's a metaphorical meaning to this word "prisoner." It can mean "binding as with a spell." Paul was literally *captivated* by Jesus Christ! He thought and talked about nothing else. He got up every morning determined to please Him. Some days he didn't do too well. We all have those days. But the next morning he was up and at it again, more determined and more committed than ever. Paul's sincerity wasn't based on keeping certain religious rules or trying to look good. It was based on a deep love relationship with Christ: "Whatever we do, it is…because Christ's love controls us" (2Co 5:13-14 TLB).

OVERCOME YOUR PAST!

Forgetting those things which are behind.
PHILIPPIANS 3:13

It's impossible to succeed in life without overcoming your past. When the great Paderewski first started to study piano his teacher told him his hands were too small to master the keyboard. Yet the fire in his soul drove him to become a world-renowned pianist. When Enrico Caruso first started to study voice his teacher said he sounded like the wind whistling through the window. Today Caruso is remembered as one of the world's greatest tenors. If you need inspiration to overcome your life's obstacles, look no further than Christ. Society called His birth illegitimate. He was born into a hated minority who experienced brutal oppression every day. The recognized church branded Him a heretic. The state called Him an insurrectionist too dangerous to live. One of His closest friends betrayed Him to enrich himself. He was sentenced without a fair trial and died like a common criminal. And what was His response to His suffering, and ours? "Be of good cheer; I have overcome the world" (Jn 16:33).

We spend far too much time crying over spilt milk. Rather than giving attention to the most important assignment we have every morning—our choice of an attitude—we waste our time and energy on things that cannot be changed. You cannot change the death of a loved one. You cannot change the fact that one day your spouse told you, "I want a divorce." The past is over. Look forward. Press on! God says, "The plans I have for you...are...good" (Jer 29:11 NLT). That means the best is yet to be!

WHEN IT'S GOOD TO BE ALONE

I sat alone because your hand was on me.

JEREMIAH 15:17 NIV

Being alone isn't always a bad thing. In fact there are times when it's absolutely necessary in order to hear from God. The Bible points out that Jesus: (a) "Often withdrew to lonely places and prayed" (Lk 5:16 NIV). (b) "Withdrew by boat privately to a solitary place" (Mt 14:13 NIV). (c) "Went up on a mountainside by himself to pray. When evening came, he was there alone" (Mt 14:23 NIV). (d) "When he was alone, the Twelve...asked him about the parables" (Mk 4:10 NIV). In the Old Testament, "Jacob was left alone, and a man wrestled with him till daybreak" (Ge 32:24 NIV). Your greatest spiritual victories come from the battles God calls you to fight when you're alone. Most times He outlines and clarifies His plans for your life when there's nobody else around. That's because He wants you to be more influenced by Him, than them!

When God's grooming you for a special work you'll be required to spend time outside the company of others. In Exodus God said, "Moses alone is to approach...the people may not come up with him" (Ex 24:2 NIV). When Elijah spent the night alone in a cave, God told him to "Go out and stand on the mountain...for the Lord is about to pass by" (1Ki 19:11 NIV). Daniel "was left alone, gazing at this great vision" (Da 10:8 NIV), and Jeremiah wrote: "I sat alone because your hand was on me." Learn to understand the difference between being lonely and being alone. When God sidelines you consider it an honor, glean all you can, then move to the next level.

WHY YOU BELONG IN CHURCH

*God is building a home. He's using us all—irrespective
of how we got here—in what he is building.*

EPHESIANS 2:20 TM

Paul writes: "God is building a home. He's using us all—
irrespective of how we got here—in what he is building. He
used the apostles and prophets for the foundation. Now he's
using you, fitting you in brick by brick, stone by stone, with
Christ Jesus as the cornerstone that holds all the parts together.
We see it taking shape day after day—a holy temple built by
God, all of us built into it, a temple in which God is quite at
home" (vv. 19-22 TM).

There are times when we need to be alone with God in
prayer. But there are other times when we can only experience the fullness of His presence as we come together with
His people. The church is like a corporate headquarters. When
people who are individually indwelt by the Spirit meet there for
worship, praise, instructions, encouragement and service, God's
Spirit shows up in a powerful way and we grow as we experience His presence and hear His Word.

The world and circumstances may beat us up all week and
make us feel like losers, but when we gather with other members of Christ's body we are reminded that we are on the winning side. It's hard to celebrate all by yourself. When you have
something worth celebrating you call folks together so you can
share the joy. Jesus Christ is so excited about His victory at the
cross that He calls us together each week to celebrate what He
achieved for us. And celebration, like spiritual growth, is a
group project.

YOU CAN'T ESCAPE THIS TRIAL!

Consider it all joy...when you encounter various trials.
JAMES 1:2 NAS

The Bible doesn't tell us to rejoice when we mess up and get into trouble. God can certainly use our mistakes to teach us, but that's not what James has in mind. Some of our trials just come from "living." Things aren't going right. Usually it's not one big thing but a lot of little things. We encounter physical, financial, relational or emotional trials that knock us for a loop. Peter calls this "the trial of your faith" (1Pe 1:7). What's on trial? Your faith! Whatever the size or length of our trial, there's nowhere we can go to escape the trial of our faith. Trying to avoid it is like changing schools in hopes of avoiding a test you don't want to take. But the next school will have tests too, probably harder than the ones in the school you just left, and now you're that much further behind in your studies and preparation. You can't outrun God-ordained trials. He knows where to find you!

The good news is, there's no such thing as a purposeless trial! Each trial is designed to launch us to a new spiritual level. The interesting thing about our trials is, they're custom made; they have our name on them. Paul discovered two things about his trials: *(a) The reason for the trial.* "To keep me from becoming conceited" (2Co 12:7 NIV). *(b) The result of the trial.* "That Christ's power may rest on me" (v. 9 NIV). Like a tailor measuring you for a suit that will fit perfectly, the Holy Spirit customizes the trials we encounter to meet our spiritual need, to mold us, and to make us more like Jesus!

DYING TO SELF

I die every day.

1 CORINTHIANS 15:31 NCV

Did you know you speak over nine million words a year, and more than half of them are *I...me...my...*and *mine?* So God's response calls for dying to self. Paul said, "I die [to self] every day." But for many of us, "Behold I live for evermore" is more in keeping with how we conduct our lives! The Bible says as followers of Jesus, "Everything connected with getting our own way...is killed off for good" (Gal 5:24 TM). But self-interest won't just roll over and die, it must be "killed off for good." It's a constant battle because we've a tendency to cling to our own interests with a death grip. Jesus told His disciples, "Whoever desires to be first...let him be your slave" (Mt 20:27 NKJV). A slave was the lowest servant on the totem pole. Seasoned followers of Christ are called to higher levels of selflessness than beginners. And when you aspire to lead others, God raises that bar even higher! Many times He'll leave you with a permanent reminder of how He managed to get through to you in an area where you were stubborn. "Moses was...a powerful speaker" (Ac 7:22 CEV), but after he hit "the big 40" and decided to do his own thing, an encounter with God left him with a stutter. A limp became Jacob's trademark. Even the apostle Paul "was given...a handicap to keep [him] in...touch with [his] limitations" (2Co 12:7 TM). What's your handicap? The habit you battle or the fear that never leaves? "Why doesn't God just take it away?" you ask. Because anything that keeps you dependent on Him is a plus, not a minus.

WHEN YOUR ENEMY IS YOUR FRIEND

Friend, do what you came for.

MATTHEW 26:50 NIV

There's no pain like betrayal. And none of us is exempt. David lamented: "My best friend, the one I trusted…has turned against me" (Ps 41:9 NLT). The truth is, God *allows* certain people into our lives to facilitate His purposes—even ones like Judas, whom Jesus called "friend," and said: "Do what you came for." Before Jesus was betrayed He told the disciples: "I know whom I have chosen…that the Scripture may be fulfilled, 'He who eats bread with Me has lifted up his heel against Me'" (Jn 13:18 NKJV). He could have fulfilled His destiny without John the beloved disciple, or impetuous Peter who was always ready to defend Him. But it was Judas' kiss of betrayal that ushered Him into His destiny. So you can't always avoid getting hurt. But God can give you the grace to reevaluate the situation and realize that the person you thought was your enemy, was a friend in disguise. God will never permit His plans for us to be sabotaged by somebody else's actions. When you're under His shield of protection He'll allow your Judas to go so far and no further. As a child of God, *His* purposes govern how much damage others can do to you. Once you understand that, it lessens the fear that stems from getting involved again when you've been burned. The Psalmist said: "It was good for me to be afflicted so that I might learn your decrees" (Ps 119:71 NIV). God loves to turn our negatives into positives. And while none of us *enjoys* suffering, it takes us to levels of understanding that, left to our own devices, we'd never reach.

WHAT DO YOU NEED TO AVOID?

Run from temptations.

2 TIMOTHY 2:22 CEV

According to Greek mythology, sirens living along the Mediterranean coast made such compelling music that passing sailors were mesmerized and jumped overboard to their death. So the hero Odysseus ordered himself to be tied to the mast and the crew's ears filled with wax to block the music; that way they sailed past in safety. A wise sailor knows when the storm is more than his boat can handle. An ocean liner can withstand winds that will sink a small boat. Look at Joseph. When Potiphar's wife tried to seduce him he didn't: (1) try to counsel or convert her; (2) think, "I'm young, lonely, far from home, and her husband's out of town; maybe just this once;" (3) hang around to see how strong he was. No, he fled the scene saying, "How...could I do such a wicked thing...against God?" (Ge 39:9 NIV).

It's good to stretch yourself. It's how you mature. But be aware of your danger zones and don't knowingly put yourself in harm's way. Paul said, "If you think you are strong...be careful not to fall" (1Co 10:12 NCV). He told Timothy: "Run from temptations that capture young people...do the right thing." And James said: "Don't let anyone under pressure to give in to evil say, 'God is trying to trip me up.' God...puts evil in no one's way. The temptation...comes from us and only us" (Jas 1:13-15 TM). The bottom line is this: when you're weak in certain areas you need to steer clear of anything that feeds into them. The Psalmist said: "You are my safe refuge...where my enemies cannot reach me" (Ps 61:3 NLT). So, what do you need to avoid?

STAY TEACHABLE (1)

The discerning heart seeks knowledge.
PROVERBS 15:14 NIV

If you're talented, you may have difficulties when it comes to staying teachable. Gifted people sometimes act like they know it all. That makes it hard for them to keep developing. Teachability is not so much about competence and mental capacity as it is about *attitude;* it's the hunger to discover and grow. It's the willingness to learn, unlearn, and relearn. John Wooden said, "It's what you learn after you know it all that counts." When you stop learning, you stop leading. Only as you remain teachable will you keep growing and continue to make an impact.

Besides being an astonishing painter and sculptor, Leonardo da Vinci was a genius in more fields than any scientist of any age. His notebooks were hundreds of years ahead of their time. He anticipated submarines, helicopters and other modern inventions. In one notebook he wrote: "Iron rusts from disuse; stagnant water loses its purity and in cold weather becomes frozen; even so does inaction sap the vigor of the mind." He was driven by his desire to know more. He was learning and writing discoveries in his notebooks until the very end of his life. And the good news is, you don't have to have the mind or talent of a Leonardo da Vinci to be teachable. You just have to have the right attitude.

The most important skill to acquire is—learning how to learn. Try this for the next week: ask others for their advice and deliberately withhold the advice you'd normally give. At each day's end write down what you've learned by being attentive to others. You'll be amazed!

STAY TEACHABLE (2)

Wise men and women are always learning,
always listening for fresh insights.
PROVERBS 18:15 TM

When it comes to staying teachable, understand two things: *(1) Nothing is interesting if you are not interested.* Philip B. Crosby writes: "There is a theory of human behavior that says people subconsciously retard their own growth. They come to rely on clichés and habits. Once they reach the age of their own personal comfort with the world, they stop learning and their minds run on idle for the rest of their days. They may progress organizationally, they may be ambitious and eager, and they may even work night and day, but they learn no more." It's a tragedy when we allow ourselves to get in a rut and never climb out. We miss the best God has to offer. In contrast, teachable people are fully engaged in life. They get excited about things. They are interested in discovery, discussion, application and growth. *(2) Successful people view learning differently than those who are unsuccessful.* That doesn't mean that unsuccessful people are unable to think the way successful people do. If you have the desire and the discipline, you can retrain yourself to think differently. Teachable people are always open to new ideas and are willing to learn from anyone who has something to offer. Sidney J. Harris wrote: "A winner knows how much he still has to learn, even when he is considered an expert by others. A loser wants to be considered an expert by others, before he has learned enough to know how little he knows." It's all a matter of attitude. Bottom line—it's truly remarkable how much a person has to learn, before he realizes how little he knows. So, stay teachable.

STAY TEACHABLE (3)

Blessed is the man who finds wisdom.
PROVERBS 3:13 NIV

One of the paradoxes of life is that the things which initially *make* you successful, are not necessarily the things that *keep* you successful. You have to remain open to new ideas and be willing to learn new skills. Dr. J. Konrad Hole says: "If you cannot be teachable, having talent won't help you. If you cannot be flexible, having a goal won't help you. If you cannot be grateful, having abundance won't help you. If you cannot be mentor-able, having a future won't help you. If you cannot be durable, having a plan won't help you."

Confined to a dungeon and facing the certainty of an executioner's chopping block, Paul writes to Timothy and asks him to bring: (1) Writing paper. "I still have something to say." (2) Books. "I still have more to learn" (See 2Ti 4:13). Learning should be your lifelong pursuit. The Roman scholar Cato started to study Greek when he was eighty. When asked why he was tackling such a difficult task at his age he replied, "It's the earliest age I have left." Unlike Cato, too many of us regard learning as an event instead of a process. It's estimated that only one-third of all adults read an entire book after their graduation. Why? Because they view education as a *period* of life, not a *way* of life. Learning is an activity that is not restricted by age. Every stage of life presents lessons to be learned. We can choose to be teachable and continue to learn them, or we can be closed-minded and stop growing. The decision is ours.

MARCHING TO ZION

The Lord has chosen Zion,
he has desired it for his dwelling.
PSALM 132:13 NIV

Before David became qualified to rule as King in Zion, he first had to be found faithful in three places. Examine them carefully, for you too must pass these three tests:

(1) At home in Bethlehem. That's where David learned to be responsible, to earn a living and support his family, to develop his relationship with God, and to overcome the resentment of others because of God's favor on his life. "Charity begins at home." It's here you become qualified to handle bigger assignments by being faithful in smaller ones. It's here your character is developed and your dependability proven.

(2) In the cave of Adullam. By living among the misfits and rejects of society David learned to give of himself to others without expecting anything in return; to love and serve others even when his own life was under attack. "Adullam" is where our kingdom dies and God's kingdom is showcased through us. It's here that God deals with every self-seeking, self-serving motive in our hearts. Sadly, some of us never make it out of this cave.

(3) On Mount Hermon. The word "Hermon" means "covenant." It was the highest mountain in Israel and there was no easy road to the top; it was uphill all the way. And it's that way with covenant relationships! They require loyalty regardless of circumstance, truthfulness regardless of cost, and forgiveness regardless of pain. When we begin to live this way the world will look again to Zion (the church) for answers, because they'll see God working in us.

PAY YOUR WAY!

Give everyone what you owe him.

ROMANS 13:7 NIV

At Thanksgiving, a barber whose business was prospering decided that for the next week he'd give the first customer of the day a free haircut. The first recipient was a baker. Next morning he presented the barber with a dozen donuts. The second day it was a florist, who thanked him by leaving a dozen roses on his doorstep. The third day a pastor received a free haircut. Guess what? Next morning there were a dozen more preachers all waiting for free haircuts!

Do you expect a "free haircut?" If so, who's supposed to pay the barber? The Bible teaches that congregations should honor and be generous to pastors who serve them well (See 1Ti 5:17 NLT). But problems arise when someone develops "a sense of entitlement." Those called to leadership in God's kingdom should create a standard of excellence. They should be known for paying their bills, and paying them on time. It's wrong to live beyond our means because we want to present a certain image or set an example of success. We hurt God's work when we "step out in faith" and purchase things we know we can't pay for, then leave someone else holding the bag. Think this doesn't happen? Talk to those around you who say "never do business with Christians!" If there's no money to pay for it—God didn't order it!

There was a time in Paul's ministry when he preached weekends and supported himself as a tentmaker (See Ac 18:3). And when it came to the subject of "paying your way" he minced no words: "Give everyone what you owe him."

KEEP PERSEVERING!

Blessed is the man who perseveres.
JAMES 1:12 NIV

On June 1, 1965, a thirteen-foot boat slipped quietly out of Falmouth, Massachusetts. Its destination? Falmouth, England. It would be the smallest craft ever to make the voyage. Its name? *Tinkerbelle.* Its pilot? Robert Manry, a copy editor for the *Cleveland Plain Dealer* newspaper who felt that ten years at a desk was enough boredom for anyone. Manry was afraid, not of the ocean but of all the people who would try to talk him out of the trip. So he only shared it with some relatives and his wife Virginia, his greatest source of support. The trip? He spent harrowing nights of sleeplessness trying to cross shipping lanes without getting run over. Weeks at sea caused his food to become tasteless. Loneliness led to hallucinations. His rudder broke three times. Storms swept him overboard. Had it not been for the rope around his waist he would never have been able to pull himself back on board. Finally, after seventy-eight days alone at sea he sailed into Falmouth, England. During those nights at the tiller he had fantasized about what he would do once he arrived. He expected to simply check into a hotel, eat dinner alone, then next morning see if perhaps the Associated Press might be interested in his story. What a surprise! Word had spread far and wide. To his amazement, three hundred vessels with horns blasting escorted *Tinkerbelle* into port. And 47,000 people stood screaming and cheering him to the shore.

One of the great themes of Scripture is perseverance. No matter how great your calling, your talent, your cause or your goal, without perseverance you won't make it. Hence James writes, "Blessed is the man who perseveres."

SELF-CONTROL

Do not let sin control the way you live.
ROMANS 6:12 NLT

Restraining ourselves—self-control—is listed in the Bible as proof that God's Spirit lives within us (See Gal 5:22-23). Living without restraint is like removing the brakes from your car. It may be exciting for a while, but inevitably you'll pay a high price for the ride. Take away the brakes, and your life, like your car, is transformed into an unguided missile—headed for disaster.

It's impossible to live a lifestyle of moral purity without dealing with some practical facts related to our flesh-and-blood appetites that constantly crave satisfaction. The Bible says: "Do not let sin control the way you live; do not give in to sinful desires. Do not let any part of your body become an instrument of evil to serve sin. Instead, give yourselves completely to God... realize that...whatever you choose to obey...[becomes your master]" (Ro 6:12-16 NLT). If you let it, your body will lead you off course. It isn't that your body is evil; it's just that it possesses a number of appetites that are always ready to respond to the surrounding stimuli, all of which are terribly appealing and temporarily satisfying. One Bible scholar writes: "Life on earth is really nothing more than a string of moments, one after another. And I do not want my testimony for Jesus Christ to be shattered by a single moment of indulging my flesh. I don't want one moment of rage or pride or lust to cast a shadow over a lifetime of walking with my Lord. Frankly, I fear that possibility. And do you know what? I *want* to fear that possibility. When I stop fearing it, I'm in grave danger."

BUILDING STRONG CHARACTER (1)

[It is] better to have self-control than to conquer a city.
PROVERBS 16:32 NLT

First and foremost, building strong character requires *self-discipline*. Self-discipline is the ability to do what's right, when you don't feel like it. Plato asserted, "The first and best victory is to conquer self." Yes, your greatest victories are internal ones. Bobby Jones was winning golf tournaments by age twelve. But he had a temper. His nickname was "club-thrower." An older gentleman called Grandpa Bart recognized Jones' talent *and* his character issues. He said, "Bobby, you're good enough to win, but you'll never win big until you control that temper of yours." Jones did master his temper, and went on to win his first U.S. Open at twenty-one. Grandpa Bart used to say, "Bobby was fourteen when he mastered golf, but he was twenty-one when he mastered himself." English theologian Henry Parry Liddon observed: "What we do on some great occasion will probably depend on what we already are; and what we are will be the result of previous years of self-discipline."

If you're serious about building strong character, set higher standards for yourself and refuse to lower them. Need a role model? You won't find a better one than Jesus. He said, "If anyone would come after me, he must deny himself" (Mt 16:24 NIV). Each day look for an opportunity to say no to yourself in some *small* area. Try it; you'll be surprised how hard it is. But the payoff will come when you need to say no to yourself in some *big* area of life. Like saving for a rainy day, you'll have spiritual strength to draw on when you need it.

BUILDING STRONG CHARACTER (2)

God determined...the way to bring out his best in us.
1 CORINTHIANS 2:7 TM

Building strong character requires having a clear *sense of purpose*. Paul writes: "I thank Christ Jesus our Lord...[for] appointing me to his service" (1Ti 1:12 NIV). So, what do you see as your life's purpose? You have only two options: *(a) Speculation.* Dr. Hugh Moorhead, a philosophy professor at Northeastern Illinois University, wrote to 250 of the best known philosophers, scientists, writers and intellectuals, asking them, "What is the meaning of life?" He then published their responses in a book. Some offered their best guesses, some admitted that they had just made up a purpose for life, and others were honest enough to say they were clueless. In fact, a number of famous intellectuals asked Professor Moorhead to write back and tell them if *he* discovered the purpose of life! Fortunately, there is an alternative to speculation about the meaning and purpose of life. *(b) Revelation.* We can turn to what God has revealed about life in His Word. It is our Owner's Manual explaining why we are alive, how life works, what to avoid, and what to expect in the future. It explains what no self-help or philosophy book could know. The Bible says: "God's wisdom ...goes deep into the interior of his purposes...It's not the latest message, but more like the oldest—what God determined as the way to bring out his best in us." God is not just the starting point of your life, He is the source of it. To discover His purpose for your life you must turn to God's Word, not the world's wisdom. You must build your life on eternal truths, not pop psychology, success, motivation, or inspirational stories.

BUILDING STRONG CHARACTER (3)

The integrity of the upright guides them.
PROVERBS 11:3 NIV

Building strong character requires having *integrity*. The word "integrity" simply means "to integrate, to become one with." It requires being consistent in your values, thoughts, and actions. Margaret Mead stated, "What people say, what people do, and what people *say* they do, are entirely different things." Amazingly, there are some who actually promote this inconsistency. A popular fashion designer recently said: "The crux of a person's identity…resides in the trappings, not in the person himself …one needn't be well-read, so long as one surrounds himself with books…In short…one can seem to be what one wants to be." The trouble is, while you may make an *impression* with "trappings," the real you always comes through! Impressions are like shadows—they disappear when a strong enough light is shone on them. Integrity is the genuine article—the more you shine the light on it, the more of its details you can see. Integrity shows that you truly are who you appear to be.

People of integrity always stand out. Author Pat Williams tells of Gandhi's trip to England to speak before Parliament. The British Government had opposed India's independence and as a result Gandhi had often been threatened, arrested and jailed. Gandhi spoke eloquently and passionately for two hours, after which the packed hall gave him a standing ovation. Afterward, a reporter asked Gandhi's assistant how the statesman had been able to deliver such a speech without notes. "You don't understand Gandhi," he responded. "What he thinks is what he feels. What he feels is what he says. What he says is what he does. What Gandhi feels, thinks, says and does, are all the same. So he doesn't need notes." Now, *that's* integrity!

SPIRITUAL SOUL MATES

The baby leaped in her womb.
LUKE 1:41 NIV

After telling the Virgin Mary, "The Holy Spirit will come upon you," the angel of the Lord announces, "Elizabeth your relative is going to have a child in her old age...For nothing is impossible with God" (vv. 35-37 NIV). Next we read: "Mary got ready and hurried...she entered Zechariah's home and greeted Elizabeth. When Elizabeth heard Mary's greeting, the baby leaped in her womb, and Elizabeth was filled with the Holy Spirit. In a loud voice she exclaimed: 'Blessed are you among women, and blessed is the child you will bear!...As soon as the sound of your greeting reached my ears, the baby in my womb leaped for joy. Blessed is she who has believed that what the Lord has said to her will be accomplished'" (vv. 39-45 NIV).

What a story! When Mary greeted Elizabeth, the child of destiny within her (John the Baptist) leaped for joy. *Every Mary needs an Elizabeth—and vice versa!* Notice: when Mary heard what God had done in Elizabeth's life she "got ready and hurried" (v. 39 NIV) to meet her. She also "stayed with Elizabeth for about three months" (v. 56 NIV). When God introduces you to someone who's been touched by His Spirit and carries within them the same vision you do, reach out to them, treasure them and spend time with them. They are spiritual soul mates! The connection between these two women didn't take place because they were cousins. The truth is, sometimes our own families are the first to criticize and the last to understand us. "How will I recognize a spiritual soul mate?" you ask. When you're around them something within you will leap for joy, and you will be "filled with the Holy Spirit."

"GET OVER IT!"

In every thing give thanks.

1 THESSALONIANS 5:18

Consider Moses, the lawgiver and liberator to whom God gave the Ten Commandments. His name is still known all over the earth 4,000 years after his death. But remember, this same Moses was a murderer. He was listed in Egypt as public enemy number one. He was a fugitive from justice who fled to the wilderness where he lived for forty years as a shepherd. Yet with the chisel of adversity God was shaping Moses to stand in Pharaoh's majestic palace and announce, "Let my people go!" A nation was born because this man refused to stop struggling to achieve his divine destiny.

Don't be paralyzed by your past. If God used Moses, He'll use you. Everyone goes through adversity. The phrase to remember when things go wrong is: "Get over it!" Have you been hurt? Get over it! Have you been betrayed? Get over it! Have you failed? Get over it! Paul writes: "In every thing give thanks." In reversal, give thanks. In heartache, give thanks. In poverty and in prosperity, give thanks. God is greater than the criticism you're getting. He's greater than the giants you're facing. He's greater than the mountain you're climbing. He's greater than the burdens you're carrying. Look at the Bible record of men and women who chose to focus on the silver lining, not the dark cloud. These people didn't curse the darkness, they shone a light and scattered it. They chose the right attitude, an attitude of faith. Come on, stop hiding from success because you're afraid to fail. Failure means you're a learner, not a loser. Stop fearing risk! Take God's hand, step out and fulfill His purpose for your life.

WALKING STICKS AND BEDPANS!

The Lord said…"What is that in your hand?"

EXODUS 4:2 NIV

One of the biggest mistakes we make is comparing ourselves with someone else and concluding that because we don't have their particular talents, we "don't have what it takes." One day God said to Moses, "What is that in your hand?" Moses replied, "A rod" (Ex 4:2). Just a walking stick, no big deal. Really? God used it to dry up the Red Sea! Understand this: God can take something you've had all your life and thought was of little importance, and use it to accomplish great things. But that only happens when you are willing to acknowledge its potential, and place it in His hands.

There's a hilarious story about a couple of nuns who worked in a hospital, who ran out of gas while driving to work one morning. A service station was nearby but they had no gas container. Suddenly, one of them remembered a bedpan in the trunk of their car. The gas was put into the pan and they carried it very carefully back to the car. As the nuns were pouring the gasoline from the bedpan into the gas tank, two men were driving by. Staring in disbelief, one said to the other, "Now, Fred, that's what I call faith!" It appeared to be foolish. The trouble was, those doubters just didn't "know the truth." And were they ever surprised when those two nuns went roaring by them on the freeway! The Bible says, "Without faith it is impossible to please God" (Heb 11:6 NIV). It takes faith to see walking sticks and bedpans as "the tools needed to do the job!" But when you give God what you've got, amazing things happen in your life!

SPIRITUAL INTIMACY

*That I may...become more deeply and
intimately acquainted with Him.*

PHILIPPIANS 3:10 AMP

In Genesis 2:25 we read: "The man and his wife were both naked and were not ashamed" (NAS). That's intimacy! But the ultimate intimacy is not with your husband or wife; it's with God! And Paul didn't just pray for it, he pursued it: "[For my determined purpose is] that I may know Him [that I may progressively become more deeply and intimately acquainted with Him, perceiving and recognizing and understanding the wonders of His Person more strongly and more clearly]" (Php 3:10 AMP). Can you say that? Or do you sing His praises with a mind that's elsewhere? Are you so critical, you sound like an unbeliever? Paul would respond this way: "My aim is for that never to be true of me. I'll pursue a relationship with God that's so close, He and I will walk together whatever comes." That should be our goal too! Our tendency is to get busier and busier. As a result our walk with God stays shallow and our tank runs low. Spiritual intimacy offers a full tank that can only be found by pulling up closer to God, which requires taking the time and effort to *make* it happen.

Intimacy with God doesn't take place overnight. Your friends and family will misunderstand you. Your flesh will work against you. Adverse circumstances will come to discourage you. If it came easily everyone would be experiencing it. No, the prize goes to those who can say, "[For my determined purpose is] that I may know Him [that I may progressively become more deeply and intimately acquainted with Him]."

FORGIVE, BECAUSE YOU'VE BEEN FORGIVEN!

God put his love on the line...
ROMANS 5:8 TM

Telling of his experience as a POW, Ernest Gordon related how after work one evening a guard noticed a shovel missing. Insisting one of the prisoners had stolen it, he screamed for the guilty party to come forward. Then he prepared to kill them one by one till someone confessed. Suddenly a Scottish soldier broke rank, stood to attention and said, "I did it." The guard beat him to death on the spot. When he'd exhausted his fury the other POW's picked up their friend's body along with their tools and returned to camp. At that point the shovels were recounted. The guard was wrong. *None was missing!*

What kind of person would take the blame for something he didn't do? Christ! "We can understand someone dying for a person worth dying for...how someone...noble could inspire us to selfless sacrifice. But God put his love on the line for us by offering his Son...while we were of no use whatever to him" (vv. 7-8 TM). Think about it: "God...piled...everything we've done wrong, on him" (Isa 53:6 TM), hence, the only "Mediator who can reconcile God and [man]...Jesus" (1Ti 2:5 NLT). A mediator reconciles differences and negotiates agreement. At Calvary, Jesus stood between God's anger and the punishment for our sins. Having lived the life we couldn't live and taken the punishment we couldn't escape, He offers us redemption we couldn't afford. Now the question we must answer is: If He so loved us, can we not love each other? Having been forgiven, can we not forgive?

THAT'S HOW MUCH HE LOVES YOU!

I could ask my Father for thousands of angels...
and he would send them.

MATTHEW 26:53 TLB

The cross is the universal symbol of Christianity. It's almost impossible to go anywhere without seeing it on a steeple or headstone. So how did an instrument of torture come to represent forgiveness and hope for so many? After all, we don't wear little gold guillotines round our necks or display replicas of firing squads on our church walls. The answer can be found in the cross itself. Its horizontal beam symbolizes the breadth of God's love—it includes us all. Its vertical beam symbolizes the height and depth of His love—it reaches from the highest to the lowest of us. It's why God can be just *and* merciful without lowering His standards, and why He can redeem us *without* sanctioning our sin. "God so loved the world, that he gave his only begotten Son, that whosoever believeth in him should not perish, but have everlasting life" (Jn 3:16). Thankfully it doesn't say God loved only the wealthy or the famous or the beautiful or the sober, or we'd all be in trouble! No, if you live in the "world" you're included!

Jesus didn't have to die, He *chose* to! He told His captors: "I could ask my Father for thousands of angels...and he would send them instantly...But if I did, how would the Scriptures be fulfilled that describe what is happening now?" Max Lucado writes: "The force behind the hammer wasn't an angry mob... the hand squeezing the handle wasn't a Roman infantryman... the verdict...wasn't decided by jealous Jews. Jesus himself chose the nails...Had the soldier hesitated Jesus himself would have swung the mallet." *That's* how much He loves you.

TESTIFYING WITHOUT A TOUCH

Blessed are those who believe without seeing.

JOHN 20:29 NLT

Asking for proof before you believe something can stop you from receiving what God wants you to accept based on His Word. Thomas watched Jesus die. That's hard evidence to refute. As a result Thomas decided to believe only what he could see and verify. When your faith's been shaken you're inclined to cling to things that are practical, absolute and tangible. Jesus graciously gave Thomas the proof he needed, and said: "You believe because you have seen...Blessed are those who believe without seeing." The fact remains, however, if Thomas hadn't been permitted to see and touch Jesus, it wouldn't have changed the reality of the Resurrection one iota. Thomas' problem wasn't *lack* of faith, it was *misdirected* faith. He trusted only what he could process on a human level. Sound familiar?

By contrast, when Mary Magdalene met Jesus at the tomb He told her, "Don't touch me...But go find my brothers and tell them" (v. 17 TLB). Mary once washed Jesus' feet with her tears and dried them with her hair; touch was important to her. And touching Jesus at that moment would have confirmed what she'd seen and heard. This time, however, Jesus asked her to trust His *Word* and not His flesh; to be willing to testify without a touch. It's wonderful when we "feel the touch of God" calming us, strengthening us, reassuring us He's still in control. The truth is, His touch has often kept us from giving up or going over the edge. But sometimes He asks us to trust Him without the crutch of sensory perception, to testify without a touch. *That's faith at its highest level.*

KEEP YOUR DREAM ALIVE

Now to him who is able to do immeasurably more than all we ask or imagine.

EPHESIANS 3:20 NIV

When God gives you a dream He places within you—or within reach—all the resources needed to fulfill it. Do you have an unthinkable, scary, absolutely wild idea that won't let you sleep? That's the way it is with dreams, especially when God's in them. They appear crazy. (Humanly speaking, they *are* crazy!) Placed alongside the triangle of logic, cost and timing, such dreams usually seem beyond our reach. They won't fly when you test them against the gravity of reality. And the strangest part is the more they are told "can't" the more they pulsate "can" and "will" and "must." What's behind great accomplishments? Inevitably, great people. But what is in those great people that makes them different? It's certainly not their age or gender or heritage or talent or environment. It's faith! They are people who *think* and *believe* differently.

Are you dreaming about writing a book? Don't wait for a publisher, start writing! Are you wondering if all that work with the kids is worth it? It is! Want to go back to school and finish your degree? Do it. Pay the price, even if it takes years! Trying to master a skill that takes time, patience and energy (not to mention money)? Press on! Thinking about going into business? Why not? It's hard to find satisfaction halfway up someone else's corporate ladder. Without a dream and the determination to fulfill it, life is reduced to bleak black and wimpy white, a diet too bland to get anybody out of bed in the morning. So go after the quest that fuels your fire. Keep your dream alive!

STAY IN STEP WITH GOD!

*For we are…created in Christ Jesus to do good works,
which God prepared in advance for us to do.*
EPHESIANS 2:10 NIV

Our fixed attitude must always be, "Lord, show me *Your* plan." Then when we know what God desires, to do it! When we say yes to God, He imparts the ability we lack to perform His will. Note, the Lord doesn't impart His ability first, then call us. No, He calls us, and as we step out in faith and obey Him, He imparts His ability.

The Bible says, "Walk worthy of the vocation wherewith ye are called" (Eph 4:1). This word "walk" does not refer to some sort of meandering stroll. It means to stay in step with the Lord, to catch the beat of the Holy Spirit, and to move precisely as He moves. When God acts, we act. When God pauses, we pause. We must never think we can compartmentalize our life to the point where we say, "In this category, in this season, in this circumstance, I am operating on my own. In this other category, or season, or circumstance, I am operating according to the power of the Holy Spirit within me." The Holy Spirit does not come and go from our lives. He is *always* with us! "In him we live, and move, and have our being" (Ac 17:28). Once you begin to walk to the rhythm of the Holy Spirit, nothing is going to matter as much to you as keeping pace with Him. You will find that the direction He takes you in is always the right direction, His timing is always the right timing, and the results you get are always the right results.

SET HIGHER STANDARDS FOR YOURSELF!

The Lord tested Joseph's character.

PSALM 105:19 NLT

The life of Joseph teaches us that the road to success isn't easy. It involves having a dream nobody else believes in, and holding onto it through the hardest of times. It involves handling resentment from those closest to you and keeping a good attitude. It involves maintaining your integrity when faced each day with temptation. It involves being so honest, the prison warden would trust you with the keys. It involves being gracious when you have the power to retaliate. It involves saying the right things to yourself, when those around you are saying the opposite. It involves staying so prepared that even though your dreams are delayed, when God opens the door you're ready to walk through it. That's what the Bible means when it says, "Until the time came to fulfill his dreams, the Lord tested Joseph's character."

Take a moment and read these profound words by Dianne Snedaker: "If you are interested in success, it's easy to set standards in terms of other people's accomplishments and then let other people measure you by those standards. But the standards you set for yourself are always more important. They should be higher than the standards anyone else would set for you, because in the end you have to live with yourself, and judge yourself, and feel good about yourself. And the best way to do that is to live up to your highest potential. So set your standards high and keep them high, even if you think no one else is looking. Somebody out there will always notice, even if it's just you."

THE "DIOTREPHES SPIRIT"

Diotrephes, who loves to be first.

3 JOHN V. 9 NIV

In the movie *Rocky,* boxer Rocky Balboa describes his relationship with his girlfriend Adrienne: "I've got gaps. She's got gaps. But together we've got no gaps." It doesn't matter how gifted you are—you've got gaps. What's the best way to handle your weaknesses? By working with others who have strengths in those areas. The New Testament Christians did this; as a result, "Much grace was upon them all" (Ac 4:33 NIV).

So why don't we work together more? Because of the "Diotrephes spirit": "But Diotrephes, who loves to be the leader, refuses to have anything to do with us...Not only does he refuse to welcome the traveling teachers, he also tells others not to help them. And when they do help, he puts them out of the church" (3Jn vv. 9-10 NLT). What did Diotrephes want? Control! He wasn't service-driven, he was ego-driven. He was afraid to have anyone challenge him. With him it was "my way or the highway." He didn't want a team, just a supporting cast. But "stars" are insecure; they hold the reins tightly. The trouble is, people who are afraid to trust others end up not being trusted. There's a level of success they never get beyond because they can't work with anybody. And when they stumble they have no one to help them up. They stay weak in certain areas; they can't reach for the strength in others because they believe others "are only out for what they can get." Whoa! That's the person in the mirror talking to you! Will others disappoint you? Yes. But you'll get further with the help of others than you'll get without it.

MAKE YOUR MONEY—HIS SERVANT!

Whoever loves money never has money enough.
ECCLESIASTES 5:10 NIV

If your goal is to prosper in order to fulfill God's purposes, God will bless you. If it's just to be rich, you're on your own! Notice: *(1) Money will buy people, but not true friends.* Christina Onassis, one of the richest women in the world, had to hire someone to play tennis with her and go to supper with her. She'd so much money she couldn't spend it all, yet she lived an empty, lonely life. Yes, money will buy people, but not true friends. They'll be takers but not givers, and as soon as your money is gone they will be too. *(2) Money will buy books, but not brains.* In his book *The Seven Secrets,* John Hagee writes: "A beautiful prayer tower was erected in the center of Trinity University. Every day the chimes echoed across the campus. But that prayer tower had to be locked with an iron gate. Why? Because some students who could not achieve the academic dreams of their wealthy fathers climbed the stairs of the prayer tower to leap to their deaths." Yes, money will buy books, but not brains. *(3) Money will buy food, but not a healthy appetite.* Ever thought of an empty plate as beautiful? An empty plate becomes beautiful when you have a sick loved one with a deadly disease. You prepare the finest foods only to watch them push it away, nauseated by the sight. Next time you see a dirty plate on your table, thank God for the food He has given you and the appetite to want it. Money can't buy that. Bottom line: make Jesus Lord of your life, and make your money—His servant!

TAKE THE INITIATIVE (1)

Look at an ant.

PROVERBS 6:6 TM

Too many of us are waiting for someone to come along and tell us what to do next. The story's told of a man who was employed by a duke and duchess. One day he was called in to speak to his employer. "James, how long have you been with us?" said the Duchess. "About thirty years, Your Grace," he replied. "As I recall you were employed to look after the dog," she said. "Yes, Your Grace." "James, that dog died twenty-seven years ago," said the Duchess. "Yes, Your Grace," said James, "What would you like me to do now?"

Why do we fail to take the initiative? Because we don't realize the consequences of our inaction. Solomon writes: "Look at an ant...Nobody has to tell it what to do. All summer it stores up food...So how long are you going to laze around doing nothing? How long before you get out of bed? A nap here, a nap there, a day off here, a day off there, sit back, take it easy—do you know what comes next?...a dirt-poor life, poverty your permanent houseguest" (vv. 6-11 TM). Whatever we do—or neglect to do—always catches up with us. Those who procrastinate end up like the man in playwright James Albery's verse: "He slept beneath the moon, he baked beneath the sun. He lived a life of going-to-do; and died with nothing done." Paul writes: "God has given each of us the ability to do certain things well" (Ro 12:6 TLB). Knowing your ability is one of the keys to understanding life's assignment. But you can only plan and prepare for so long, then you've got to take action!

TAKE THE INITIATIVE (2)

*Act with courage, and may
the Lord be with those who do well.*

2 CHRONICLES 19:11 NIV

One of the last obstacles between Israel and the Promised Land was the River Jordan. But God had a plan. He told the priests carrying the Ark that when they stepped in the river, the waters would roll back. There are two important lessons here for you: *(1) Nothing happens until you quit holding back!* You can't wait for everything to be perfect. You can't wait until your fear subsides. You must take the initiative. Overcomers understand that momentum is your friend. As soon as you start moving forward, certain things become clearer and easier. And when the momentum gets strong enough, many of the problems actually take care of themselves. Maybe you've heard the story of the tourist in a small town who asked an old man, "Can you tell me something this town is noted for?" After a moment's hesitation he replied, "Well, you can start here and go anywhere in the world you want." That's true of you too. Where you finish in life isn't determined so much by *where* you start, as by *whether* you start. If you're willing to get started, there's no telling how far you'll go. *(2) You must be willing to persevere.* The Jordan River didn't dry up the moment the priests stepped into it. God dried it up twenty-six miles upstream, so they had to wait till all that water passed by (See Jos 3:14-17). Why did God do it that way? Because He sees the big picture. God planned an opening wide enough for not just one or two, but for more than a million people to cross. So trust God, and take the initiative!

TAKE THE INITIATIVE (3)

Do not be afraid...The Lord...is going before you.
DEUTERONOMY 1:29-30 NIV

Notice two things about taking the initiative: *(1) Taking the initiative closes the door to fear.* We all have fears. The question is, are we going to control them or allow them to control us? Norman Vincent Peale said: "Action is a great restorer and builder of confidence. Inaction is not only the result, but the cause of fear. Perhaps the action you take will be successful; perhaps different action or adjustments will have to follow. But any action is better than no action at all." To have any chance at getting what we desire, we need to work for it. Nothing is as discouraging or draining as hanging on to an uncompleted task. The longer we let things slide, the harder they become. The hardest work is often the accumulation of many easy things that should have been done yesterday, last week or last month. The way to get rid of a difficult task is—do it! *(2) Taking the initiative opens the door to opportunity.* People who take the initiative and work hard may succeed, or fail. But anyone who doesn't take initiative is guaranteed to fail! So, ask God, "Is there a decision I should be making? Is there a problem I should be solving? Is there a project I should be starting? Is there a goal I should be setting or striving toward? Is there an opportunity I should be seizing?" Solomon writes: "If you wait for perfect conditions, you will never get anything done" (Ecc 11:4 TLB). It's better to be 80 percent sure, and start, than to wait until you're 100 percent sure, because by then the opportunity may have passed you by.

TAKE THE INITIATIVE (4)

*Make a careful exploration of…the work
you have been given…then sink yourself into that.*
GALATIANS 6:4 TM

There's a story about a great fisherman who always came home with a load of fish. One day a stranger asked if he could accompany him the next time he went out. "Sure," the fisherman said. The next morning the two made their way to a remote cove. The stranger noticed that the fisherman didn't have any poles or other equipment, just a rusty tackle box and a scoop net. After the fisherman shut off the motor he opened the tackle box and pulled out a stick of dynamite. He struck a match, lit it, and then tossed it into the water. After a deafening explosion, he grabbed his net and began scooping up fish. With a hard look, the stranger reached into his pocket and pulled out a badge with the words *Game Warden.* "You're under arrest," he said. His words didn't faze the fisherman. He simply reached into the tackle box again, lit another stick of dynamite and held it while the fuse burned down. Then he handed it to the game warden and said, "So, are you just going to sit there, or are you going to fish?" The moral of this story is—successful people don't need a fuse lit under them. Their motivation comes from their God-given purpose within. They live for a cause greater than themselves.

If we wait for others to motivate us, what happens when "others" don't show up? We need a better plan than that. And the Bible gives us that plan: "Make a careful exploration of who you are and the work you have been given, and then sink yourself into that."

TAKE THE INITIATIVE (5)

Pay careful attention to your own work.

GALATIANS 6:4 NLT

You can only pray, plan and prepare for so long, then you must step out in faith and act. The Chinese say, "He who deliberates too long before taking a step, will spend his whole life on one leg." The reason we never get started is because we focus on tomorrow instead of today. The only time over which you have any control is the present. James writes: "Look here, you who say…'Tomorrow we are going to a certain town…We will do business there and make profit.' How do you know what your life will be like tomorrow? Your life is like the morning fog—it's here a little while, then it's gone" (Jas 4:13-14 NLT).

Edgar Guest wrote: "The greatest of workers this man would have been—tomorrow. The world would have known him, had he ever seen—tomorrow. But the fact is he died and he faded from view, and all that he left here when living was through, was a mountain of things he intended to do—tomorrow." The idea of tomorrow can be very seductive, but the promise it holds is often false. It's starting, that stops us! Dawson Trotman, founder of The Navigators, observed: "The greatest time wasted, is the time getting started." The hardest part of writing a letter is penning the first line. The hardest part of making a tough phone call is picking up the phone and making the call. So how do you overcome this difficulty? Schedule a specific time for doing what you don't like to do or fear to do, and each time you follow through and do it, it will get easier and you'll get better at it.

KEEP WATCH

Keep watch...you do not know...
what day your Lord will come.
MATTHEW 24:42 NIV

The ocean liner *Californian* was within 1,500 miles of Boston Harbor when a crew member observed flashes of light from a distant steamer. Repeated attempts to contact it failed. In fact, it appeared to be sailing away. By 1:40 a.m. its lights vanished. It wasn't till later the captain learned what had actually happened. Neither he nor his second officer considered the flashing lights alarming, or that it was coincidental that they'd even seen them. Earlier the *Californian* had parked because of oceanic ice, and the unscheduled stop gave her a ringside seat to an unimaginable event. The crew didn't realize the flares were distress signals or they would have come to her aid—because they were only nine miles away. The foundering ship also sent radio distress calls that were within answering range—except for one important detail. The *Californian's* radio operator, fresh from training school, was fast asleep! So on April 12, 1912, from his vantage point on the bridge, the liner's second officer unwittingly watched the *Titanic* sink!

Jesus said: "People were eating...drinking, marrying...to the day Noah entered the ark; and they knew nothing...until the flood came and took them...That is how it will be at the coming of the Son of Man...keep watch...you do not know... what day your Lord will come" (vv. 38-42 NIV). And Paul adds: "For the grace of God that bringeth salvation hath appeared to all men, teaching us that denying ungodliness and worldly lusts we should live soberly, righteously, and godly, in this present world; looking for that blessed hope, and the glorious appearing of the great God and our Saviour Jesus Christ" (Tit 2:11-13). So, keep watch!

FAITH AND CAREFUL PLANNING

We should make plans—counting on God to direct us.
PROVERBS 16:9 TLB

There must be a balance between faith and careful planning. Yet, talk to some professing Christians and you might think otherwise. For example, talk with some who are unemployed and they'll tell you, "I'm just waiting for the Lord to provide a job." That's fine, but have you sharpened your job skills? And where have you placed your résumé? You say, "I'm not going that route; I'm just waiting on God." Oh, really? Then you won't mind going hungry for a while. The old motto of soldiers during the Revolutionary War applies here: "Trust God, but keep your powder dry!" Place your life in God's hands, but stay at the ready. You must do all you can to prepare yourself, understanding that the favor you need comes from the Lord.

To walk by faith does not mean you stop thinking, planning, taking advice, and self-correcting. And it definitely doesn't imply becoming lazy or apathetic. What a distortion of biblical faith! Trust God for your finances, but don't "blow your budget." Trust God for safety in the car, but don't pass on a blind curve. Trust God for your health, but don't chain-smoke, stay up half the night and subsist on potato chips and carbonated drinks. Acting foolishly, expecting God to bail you out when things go amiss, isn't faith, it's presumption. Wisdom says do all you can, then trust God to do what you cannot do. Faith and careful planning go hand-in-hand. They always have and they always will!

LEARN TO RELAX

*[Stop allowing yourselves to be agitated...
disturbed...and unsettled].*

JOHN 14:27 AMP

A well-known Bible teacher says: "We can only walk in peace if we're willing to be adaptable and adjust to people and circumstances. When I lived in 'explode mode' it never failed that one of my children spilled something at the dinner table every night...and every night I had a fit. One night I was under the table because the milk had made it to the crack in the middle and was running down...The kids were upset and somebody kicked me in the head, which made me even madder. I knew it was an accident...but somehow that that didn't seem to matter ...[Then] the Holy Spirit spoke to me—right under that table—and said: 'Once the milk's spilled, no matter how big a fit you throw you're not going to get it to run back up the table into the glass. You need to learn to go with the flow.'"

Jesus said, "[Stop allowing yourselves to be agitated...disturbed...and unsettled]." In other words, work on controlling your reactions. Stop losing your peace over every little thing that goes wrong in your life. When there's nothing you can do about the situation, learn to let it go and keep your joy. Ask God to help you get over life's little offenses and irritations quickly, whether it's a glass of spilled milk or somebody who's hurt your feelings. When you put as much energy into "letting go" as you do into "stewing and steaming" and trying to control every possible outcome, you'll find that God's peace "which is so great we cannot understand it" (Php 4:7 NCV) will start to fill your heart and your home.

BREAKING HABITS THROUGH PRAYER

I am watching over My word to perform it.

JEREMIAH 1:12 NAS

Are you struggling with a habit so stubborn that it has a life of its own? A mind that thinks for you, a voice that speaks to you, a power that keeps pulling you down? Nothing brings victory like "praying the Word," for God says, "I am watching over My word to perform it." So begin each day by praying:

"Lord, Your Word says that if I call on You, You will answer me; You will be with me in trouble, You will honor me and You will deliver me (See Ps 91:15). You said that through the power of Your indwelling Spirit I would be set free from this vicious cycle of temptation, sin and failure (See Ro 8:2). You said if I fully commit my life to You, I'd have the strength to stand up to the Devil and he would flee from me (See Jas 4:7). You said You have given me the power to pull down all my old mental strongholds and take control of every wayward thought, imagination, and impulse (See 2Co 10:5). You said that by reading Your Word each day and meditating on it, I would become a partaker of Your divine nature, and overcome the destructive tendencies of my flesh (See 2Pe 1:4). You said I'd be strengthened in my mind, my emotions and my will; that my self-worth would be based solely on Your love for me; and that You would do exceedingly abundantly above all I could ask or think—because You are at work in me (See Eph 3:14-21). Today I thank You for helping me to overcome this habit. In Christ's name, amen."

CONQUERING CREDIT CARD MADNESS (1)

Owning...things won't make your life safe.

LUKE 12:15 CEV

Half of America's families outspend their income and carry over $8,000 on credit cards. Sometimes it's due to sky-rocketing utility and medical costs, but most times it's all the extras we can't live without, like gourmet coffee, expensive hobbies, exotic vacations, and shopping to make ourselves feel good. Columnist Donna F. Savage admits: "I'm shopping for an experience...to make the occasion memorable...direction-less shopping hides the motivation behind spending decisions... A few Hallmark sentiments and a gift card will do the trick... Pizza and a new DVD should bring the family together...dinner and a movie will restore marital intimacy...contentment slips out of reach with each substitution. Since our deepest expecta-tions aren't met, we keep...spending."

Jesus said, "Don't be greedy! Owning a lot of things won't make your life safe." Curb your out-of-control spending with a few simple steps: *Think small.* Tackle one bill at a time; it's amazing what you accomplish when you're serious and stick with it: "Let us not become weary in doing good...at the proper time we will reap a harvest if we do not give up" (Gal 6:9 NIV). Remember, the power within you is bigger than the financial challenge ahead of you, so if you "get knocked down...get up ...and keep going" (2Co 4:9 TLB). *Spell out your financial goals.* Decide what's truly important—how much you'll save, how much you'll give and how much debt you can handle with-out jeopardizing your future. The reason we never reach our goals is because we don't set any. Wisdom means knowing where you're going and what it will take to get there!

CONQUERING CREDIT CARD MADNESS (2)

Grabbing whatever attracts your fancy.

COLOSSIANS 3:5 TM

Using credit cards to buy things you can't afford can land you in hot water. Paul says: "[Put] off everything connected with...doing whatever you feel like whenever you feel like it, and grabbing whatever attracts your fancy." If you're drowning in debt:

(1) Stop charging what you can't pay for and don't need. You're incurring higher interest rates and adding to your burden. Use a credit card only if you're disciplined enough not to go overboard. Your intentions may be good, but unforeseen circumstances can force you to carry your balance from month to month. And if your spending is totally out of control, perform plastic surgery—cut up your credit cards! *(2) Give more.* Ever wonder why we're "happier giving than getting" (Ac 20:35 TM), or how come "God [and everybody else] loves a cheerful giver" (2 Co 9:7 NIV)? It's because giving helps us focus on something besides our own desires and wants. Remember, "You...become rich by being generous or poor by being greedy" (Pr 11:24 CEV). Giving proves you've conquered greed! *(3) Expect disapproval.* Do what Noah did—ignore it and get on with the job at hand! For example, during one woman's second pregnancy her friends criticized her because she refused to register at a baby store for more stuff, even though she already had everything she needed. Don't expect others to understand your new approach. Anytime you try to make your mark, you'll attract erasers. Choosing how you'll react to criticism is one of life's most important decisions. If you only do things nobody can find fault with, you'll never accomplish much!

P-R-A-Y!

Look to the Lord and his strength;
seek his face always.

1 CHRONICLES 16:11 NIV

To help you remember the four parts of prayer, think of the acrostic P-R-A-Y: P—*Praise the Lord!* Not sure how? Think you'll run out of words? Not if you use the Scriptures. David gives us a beautiful example in 1Ch 29:11-13. It's one you can use: "Yours, O Lord, is the greatness and the power and the glory and the majesty and the splendor...Yours, O Lord, is the kingdom...In your hands are strength and power to exalt and give strength to all. Now, our God, we give you thanks, and praise your glorious name." R—*Repent of your sins!* Just as heat forces impurities to the surface so the metal refiner can remove them, your prayer time will reveal attitudes that must be changed, habits that must be broken, and barriers to blessing that must be removed. It's not enough to tell God about your sins. He already knows them. You must ask Him to help you turn away from them. This is true repentance. A—*Ask for yourself and others!* Your prayers invite God into the situation, and your faith activates His power to change it. There's no distance in prayer, no culture or language barrier it can't overcome. It's like throwing on a power switch—things begin to move when we pray. Jesus said, "I will give you the keys of the Kingdom of Heaven...whatever doors you open on earth shall be open in heaven" (Mt 16:19 TLB). Y—*Yield yourself to God's will!* Declaring the Lordship of Jesus Christ in your life is like signing your name to the bottom of a blank check, and inviting Him to fill in the amount.

THE IMPORTANCE OF RELATIONSHIPS (1)

Share each other's troubles and problems.

GALATIANS 6:2 TLB

Johnny Cash recorded more than 1,500 songs, had fourteen number one hits, was awarded eleven Grammies and sold 50 million albums. Much of the credit goes to his wife June, a committed Christian. At her funeral Johnny's daughter said: "In her eyes there were only two kinds of people: those she knew and loved, and those she didn't know and loved. She looked for the best in everyone; it was a way of life for her. If you pointed out that a particular person was perhaps not deserving of her love, she would say, 'Well, honey, we just have to lift him up.' She was forever lifting people up. It took me a long time to understand that what she did when she lifted you up, was to mirror the very best parts of you back to yourself. She was like a spiritual detective; she saw into all your dark corners and deep recesses, saw your potential, and the gifts you didn't even know you possessed, and she lifted them up for you to see. She did it for all of us, daily, continuously. But her great mission and passion was lifting up my dad. If being a wife were a corporation June would have been the CEO. It was her most treasured role. She'd begin every day by saying, 'What can I do for *you*, John?' Her love filled up every room he was in and lightened every path he walked. Her devotion created a sacred, exhilarating place for them to live out their married life. My daddy has lost his dearest companion, his musical counterpart, his soul-mate and best friend." *That* is the power of a great relationship!

THE IMPORTANCE OF RELATIONSHIPS (2)

Whoever walks with…fools suffers harm.

PROVERBS 13:20 NRS

In his book *High Maintenance Relationships* Les Parrott offers us ways to know whether someone is a plus or a minus in our lives:

(1) Do you feel anxious when a particular person has called and left a message for you to return? (2) Are you dealing with a relationship that drains you of energy and enthusiasm? (3) Do you dread having to see or talk to a particular person at work or in a social situation? (4) Do you always seek to give, but get nothing in return? (5) Do you keep second-guessing your own performance as a result of interacting with this person? (6) Do you become more self-critical in their presence? (7) Is your creativity blocked or is your clarity of mind hampered by the lingering discomfort of having to deal with them? (8) Do you try to calm yourself after being with this person by eating more, biting your nails, or engaging in some other unhealthy habit? (9) Do you have imaginary conversations or mental arguments in which you defend yourself or try to explain your side of a conflict? (10) Do you feel resentful that this person seems to treat other people better than they treat you? (11) Do you wonder why this person singles you out for criticism but rarely acknowledges what you do well?

If you answer yes, you're in a high-maintenance relationship, and you've three options: (1) Continue to suffer. (2) Continue to complain. (3) Do something about it. Start by heeding the Scripture: "Whoever walks with the wise becomes wise, but the companion of fools suffers harm."

THE IMPORTANCE OF RELATIONSHIPS (3)

A friend loveth at all times.

PROVERBS 17:17

Work to build solid relationships that are mutually beneficial. Here are some signs that a relationship's headed that
way: *(1) Mutual enjoyment.* In solid relationships people spend
time together just for the joy of being together. What they do is
not of significance. Unfortunately the busyness of life causes us
to forget what a joy this can be. *(2) Mutual respect.* How do
you build mutual respect? When you don't let obstacles or circumstances become more important to you than the relationship. When the pressure is on and you still treat them with
patience and kindness. When the relationship is struggling and
you're willing to work to preserve it. *(3) Shared experiences.*
Helen Keller may have been blind, but she had 20/20 vision
when it came to relationships: "My friends have made the story
of my life. In a thousand ways they have turned my limitations
into beautiful privileges, and enabled me to walk serene and
happy in the shadow cast by my deprivation." *(4) Trust.* Ralph
Waldo Emerson wrote: "The glory of friendship is not just in
the outstretched hand nor the kindly smile nor the joy of com-
panionship; it is in the spiritual inspiration that comes to one
when he discovers that someone else believes in him and is willing to trust him." Paul writes: "Love never gives up" (1Co 13:7
NLT). *(5) Reciprocity.* All relationships experience ebb and flow.
Sometimes one person is the primary giver, sometimes the other
is. But a solid relationship will always be two-sided. Friendships
are like bank accounts. You cannot continue to draw on them
without making deposits. If either of you becomes overdrawn
and it stays that way too long, the relationship won't last.

THE IMPORTANCE OF RELATIONSHIPS (4)

As iron sharpens iron, so one man sharpens another.
PROVERBS 27:17 NIV

Solid relationships keep us grounded and accountable. If we start to get off course they help keep us on track. So who are the significant people in your life, the ones you spend the most time with, the ones whose opinions really matter to you? These people are your greatest influencers. The question is, how are they influencing you? To know the answer, ask yourself the following questions: *(1) What does he/she bring out of me?* Author William Alan Ward remarked: "A true friend knows your weaknesses, but shows you your strengths. Feels your fears, but fortifies your faith. Sees your anxieties, but frees your spirit. Recognizes your disabilities, but emphasizes your possibilities." *(2) What does he/she think of me?* People tend to become what the most important person in their lives believes they can be. Indeed, that's what our children grow up to be! We embrace the opinions of those we respect. *(3) What does he/she think of my future?* Paul tells Timothy, "Don't let anyone think less of you because you are young" (1Ti 4:12 NLT). Do the most important people in your life understand God's plan for you? Do they help or hinder you? *(4) How does he/she behave toward me in difficult times?* The solid relationships in your life are those who are slow to suspect, but quick to trust. Slow to condemn, but quick to justify. Slow to offend, but quick to defend. Slow to expose, but quick to shield. Slow to reprimand, but quick to forbear. Slow to belittle, but quick to appreciate. Slow to demand, but quick to give. Slow to provoke, but quick to help. Slow to resent, but quick to forgive.

ANYBODY CAN DO IT!

Encourage one another.
1 THESSALONIANS 5:11 NIV

Chuck Swindoll writes: "The ski slopes were in perfect condition. I struck out on my first attempt at skiing with a positive attitude, thinking, 'I'm going to be the first person who learns to ski without falling down.' You've heard of the Elephant Man? On skis, I'm the rhinoceros man. It's doubtful anyone ever came down a ski slope more ways, or landed in more positions, or did more creative things in the air before landing. Working with me that humiliating day was the world's most encouraging ski instructor (yes, I had an instructor!). Never once did she lose her cool, or laugh at me, or say 'You are absolutely impossible. I quit!' That dear, gracious lady helped me up more times than I can number. She repeated the same basics time and again—like she had never said them before. Even though I was colder than an explorer in the Antarctic, irritable, impatient, and under the snow more than I was on it, she kept offering words of reassurance. That day God gave me a never-to-be-forgotten illustration of the value of encouragement. Had it not been for her spirit and her words, believe me, I would have hung 'em up and been back in the condo, warming my feet by the fire in less than an hour. What is true for a novice on the snow once a year is all the more true for people we meet every day. Harassed by demands and deadlines; bruised by worry, adversity and failure; broken by disillusionment and defeated by sin, they live somewhere between dull discouragement and sheer panic. *All* of us need encouragement, and the beautiful part about encouragement is this: *anybody* can do it!"

WHEN YOU LOSE WHAT YOU LOVE

When they walk through the Valley of Weeping...
They will continue to grow stronger.

PSALM 84:6-7 NLT

When you lose what you love you go through five stages: *(1) Denial*—"No, it can't be happening." *(2) Anger*—"God, why are You permitting this?" *(3) Bargaining*—"Please make it go away." *(4) Depression*—Silence and withdrawal. *(5) Acceptance*—"Not my will but Thine be done." Whether it's the loss of a child, a marriage, a job, your health, etc. when you turn to God He'll give you the grace to embrace it, grieve it, express it, release it, and go on to become stronger. Sometimes we seek quick relief by releasing it before we've gone through these stages. That's because we fear the *process*. We've been taught that any show of emotion is a show of weakness, so we stuff it. But we only stuff it into our emotional garbage can, then spend all our time and energy sitting on the lid, trying to keep the contents from spilling out. "You shall know the truth, and the truth shall make you free" (Jn 8:32 NKJV). It's knowing and embracing the truth, including its painful aspects, that sets you free. You must be *willing* to forgive. But until you come to grips with the enormity of your loss, including any injustice of what was done to you, you are not *ready* to forgive. When you rush to forgive, you forgive only in part and you're released only in part. Are you running from pain today? Are you trading it in prematurely for some other feeling? That's not God's way. Jesus said, "You will weep and mourn...but [eventually] your grief will turn to joy...and no one will take [it] away" (Jn 16:20-22 NIV).

LEARN TO BENEFIT FROM CRITICISM

Whoever learns from correction is wise.

PROVERBS 15:5 NLT

There are two kinds of criticism: *(1) Unjustified criticism.* One day Henry Ward Beecher went to his church to preach. As the great orator placed his Bible on the pulpit he noticed a blank sheet of paper with the word "fool" written on it. Beecher's keen sense of humor seized the moment. He lifted the paper for all to see, then his booming voice filled the church as he announced: "Generally I receive letters from people who write and forget to sign their name. This letter is different. The person has signed his name but forgotten to write the letter." Jesus said, "Offences will come" (Lk 17:1). So expect them. And remember, attack is a sign of respect. You're getting noticed. You're making a difference. So when you are criticized unjustly, forget it and move on. Jesus did! *(2) Justified criticism.* Criticism that's justified has a measure of truth in it. An old Arab proverb states, "If one person calls you a donkey, forget it. But if five people call you a donkey, buy a saddle." Dr. James G. Kerr, a management psychologist, points out that a major deterrent to gaining information about ourselves lies in our natural reluctance to discover anything about ourselves that isn't flattering. When we erect defenses against our own inadequacies and try to hide our faults from ourselves and others, we close the door to a vital source of self-knowledge and therefore deny ourselves the joy of spiritual growth. Stop hiding from the truth. Every one of us can improve what we're doing and the way in which it's being done. As they say, "The largest room in the world— is room for improvement!"

KEYS TO A STRONGER MARRIAGE (1)

Love…is not…self-seeking.
1 CORINTHIANS 13:4-5 NIV

An elderly couple celebrating their fiftieth anniversary had no secrets, except for a shoe box the wife had always kept hidden under the bed. She agreed to let her husband look inside. When he did he found two crocheted dolls and $50,000 in cash. "Years ago," she explained, "my mother told me that the secret to a happy marriage was never to argue. Instead, when I got angry I should keep quiet and crochet a doll." Her husband was delighted; she'd only been angry at him twice in fifty years! "Honey," he said, "that explains the dolls, but what about the $50,000?" "Oh," she replied smiling, "*that's* from selling dolls!"

Marriage therapy often calls for "active listening," and affirming your spouse through paraphrasing, validation, and positive feedback. But research shows that many couples aren't always happy with the results and problems still recur. Dr. John Gottman says, "That's because we're asking people to do Olympic-style gymnastics when they can hardly crawl!" Instead, Dr. Susan Boon recommends identifying the issues that *must* be resolved—and learning to live with the rest! Work around them, commit to staying together, and for every negative experience look for five positive ones to balance it out. Dirty socks, snoring, thermostat settings, unmade beds—our habits can drive our partners crazy. We must learn to "Submit to one another out of reverence for Christ" (Eph 5:21 NIV), and remember, "Love…is not rude…self-seeking…easily angered, it keeps no record of wrongs" (1Co 13:4-5 NIV). Well, how are you doing so far?

KEYS TO A STRONGER MARRIAGE (2)

*Do not let any unwholesome talk come out of your
mouths, but only what is helpful.*

EPHESIANS 4:29 NIV

Conflict in marriage isn't nearly as important as how you
handle it. Dr. Shae Graham Kosch, who's been married
thirty-two years and has counseled couples for just as long,
says: "Most marital conflicts don't ever get resolved. There are
always issues around in-laws, children, money…What's crucial
is keeping things positive…accept the other person's perspective, have an appropriate discussion without getting critical or
blaming…Your attitude plays out over the long haul. Couples
that retain mutual respect and understanding…stay together."
Solomon said: "Reckless words pierce like a sword…the tongue
of the wise brings healing" (Pr 12:18 NIV).

Marriage is a special relationship created by God. You're
"no longer two, but one" (Mt 19:6 NIV), so when conflicts
arise: (a) attack the problem, not each other; (b) stay calm and
your partner's more likely to take you seriously; (c) choose the
best time to address the issues, not when you're both tired and
the kids are hungry; (d) consider your spouse's viewpoint; men
and women see things differently; (e) remember, there'll be
times when you'll have to compromise and times your partner
will; (f) choose your words carefully. "Do not let any unwholesome talk come out of your mouths, but only what is helpful
for building others up." "Encourage one another" (1Th 5:11
NIV); "forgiving one another" (Eph 4:32 NLT); "pray for each
other" (Jas 5:16 NIV); "spur one another on toward love and
good deeds" (Heb 10:24 NIV); "Carry each other's burdens"
(Gal 6:2 NIV); "giving preference to one another" (Ro 12:10
NKJV). That about sums it up!

READ YOUR BIBLE (1)

If ye continue in my word,
then are ye my disciples indeed.

JOHN 8:31

You *cannot* be a disciple of Jesus without a regular intake of God's Word. Jesus said, "If ye continue in my word, then are ye my disciples indeed." This word "continue" means to live each day by its principles. The story's told of a man who came to pick up his wife after church: "Is the sermon over?" he asked. A turned-on member replied, "No, it has just begun. Now the rest is up to us!"

The common denominator of every great man and woman of God in history is that they disciplined themselves to spend regular time with the Lord in His Word. What made George Muller so successful? During his lifetime he read through the Bible over two hundred times—and more than half of those readings on his knees, praying over the Word while studying it. When you know God *that* well, you'll pray specifically and get specific answers. Most of us who say we *believe* the Bible from cover to cover—have never *read* it from cover to cover! We are more faithful to the advice columnists and the sports pages of the newspaper than we are to God's Word. People who are not professing Christians wouldn't dream of leaving their homes in the morning until they've read their horoscope. Imagine what would happen if *you* committed yourself with equal vigor to reading your Bible before you leave for work, school, or wherever? It would change your life, and impact those around you! So, read your Bible!

READ YOUR BIBLE (2)

Continue in…the Holy Scriptures,
which are able to make you wise.
2 TIMOTHY 3:14-15 NKJV

Why don't we read God's Word more? Three reasons: *(1)*
We don't know how! We hear the pastor preach a great
sermon and think, "Why didn't I see that?" Because the pastor
spends hours praying over it and studying the Scriptures; we
don't! *(2) We're not motivated!* That's because we haven't experienced the joy that comes from personally discovering great
truths from God's Word. We've become satisfied with getting
what we need from somebody else rather than finding it out
for ourselves. Understand this: If you ever get serious about
studying the Bible on your own, you'll never fully be satisfied
with a secondhand knowledge of the Scriptures. Dr. Paul Lyttle
once compared personal Bible study to eating peanuts: "Once
you start doing it, you're hooked! When you discover how good
Bible study 'tastes' you'll find yourself going back for more and
more. Yes, personal Bible study can be habit-forming!" *(3) We
are lazy!* Bible study is hard work. There are no shortcuts to it.
It takes time, effort, concentration and persistence. Most of its
great truths don't lie on the surface; we have to dig for them.
Dr. Howard Hendricks describes the three stages of Bible study:
(a) The "castor oil" stage—we study the Bible because we know
it's good for us, but it's not too enjoyable. (b) The "cereal"
stage—our Bible study is dry and uninteresting, but we know
it's nourishing. (c) The "peaches and cream" stage—we are
really feasting on the Word of God. Bottom line? "Continue in
…the Holy Scriptures, which are able to make you wise."

READ YOUR BIBLE (3)

They…searched the scriptures daily.

ACTS 17:11

You have to "live" with a Scripture until it takes root within you and begins to grow. Butterflies cover more ground, but bees gather more honey. Sometimes you have to stay with a particular Scripture until you extract the honey. God may work on one area of your life for several weeks, or months. It takes time to change ingrained character traits. New habits and ways of thinking are not formed in a day. We must be aware of this and let God reinforce a new truth in our lives. Don't fool yourself into thinking that just because you've read a certain truth it'll produce instant change. It must be applied, and that takes time!

Rick Warren writes: "On one occasion my application was to work on the quality of sensitivity. It took several months for God to build that into my life. I needed to see how this quality related to all areas of my life. He kept putting me into situations where I was tempted to do the opposite—to be insensitive. He may do the same with you. God may teach you to love others by putting you in the midst of unlovely people. You may have to learn patience while experiencing irritations, and learn peace in the midst of chaos. You are then discovering how to have joy even in times of sorrow and testing. You must realize that when God wants to build a positive quality into your life, He must allow you to encounter situations where you choose to do the right thing instead of following your natural inclinations." The real test is, "How will applying this Scripture to my situation help me become more like Jesus?"

YOU HAVE TO GIVE IT AWAY

Give, and it shall be given unto you.

LUKE 6:38

Legend has it that a man was lost in the desert, dying for water. He came upon a shack and saw a rusty old water pump. He stumbled over to it, grabbed the handle and began to pump up and down. But nothing came out. Then he noticed a nearby jug with these words: "My friend, you have to prime the pump with the water in this jug. P.S. Be sure to fill the jug again before you leave." As he popped the cork, suddenly he was faced with a decision. If he drank the water he could live. But if he poured it into the old rusty pump, maybe it would yield from down deep in the well all the water he wanted later. He studied his options. What should he do, pour it into the pump and take a chance on fresh, cool water, or drink what was in the jug and ignore its message? Reluctantly he poured all the water into the pump. Then he grabbed the handle and began to pump...squeak, squeak, squeak. Nothing came out! Squeak, squeak, squeak. A little bit began to dribble out, then a small stream, and finally it gushed! To his relief fresh, cool water poured out of the old rusty pump. Eagerly, he filled the jug and drank from it. He filled it another time and once again drank its refreshing contents. Then he filled the jug for the next traveler. He filled it to the top, popped the cork back on, and added this little note: "Believe me, it really works." Friend, don't ignore the message Jesus left: "Give, and it shall be given unto you."

REDEEMED!

The Lord...redeems your life from destruction.

PSALM 103:2-4 NKJV

On a winter afternoon Harry de Leyer returned from an auction with a big gray horse that his children promptly named Snowman. He was a good riding horse, but when a neighbor offered Harry twice what he'd paid for him, he agreed. Right away he regretted his decision; apparently so did Snowman. And that's when his hidden talent showed up—along with the horse himself! The neighbor's fences were high, but Snowman repeatedly scaled them to be with the master and family he loved. One day Harry made the reunion permanent by buying the horse back—and the rest is history. Snowman kept winning championships and shows until the ultimate dream, The National at Madison Square Garden, where he was named "Horse of the Year" two years running. But not because he *ran;* Snowman was a *jumper.* And nobody would ever have known had it not been for the fences that separated the grateful animal from his loving master. And the horse had every reason to be grateful, because Harry had arrived late at the auction that day after the best horses were sold. The big gray gelding that became the indomitable Snowman was rescued from the only other bidder...a man who intended him *for the glue factory!* The Psalmist said, "The Lord...redeems your life from destruction." When others write you off, He sees what you can become. Andrew Bonar said: "Kept by the mighty power of God...every day we escape dangers we're not aware of...If we...saw the snares Satan lays for us...how we'd adore the Lord who enables us to escape them all!" Take a moment today and thank the One who has redeemed your life from destruction.

WILLING TO BE A SERVANT

*He who is the greatest among you
shall be your servant.*

MATTHEW 23:11 NKJV

What do you think of when you hear the word *servant?* Someone who's pathetic, without will or purpose? Our false definition of the word servant is expressed in *The Sarcastic Beatitudes* by J. B. Phillips, who also wrote a paraphrase of the New Testament: "Blessed are the pushers, for they get their way. Blessed are the hard-boiled, for they never get hurt. Blessed are those who complain, for they get all the attention. Blessed are the blasé, for they never worry about sin. Blessed are the slave-drivers, for they get results. Blessed are the greedy, for they get what they want." How did Jesus introduce Himself? "The Son of Man did not come to be served, but to serve, and to give his life" (Mk 10:45 NIV). And He practiced what He preached. Listen to the sound of water splashing in a basin as God incarnate sponges the grime from the feet of His undeserving disciples, then says, "He who is the greatest among you shall be your servant." Some of us wish we could echo His humility. Ruth Calkin, author and poet, expressed that wish in her poem "I Wonder": "You know, Lord, how I serve You with great emotional fervor in the limelight, how eagerly I speak for You at the Women's Club, how I radiate what I promote at a fellowship group. But how would I react, I wonder, if You pointed to a basin of water and asked me to wash the calloused feet of a bent and wrinkled old woman, day after day and month after month, in a room where nobody saw and nobody knew. I wonder? Do you also wonder?!"

"BOB'S LAST LETTER"

Husbands, love your wives.

EPHESIANS 5:25 NIV

The following hilarious letter illustrates what Paul *didn't* mean by "Husbands, love your wives."

Dear friends: Men must remember that as women grow older it's harder for them to maintain the same quality of housekeeping. When men notice this, they should try not to yell. Let me relate how I handle the situation. When I took early retirement, it became necessary for Nancy to get a full time job. Shortly after she started working I noticed she was beginning to show her age. I usually get home from fishing about the same time she gets home from work. Although she knows how hungry I am, she almost always has to rest before she starts supper. I try not to yell; instead, I tell her to take her time and just wake me up when she does get supper on the table. She used to do the dishes as soon as we finished eating. Now they sit several hours after supper. I do what I can by reminding her each evening that they aren't cleaning themselves. I know she appreciates this, as it does seem to help her get them done before she goes to bed. It also gives her more time to do things like shampooing the dog, vacuuming and dusting. And if I have had a good day fishing, it allows her to gut and scale the fish at a more leisurely pace. Now I know that I probably look like a saint in the way I support Nancy. However, guys, if you just yell at your wife a little less often because of this letter, writing it was worthwhile. Signed, Bob. P.S. Bob's funeral was on Saturday. P.P.S. Nancy was acquitted on Monday.

FIND YOUR STRENGTH ZONE

He alone decides which gift each person should have.
1 CORINTHIANS 12:11 NLT

We all have equal value in God's eyes, but we don't have equal giftedness. In their book *Now, Discover Your Strengths,* Marcus Buckingham and Donald O. Clifton state that every person is capable of doing something better than the next 10,000 people. And they support that with research. They call this area your *strength zone,* and they encourage you to find it and make the most of it. It doesn't matter how aware you are of your abilities, how you feel about yourself, or whether you have previously achieved success. You have talent, and God requires you to develop it! But you can only develop the talent you have, not the one you want. When it comes to your character, you must never stop working on your areas of weakness. But when it comes to fulfilling your God-given assignment, you must recognize your *strength zone* and give yourself to it. Dr. John Maxwell writes: "It's been my observation that people can increase their ability in an area by only two points on a scale of 1-10. For example, if your natural talent in an area is 4, with hard work you may raise it to a 6. In other words, you can go from a little below average to a little above average. But let's say you find a place where you are a 7; you have the potential to become a 9, maybe even a 10, if it's your strength zone and you work hard! That helps you advance from 1 in 10,000 talent to 1 in 100,000 talent—but only if you do the other things needed to maximize your talent." So, find your strength zone!

A MOTHER'S INFLUENCE

Direct your children onto the right path.
PROVERBS 22:6 NLT

When Harry and Ada Mae Day brought their first child, Sandra, home from the hospital, it was to a tiny ranch house without running water, electricity, or a school within driving distance. But they refused to let their surroundings limit them. His father's death had kept Harry from attending Stanford University, but he never lost hope that his daughter would study there. Ada Mae subscribed to educational newspapers and magazines, home-schooled her daughter and later sent her to the best boarding schools. One summer the entire family climbed to the dome of every state capitol west of the Mississippi! Sandra *did* attend Stanford, then law school, and eventually became the first woman Supreme Court justice in America. The day she was sworn in she donned her robes and took her place among the other justices. Then she locked eyes with her family, and the tears began.

Solomon said, "Direct your children onto the right path, and when they are older, they will not leave it." What made Sandra Day O'Connor successful? Intelligence and ambition undoubtedly played a part. But much of the credit goes to a determined little woman sitting in a four-room adobe house reading to her kids hour after hour, and to parents who climbed the stairways of capitol domes alongside them. Chuck Swindoll says: "As significant as political, military, educational or religious figures may be, none compare to the impact made by mothers. Their words are never fully forgotten, their touch leaves an indelible impression...the memory of their presence lasts a lifetime. *I ask you, who else has that kind of influence?*"

RECOGNIZING GOD'S VOICE

Speak, Lord, for your servant is listening.

1 SAMUEL 3:9 NIV

Learning to recognize God's voice is not a skill that's acquired overnight because He speaks to us at different times, in different settings and in different ways. *(1) It requires you to mature spiritually.* Jesus said His sheep follow Him because they know His voice (See Jn 10:4 NIV). Notice, Jesus said that His "sheep," not His lambs, know His voice. Baby sheep just follow adult sheep until their senses are trained. Thank God there's grace for the immature. If your spiritual ears are not yet developed, God will work with you until you learn to recognize His voice. *(2) It requires guidance and confirmation from godly leadership.* "Obey your spiritual leaders, and do what they say. Their work is to watch over your souls" (Heb 13:17 NLT). Who's your spiritual upline? *(3) It must not be limited to your previous experiences.* God spoke to Moses on a mountain that shook, and to Elijah through a still, small voice. Don't limit God; He will speak to you through the Scriptures, through those qualified to teach you His Word, through a song, through a painful situation, and even your own thoughts and desires when you're submitted to Him. The key is to stay close to God and keep your receiver on. *(4) Above all else, it requires obedience.* The Psalmist said, "When thou saidst, Seek ye my face; my heart said...Thy face, Lord, will I seek" (Ps 27:8). When it comes to hearing from God, how's your response time? "When I get around to it?...I'll see if I can fit You in!...I'll think about it!" Wrong! God speaks, and continues to speak, to those who obey, and continue to obey.

TAKING RESPONSIBILITY (1)

Much is required from those to whom much is given.

LUKE 12:48 TLB

Responsibility is a two-sided coin. On one side is responsibility; on the other side is reward. Too many of us are focused on one side of the coin only—reward. Taking responsibility means three things: (1) Acknowledging what you are responsible for. (2) Acknowledging who you are responsible to. (3) Acting responsibly at all times. All the excuses you give yourself, and others, won't let you off the hook. Jesus said, "Much is required from those to whom much is given." At their annual conference the manager of a dog food company asked his sales team how they liked the company's new advertising program. "Great!" they replied. "The best in the business." "What do you think of the product?" he asked. "Fantastic," they replied. "How about the sales force?" he asked. They *were* the sales force, so of course they responded positively, saying they were the best. "Okay then," the manager said, "so if we have the best brand, the best packaging, the best advertising program and the best sales force, why are we in seventeenth place in our industry?" After an awkward silence one of the salesmen shouted, "It's those dogs—they just won't eat the stuff!"

Guess what? Your problem is not the dogs, or your job, or your spouse, or society at large, or whatever. Be honest, your biggest challenge in life is *you*. If your life's not going the way you want it to, *you* are responsible for changing it. And God will help you if you turn to Him. But you must *want* to change, *decide* to change, and *work* each day toward that end.

TAKING RESPONSIBILITY (2)

A man reaps what he sows.

GALATIANS 6:7 NIV

Our values today are badly messed up. We overlook the poor grades and irresponsible acts of high school and college athletes. Why? Because they win tournaments and make us look good! And how about "celebrity justice?" Someone famous gets a free pass, while the less fortunate do the time because they did the crime? Wrong! We need to teach our children that unless they accept responsibility, life won't be good to them: "A man reaps what he sows." Parent, taking personal responsibility means holding your child accountable when they violate the rules; mix with the wrong crowd; try "cool" stuff like drinking, drugs and premarital sex; cheat on a test; or stay out beyond curfew. Sound straitlaced? So is gravity. So is the harvest law. Your sincere but naïve sentiment, "I want them to have all the things I didn't have growing up," will turn spoiled children into spoiled adults. Practice prevention: build a fence at the top of the cliff, not a hospital at the bottom! You say, "By the time I get home at night I'm too tired to discipline them." Wake up: when they get arrested for DUI the judge won't cut them any slack. Nor will the banker when he repossesses their car and their house because they didn't pay the note. Kindness is cruelty in disguise when it's not accompanied by responsibility.

Eli the High Priest rose to the top of his profession. Only one problem: he didn't take responsibility for his family. As a result, he and his sons died prematurely. God said, "I told him that I would judge his family...because...he failed to restrain them" (1Sa 3:13 NIV). So, take responsibility!

TAKING RESPONSIBILITY (3)

*Now, a person who is put in charge
as a manager must be faithful.*

1 CORINTHIANS 4:2 NLT

In any great endeavor you'll face: (a) nay-sayers who think it can't be done; (b) road-blockers who place obstacles in your way; (c) a high probability you'll fail before you succeed. Who wants to endure such things? Winners! It takes courage to leave Egypt, walk through the wilderness wondering, "Am I making any progress at all?" and stand at the Red Sea knowing that without a miracle you'll drown, thinking, "Nobody's ever been in this situation before. What if it doesn't work?" Taking responsibility means stepping out in faith when there's no precedent to go by, no logic to stand on, and your friends are questioning your sanity.

The one quality all successful people have is the ability to accept ultimate responsibility. General Eisenhower was given responsibility for planning the D-Day invasion. Giving the okay was a painful decision, one he knew would lead to many deaths. Yet if it was successful, it would guarantee victory over the Nazis. In the hours prior to the assault Eisenhower wrote a press release that he would use in the event of the invasion's failure. It read: "Our landings have failed…and I have withdrawn the troops. My decision to attack at this time and this place was based on the best information available. The troops, the Air Force and the Navy did all that bravery and devotion to duty could do. If any blame or fault attaches to this attempt, it is mine alone." If you want others to trust you, to give you greater opportunities and resources, to partner with you—then embrace responsibility and practice it faithfully in *every* area of your life!

TAKING RESPONSIBILITY (4)

I have a great sense of obligation.
ROMANS 1:14 NLT

Taking responsibility means giving back what was given to you. Paul focused on: (a) making Christ known; (b) building a church that would continue to make Christ known. And he took his responsibility seriously: "I have a great sense of obligation to people in both the civilized world and the rest of the world...to preach the Good News" (vv. 14-15 NLT). That's called "living beyond yourself!" *Self-serving* people regard their talents and resources as something they own. *Serving* people see themselves as executors of God's estate; they know they don't own it, they just administer it for Him.

After his time in Nazi concentration camps, Elie Wiesel lived for one thing—to give back to others. He taught as a professor at Boston University, and traveled extensively, sharing the wisdom gained from his life experiences. A question he often asked young people was, "How will you cope with the privileges and obligations society will feel entitled to place on you?" As he tried to guide them, he shared his sense of responsibility: "What I receive I must pass on to others. The knowledge that I have must not remain imprisoned in my brain. I owe it to many men and women to do something with it. I feel the need to pay back what was given to me. Call it gratitude...To learn means to accept that life did not begin at my birth. Others have been there before me, and I walk in their footsteps."

Your life is a story. Each day you get to write a new page. So fill those pages with responsibility to God, to others, and to yourself. If you do, in the end you will not be disappointed.

WALKING IN HUMILITY

Walk...with all lowliness and meekness.
EPHESIANS 4:1-2

Think carefully about the words "walking with God." *Whose* company are you in? God's! Can you think of a higher calling? Yet, the higher your calling, the lower you must become in your own eyes. Paul had one of the greatest callings the world has ever known. Can you imagine the world without his Epistles? We would know far less about how the church is to function, or how to walk out our faith each day. Yet Paul said of himself, "Christ Jesus came into the world to save sinners; of whom I am chief" (1Ti 1:15). If you believe God has called you to greatness, your response to that call should be to fall on your face before Him. That's how every great man and woman of God in Scripture responded. When an angel of the Lord appeared to Zacharias telling him he would have a son named John, Zacharias hit the floor and didn't move, to the point that people wondered if he was dead. The prophet Ezekiel said that in the presence of the Lord and at the vision God gave him, he collapsed on the floor. God had to tell him to get up, saying, "Son of man, stand upon thy feet, and I will speak unto thee" (Eze 2:1). When John the Revelator saw Jesus standing in the midst of the seven churches, he wrote: "And when I saw him, I fell at his feet as dead" (Rev 1:17). Those who exalt themselves are humbled by the Lord. Those who humble themselves before the Lord are those whom the Lord raises up. Humility doesn't mean thinking less of yourself, it just means thinking of yourself less.

THE SPIRIT OF CALEB

My servant Caleb has a different spirit.
NUMBERS 14:24 NIV

Caleb wasn't into "safe living." As a young man he came back from the Promised Land, stood with the minority and announced, "With God on our side we'll take it!" At eighty-five, he was still slaying giants and claiming mountains. That's because he had "a different spirit." He wasn't a "go with the flow and expect the status quo" guy. Richard Edler writes: "Safe living generally makes for regrets later on. We are all given talents and dreams. Sometimes the two don't seem to match. But usually we compromise both before ever finding out. Later on, we find ourselves looking back longingly to that time when we should have chased our *true* dreams and our *true* talents for all they were worth. Don't let yourself be pressured into thinking that your dreams or your talents aren't prudent. They were never meant to be prudent. They were meant to bring joy and fulfillment into your life." If a caterpillar refuses to get into its cocoon it'll never transform and will be forever relegated to crawling on the ground, even though it had the potential to fly.

What do you believe God's called you to do? Do it! God's not limited by your IQ, He's limited by your "I can't." The poet said: "If you think you are beaten, you are. If you think you dare not, you don't. If you'd like to win but you think you can't, it's almost certain you won't. Life's battles don't always go to the stronger or faster man, but sooner or later the man who wins, is the man who believes he can." The spirit of Caleb is the "can do" spirit! Have you got it?

DON'T MISS THE BOAT!

Then he got into the boat
and his disciples followed him.
MATTHEW 8:23 NIV

There are "destiny moments" when you have to make life-changing choices. One day Jesus invited two people to join His team, but they both had their reasons for putting it off. One had a funeral to attend, another wanted to go home to explain his decision. That's the last we hear of them. Matthew records, "Then [Jesus] got into the boat and his disciples followed him." And those two missed the boat!

You'll never be successful if you're forever putting things off. If you take too long to make up your mind about an opportunity, you'll miss out on seizing it. One of the best illustrations of this is the story about the patent of the telephone. In the 1870s two men worked extensively on modifying and improving telegraphy, which was the current technology. Both had ideas for transmitting sound by wire, and both explored the transmission of the human voice electronically. What's remarkable is that both men—Alexander Graham Bell and Elisha Gray—filed their idea at the patent office on the same day, February 14, 1876. Bell was the fifth person that day who filed for a patent. Gray, on the other hand, got busy with other things so he sent his attorney. Unfortunately the attorney arrived more than an hour after Bell, to apply for a caveat, a kind of declaration of intention to file for a patent. Those minutes cost Gray a fortune. Bell's claim was upheld in court, even though Gray complained that he had come up with the idea first. So it's not enough to see your God-given opportunities, you have to seize them. In other words—don't miss the boat!

DON'T SETTLE FOR A "B"

I can do everything through him who gives me strength.
PHILIPPIANS 4:13 NIV

Harvey MacKay tells the story of a professor who stood before his class of thirty senior molecular biology students. Before passing out the final exam he said: "I have been privileged to be your instructor this semester, and I know how hard you have worked to prepare for this test. I also know most of you are off to medical school or graduate school next fall. I am well aware of how much pressure you are under to keep your grade point averages up. Because I am confident that you know this material, I am prepared to offer an automatic B to anyone who opts to skip taking the final exam." The relief was audible. A number of students jumped up from their desks, thanking the professor for the lifeline he had thrown them. "Any other takers?" he asked. "This is your last opportunity." One more student decided to go. The instructor then handed out the final exam, which consisted of two sentences. It read: "Congratulations, you have just received an A in this class. Keep believing in yourself." It was a just reward for the students who had worked hard and believed in themselves.

The apostle Paul experienced more headaches and heartaches in a month than most of us will see in a lifetime. Yet he wrote: "I can do everything through him who gives me strength." Come on, start believing in yourself, in the Christ who lives within you, in the gifts He's placed at your disposal, and the destiny to which He's called you. Refuse to settle for a B when God has promised and called you to an A.

SOMETIMES IT'S WISE TO COMPROMISE

Honor one another above yourselves.

ROMANS 12:10 NIV

Compromise is not always bad. Obviously there are moral and ethical standards taught in Scripture that leave no room whatsoever for compromise. But compromise is much broader than that. Sometimes it's wise to compromise. Without compromise, disagreements cannot be settled, so negotiations grind to a halt. A good marriage is maintained and strengthened by compromise. Moms and dads who give their children no wiggle room are asking for trouble when teenage years surface. Siblings who do not compromise, fight. Nations with differing ideologies that refuse to listen to each other and won't compromise at various points, go to war.

Are we saying this is easy? Or free from risk? Or that it comes naturally? No. It's much easier (and safer) to stand your ground, to keep on believing that your way is the only way to go and that your plan is the only plan to follow. One major problem, however, is that you wind up narrow-minded and alone, or surrounded by a few non-thinkers. That may be safe, but it isn't very satisfying.

While pursuing true character, don't miss wise compromise. Give your heart permission to flex! Be tolerant of those who don't think like you, don't dress like you, don't care about the things you care about, and don't vote like you. Be tolerant of those whose fine points of theology differ from yours, whose worship style is different. Be tolerant of the young if you are older, and tolerant of the older if you are young. Jesus wanted His followers to be people of simple faith, modeled in grace, based on truth. It's what Paul meant when he wrote: "Honor one another above yourselves."

"NEVERTHELESS..."

Nevertheless David took the stronghold of Zion.

2 SAMUEL 5:7 NKJV

When David spied out Jerusalem in 1000 BC, it was a forbidding fortress inhabited by an old enemy who declared, "You'll never get in here...Even the blind and lame could keep you out!" (v. 6 NLT). End of story? No, just the beginning! The walls were high, the enemy daunting and the voices intimidating, "Nevertheless David took the stronghold...dwelt in [it]... and called it the City of David" (vv. 7-9 NKJV). Now *that's* what you call turning the tables!

What's *your* stronghold, the one area where Satan's strong enough to hold you? A sharp tongue? A judgmental attitude? Low self-esteem? A losing battle with a stubborn habit? When the enemy says, "You're stuck, you'll never get out," God says, "*Nevertheless* [even so...despite how it looks on the surface]." Strongholds mean nothing to God; His "mighty weapons... knock down the devil's strongholds" (2Co 10:4 TLB). And He will do for you what He did for David once you understand two important principles: (1) There are two voices continually competing for your attention. One says, "You can do it; don't give up!" The other says, "It's hopeless; you'll never make it!" Follow David and practice selective hearing. Tune out the voices that taunt you from your stronghold. Instead of dialoging with the Devil, say what Jesus said: "Get thee behind me, Satan" (Mt 16:23). (2) Look through eyes of faith. Where others saw walls, David saw tunnels; they focused on the problems while he looked for the possibilities. And because he did what nobody expected, he accomplished what nobody envisioned—and with God's help you can too.

ROOTS OF REJECTION

Rooted deep...and founded securely on [God's] love.
EPHESIANS 3:17 AMP

Are you struggling with *rejection?* When your roots spring from the soil of rejection, it's like living in a house with a faulty foundation; every storm brings new problems. You can employ all kinds of tricks from people-pleasing to workaholism to make yourself feel better, but without a healthy root system nothing works. Flawed roots always produce flawed fruit. And your roots were diseased long before you started producing such fruit. What's the answer? Being "rooted deep...and founded securely on [God's] love." God wants to pick you up, shake off the old soil and replant you securely in His love and acceptance. And He doesn't just replant you, He "re-parents" you. That means you no longer draw your self-worth from your family of origin. "Now are we the sons of God" (1Jn 3:2). But remember, it's a process. Strong roots require three things: *(1) Time to develop.* Becoming confident in your identity as God's child is like breaking in new shoes. You must walk in them till they become comfortable. *(2) Protection from predators and harsh elements that can kill.* You need to surround yourself with people who "have obtained like precious faith" (2Pe 1:1). Christian fellowship is your protective shield! *(3) Being fed and watered regularly.* Once-a-week in church won't cut it; you must learn to feed yourself regularly on God's Word!

The cure for rejection is—being able to see yourself as God sees you. It means announcing, "I am what God says I am, I have what God says I have, therefore I can do what God says I can do." So even if you didn't get off to a great start, you can still have a great finish!

YOU HAVE ACCESS TO GOD

Let's walk right up to him
and get what he is so ready to give.

HEBREWS 4:16 TM

If you've been to an amusement park you know that it's designed to transport you to another world. The goal of the entire experience is to help you lose yourself in its joy and excitement. In prayer, we're transported to another world. Now, a theme park is all make-believe; you have to leave it and come back to the real world. But there is no make-believe with prayer. It takes us into the heavenly realm where Jesus is sitting at the right hand of God. It positions us to hear from God. Hear what? Hear God's voice applying His Word to our specific needs and circumstances. But let's admit it, prayer can be hard work; it requires discipline. It's not as easy as running around having fun at an amusement park. All of us know what it's like to get down on our knees with the best of intentions, and either fall asleep, run out of things to say, or find our minds wandering after just a few minutes.

"Prayer changes things," as the old saying goes, but it first has to change *us:* to turn us from a self-focus to a God-focus so we can understand and do His will. The writer to the Hebrews puts it this way: "We don't have a priest who is out of touch with our reality. He's been through weakness and testing, experienced it all—all but the sin. So let's walk right up to him and get what he is so ready to give. Take the mercy, accept the help" (vv. 14-16 TM). Today you have access to God through prayer. Use it!

STOP WORRYING!

It begins and ends with faith...
those who are right with God...live by faith.
ROMANS 1:17 NCV

A man who maintained he'd swallowed a horse was referred to a psychiatrist, who recommended surgery. The surgeon agreed to bring a horse into the operating room so that when the man woke up he'd know the operation was a success. But after regaining consciousness the man opened his eyes and announced, "That's the wrong horse. It's white. The one I swallowed was black!" Too much anxiety and not enough reality—it's why Christ talks to us so much about worry (which means to be *divided* or *distracted*). Understand this. Worry:

(a) Wastes your time and energy. Jesus said, "Who of you by worrying can add a single hour to his life?" (Mt 6:27 NIV). It's a medically proven fact that worry won't lengthen or enrich your life, but it can shorten it. *(b) Stops you from enjoying what you have.* How? By creating burdens God never intended you to carry—because they're His. *(c) Makes you feel less-than.* Jesus pointed out that you're worth much more than the birds of the air, and they don't worry or die from hunger; they simply enjoy life. Come on, if God takes care of them, don't you think He'll take care of you too? *(d) Makes you overlook God's promises.* "If God didn't hesitate to put everything on the line... by sending his...Son, is there anything else he wouldn't...do for us?" (Ro 8:32 TM). Note the word "anything." That covers whatever you're going through right now, plus whatever comes up in the future. So stop worrying.

FINANCIAL AMNESIA

Remember...the Lord...gives you power to become rich.
DEUTERONOMY 8:18 TLB

Can God trust you with money? Do you have the courage to thank Him publicly for what He's given you? Ever noticed how some of us who praised Him when we had very little, suddenly become "image conscious" when we start to prosper? We call on God when we're in trouble, but when we get back on our feet we stop counting our blessings and start counting our money. What's happened? We've become so self-sufficient that we're reluctant to mention the name of Jesus when we talk about our blessings! Israel's financial amnesia was nothing new; it happens once you start believing "it was [my] own power and might that made [me] wealthy" (v. 17 TLB).

Never get so dazzled by success that you forget the source of everything you have, or become so caught up in your blessings that you fail to acknowledge the One who blessed you. God told the Israelites: "When you have become...prosperous ...built fine homes...and your silver and gold have multiplied... don't become proud and forget the Lord...who brought you out of...slavery" (vv. 12-14 TLB). God doesn't condemn success, He condemns arrogance! When you've had very little and suddenly enter the "Promised Land," it's easy to forget where you came from. A few gourmet meals, a designer suit and a house in "the right neighborhood" can make you forget about yesterday's hand-me-downs! God *constantly* had to remind His people not to overlook His goodness to them. And the same applies to us. "Remember...the Lord...gives you power to become rich, and...just as [He]...caused other nations in the past to perish...That will be your fate...if you don't obey...God" (vv. 18-20 TLB). Bottom line—you don't have *anything* God didn't give you!

LEARN TO WORK WITH OTHERS (1)

We rebuilt the wall.

NEHEMIAH 4:6 NIV

When Nehemiah talks about *himself,* he talks openly and honestly about crying over the ruins of Jerusalem, praying for guidance, and the days when he wondered how he'd survive. But when it came to the amazing feat of rebuilding the walls of Jerusalem in a record fifty-two days, he gives the credit to *others.* "We rebuilt the wall...for the people worked with all their heart." There's no limit to what can be done—when nobody cares who gets the credit.

In recent years Bono has expanded his efforts beyond the world of music and has become a passionate advocate for the helpless and downtrodden. Interestingly, he's a Bible reader, and he's learned to partner with others to further his cause. He has met with heads of state, economists, industry leaders, celebrities—anyone who has the potential to help the people he's trying to reach. Where did Bono learn to rely on others, to be part of a team and enlist the aid of others? Rock stars are usually seen as self-absorbed, isolated, and indifferent to others. It's the reason many music groups don't stay together. Bono comments: "There are moments when people are so lost in themselves and the demands of their own life, that it's very hard to be in a band... people want to be lords of their own domain. I mean, everybody, as they get older...rids the room of argument. You see it in your family, you see it with your friends. They get a smaller and smaller circle of people around them who agree with them. And life ends up with a dull sweetness." Bottom line: if you want to succeed, learn to work with others.

LEARN TO WORK WITH OTHERS (2)

My co-workers in the ministry.

ROMANS 16:3 NLT

God works with people—who know how to work with people! Not "users" who burn through them and discard them. Not "prima donnas" who manipulate them for their own purposes. Not "ranch bosses" who herd them around like cattle. No, God works with people who honor people; who recognize and develop the talent in them, honor and reward them appropriately, encourage them to rise to their full potential, and when the day comes, send them off blessed and better prepared for their next assignment.

It's healthy to stop and reflect with gratitude on those who got you to where you are today; to remind yourself you're not a sole trader; that you'll need people to help you fulfill God's purpose for your life and get you to where you need to go next. Paul dedicates an entire chapter to such people: "Give my greetings to Priscilla and Aquila, my co-workers in the ministry...In fact, they once risked their lives for me. I am thankful to them, and so are all the Gentile churches...Greet my dear friend Epenetus. He was the first person from the province of Asia to become a follower of Christ. Give my greetings to Mary, who has worked so hard for your benefit. Greet Andronicus and Junia, my fellow Jews, who were in prison with me. They are highly respected among the apostles and became followers of Christ before I did. Greet Ampliatus, my dear friend in the Lord. Greet Urbanus, our co-worker in Christ, and my dear friend Stachys. Greet Apellas, a good man whom Christ approves... and all the believers who meet with them" (vv. 3-15 NLT). Bottom line—open up, reach out, sharpen your people skills!

LEARN TO WORK WITH OTHERS (3)

Thus far has the Lord helped us.

1 SAMUEL 7:12 NIV

It was a dream come true. The Ark of the Covenant, the ultimate symbol of God working among His people, had been brought back from captivity, and the Philistines who took it, defeated in battle. It was a time to celebrate. So Samuel erected a monument called Ebenezer, meaning "The Lord helped us." Note the word "us." Samuel recognized that to fulfill a dream you need a team!

In his book *Jesus on Leadership*, C. Gene Wilkes describes why teamwork is superior to individual effort: (a) Teams involve more people, thus affording more resources, ideas and energy than any one individual possesses. (b) Teams maximize a leader's potential and minimize his or her weaknesses. Strengths and weaknesses are more exposed in individuals. (c) Teams provide multiple perspectives on how to meet a need or reach a goal, thus devising several alternatives to each situation. Individual insight is seldom as broad and deep as a group's when it takes on a problem. (d) Teams share the credit for victories and the blame for losses. This fosters genuine humility and strong bonds. When individuals take the credit or the blame alone, it tends to foster pride, and sometimes a sense of failure. (e) Teams keep leaders accountable. Individuals connected to no one can jeopardize or change the goal without accountability. So why are we reluctant to engage in teamwork? Because team-building is tough, and the more talented the team members, the tougher it is. The true measure of a leader is not getting people to work; neither is it getting them to work hard. The true measure of a leader is getting people to work hard *together!*

DEPEND ON GOD

Jacob was left alone.
GENESIS 32:24

Like Jacob, many of us know how it feels to be "left alone." When a loved one dies or a friend leaves, or you walk through the fire of separation and divorce, no matter how "spiritual" you are it still hurts! Emotional pain is to the soul what physical pain is to the body; it tells you something's wrong, that you need God to guide you through the challenges and upheavals of realigning your life to cope with what has happened. And the struggle doesn't begin in earnest while you're surrounded by people, it starts when you've been left alone. The fact is you can survive without others, but you can't survive without God. That's why He sometimes strips away everything that makes us dependent on people. He sends certain individuals into your life to help build your faith and develop your character, and when they're gone, to leave you with the assurance that God's in control. The loss of loved ones: (a) develops our spiritual muscle; (b) tests our resilience; (c) shows us the scope of God's power. When Moses died and Joshua was left in charge, God told him, "As I was with Moses, so I will be with thee" (Jos 1:5). That's something Joshua could never have learned while Moses was in the picture. And it's a lesson you can't learn while you're looking to other human beings for all your answers.

In Mark 4:39 when Jesus "ordered the wind and waves to be quiet" the Bible says "everything was calm" (CEV). In the midst of the storm, ask Him to come and stand in the bow of *your* boat, and to speak peace to the thing that's upsetting you. He'll do it!

DON'T JUST SAY IT, ENFORCE IT!

Those whom the Lord loves He disciplines.

HEBREWS 12:6 NAS

The Bible asks: "What kind of father is it who doesn't correct his son?" Answer: "Not much of a father!"

We don't know if that's how Eli, the High Priest, got started with Hophni and Phinehas, his two sons. We simply read: "His sons made themselves vile, and he did not restrain them" (1Sa 3:13 NKJV). Perhaps Eli heard about the terrible things his sons were doing and said, "Now, boys, you know you shouldn't do that." And the boys said, "Yes, Daddy," then went right back to defrauding the worshippers who came to the temple and seducing the women. The issue wasn't that Eli didn't *tell* his children the right things, it's that he didn't *enforce* what he was telling them. No doubt you don't know of any parents who tell their kids, "Go rob a bank; ten or twenty years in prison will do you good." No, those parents probably said all the right things. A lot of prison inmates' parents said the right things too. But what's missing in so much well-intentioned parenting is enforcement. Eli was not enforcing the truth, he was only stating it. He didn't pull his boys from their posts and strip them of their privileges. He let them keep doing it—while telling them they ought not to do it. Parent, don't just say something—do something! If your children are going astray and you keep quiet, you're sparing yourself and sacrificing them. The most caring thing you can do as a parent is to discipline your children in love.

THE POWER OF ENCOURAGEMENT (1)

Pleasant words are...health to the bones.
PROVERBS 16:24 NKJV

Everybody needs encouragement. None of us achieves anything without help. The great achievers in history became all that they were because of the people in their lives.

We've seen *The Chronicles of Narnia* and *The Lord of the Rings*. But did you know that their authors, C. S. Lewis and J. R. R. Tolkien, were professors at Oxford University and maintained a close friendship? Every week they'd meet to eat, talk about their fiction-writing endeavors and read passages of their yet unpublished works. It was Tolkien who encouraged Lewis, an avowed atheist, to explore Christianity, ultimately leading to his conversion. And it was Lewis who encouraged Tolkien to continue writing fiction and to seek publication. Were it not for their friendship and mutual encouragement, the world wouldn't have received the finest writing in apologetics of the twentieth century, nor one of the finest fantasy works ever written.

Everyone—young and old, successful and less-than-successful, famous and unknown—who receives encouragement is changed by it. Mark Twain said, "One compliment can keep me going for a whole month." A word of encouragement from a teacher can change a child's life. A word of encouragement from a spouse can strengthen or even save a marriage. A word of encouragement from a leader can inspire a person to reach his or her potential. Zig Ziglar says, "You never know when a moment and a few sincere words can have an impact on a life." The Bible says, "Pleasant words are like a honeycomb, sweetness to the soul and health to the bones."

THE POWER OF ENCOURAGEMENT (2)

Pleasant words are...health to the bones.

PROVERBS 16:24 NKJV

Goethe said: "Treat a man as he appears to be, and you make him worse. But treat a man as if he already were what he potentially *could* be, and you make him what he *should* be."

One day a principal called in three teachers and said, "You three are the finest in the system, so we're giving you ninety high-IQ students to see what you can do with them." Those students achieved *30 percent more* than the other students in the school. At the end of the year the principal called the three teachers in and said, "I've a confession to make. You didn't have ninety of the most promising students; they were run-of-the-mill. We picked them at random and gave them to you." The teachers naturally concluded that their exceptional teaching skills must have been responsible for the students' great progress. "I've another confession," said the principal. "You're not the brightest teachers; your names were the first three drawn out of the hat." So, why did those students and teachers perform at such a level? *Because they were encouraged to believe they could!* Baseball star Reggie Jackson said, "I'll tell you what makes a great manager; a great manager has a knack for making ball-players think they are better than they are. He forces you to have a good opinion of yourself. He lets you know he believes in you. He makes you get more out of yourself. And once you learn how good you really are, you'll never settle for playing anything less than your very best." Today, go out and encourage somebody!

COMFORT IN TROUBLED TIMES

God will help her at break of day.

PSALM 46:5 NIV

When your world is suddenly turned upside down, remember, God's plans for your life haven't been canceled! When you feel trapped with no way out, here are some things to remember:

(1) Look for the river. "There is a river whose streams make glad" (v. 4 NIV). In Old Testament symbolism, rivers represent God's supply for your every need. When every human source of supply seems to have dried up, don't fear, look for the river. *(2) Look for the city.* God has planted His "city…the holy place where the Most High dwells" (v. 4 NIV), right in the middle of your circumstances. God's city, the symbol of His presence and power, guarantees He's still in control and that He will restore peace and order to your troubled world. *(3) Look for the signs of God's presence.* "God will help [you] at break of day" (v. 5 NIV). Daybreak, a symbol of new beginnings, gives you confidence that beyond this time of trouble and testing, a new day is at hand. "Great is his faithfulness; his mercies begin afresh each morning" (La 3:23 NLT). *(4) Look at God's track record.* "Come…see the works of the Lord" (Ps 46:8 NIV). Reviewing the record of His mighty acts builds your faith and reminds you that He is the "same yesterday and today and forever" (Heb 13:8 NIV). If He took care of you then, He will take care of you now. *(5) Look to God and be at peace.* Based on the tested and proven foundation of His power and faithfulness, you can live by the Scripture: "Be still, and know that I am God" (Ps 46:10 NIV).

THE GREAT EXCHANGE

God made him...to be sin for us.

2 CORINTHIANS 5:21 NIV

The Bible says: (1) "You must not steal" (Ex 20:15 TLB). Ever stolen anything? A paper clip, a parking space, the credit for someone else's idea? (2) "You must not lie" (v. 16 TLB). You say you haven't—you just did. (3) "You must not commit adultery" (v. 14 TLB). Jesus said if you look at someone with lust, you've committed adultery in your heart (See Mt 5:28)—ouch! (4) "You must not murder" (Ex 20:13 TLB). Before you claim innocence, remember that Jesus equates anger with murder. "Anyone who is so much as angry with a brother or sister is guilty of murder" (Mt 5:22 TM). We assassinate a dozen drivers on our way to work every morning. Bad news: on your best day, you still fall far short of the divine standard required to get into heaven. Good news: "The Lord has put on him the punishment for all the evil we have done" (See Isa 53:5). A Chinese convert to Christianity understood this. Before her baptism the pastor asked her a question to ensure she understood the meaning of the cross: "Did Jesus have any sin?" "Yes," she replied. Troubled, he repeated the question. "Yes, He had sin," she answered again. The pastor set out to correct her, but she insisted, "He had mine." And she was right! "God made him who had no sin to be sin for us, so that in him we might become [righteous in God's eyes]." This is the great exchange. The holy and the vile change places. God makes right what was wrong, and straight what was crooked. Aren't you glad?

"RICH TOWARDS GOD"

Rich towards God.

LUKE 12:21

We're supposed to offer God our acts of service, but the gift He desires most is *us*. Think of Jesus' last conversation with His friend Peter. Peter was so human: he followed Jesus, learned from Him, served Him, doubted Him, misunderstood Him, praised Him, and denied Him. Yet Jesus' final question to His friend was relational: "Peter, do you love Me?" Three times He asked Peter that question. St. Augustine said all ethics could be summed up in this: "Love God, and do what you will," for when you love God you'll want to do what God loves. Though flawed like the Psalmist, you can say, "I delight to do Your will, O my God" (Ps 40:8 NKJV).

God created us so that He could be with us. In Eden He came and walked with the man and woman He had made, just to be with them. When He formed the nation of Israel He said, "I will walk among you and be your God" (Lev 26:12 NKJV). Heaven announced the birth of Jesus, saying, "Immanuel" which means "God with us" (See Mt 1:23). It's as if God says each morning, "I'd like to spend this day with you." One author writes: "I can't make myself love God, but I can come to know Him better. And because God is love, the more I come to know Him, the more my love for Him will grow. Love is a by-product of knowing. So I can spend this day loving God. And tomorrow I can seek to love Him a little more." That's what it means to be "rich towards God."

YOU CAN REKINDLE THAT FLAME!

Husbands, love your wives.

EPHESIANS 5:25 NAS

When you care more about pleasing yourself than pleasing your mate, your marriage is in trouble. Most marriages fail for one reason—selfishness. "Just give me a few more months. I'll have this project at work behind me and things will get back to normal." How many wives have heard this from their husband when they try to let him know they need more of his time and attention? And what happens? The project gets finished and he gets involved in something else just as demanding. Because her needs keep going unmet, hopelessness and resentment set in and she forms a protective shell. Often at this point the husband is clueless. He says things like, "I work hard. I bring my money home. I'm not running around on you." And then the big one: "I'm doing all this for *you.*" But his wife didn't marry a business or a paycheck, she married *him.* And there is absolutely nothing he can do to replace himself in her life, no matter what he gives her. That's why when many couples had less, they had *everything* because they had each other. Now they have everything, but they have *nothing.* Once that hard shell forms it's hard to penetrate. And worse, the statistics of divorce prove that very few men have the patience to do it. That's when they get attracted to other women. But the flame of love can melt that hard shell. If you start where you are and commit yourself to loving your wife [or husband] all over again, God will help you to rekindle that flame.

"BATHSHEBA-GATE"

Then it happened.

2 SAMUEL 11:2 NKJV

David's "Bathsheba-gate" began when he let down his guard. The Bible says, "Then it happened." What an opening line! David was fifty-two. Like a lot of us in middle age, maybe he wondered, "Do I still have it?" Whatever he thought, he wasn't on guard—and the Devil knew it. David had lived victoriously for twenty years, "Then it happened." Be careful, yesterday doesn't guarantee your success today. David saw Bathsheba that night, but it's what he *didn't* see that shipwrecked him. He didn't see that his sin would cause four of his children to die (the baby, Amnon, Absalom, and Adonijah), or that it would split his kingdom in half and make him a murderer. That's the problem with sin. If you're looking at things you ought not to look at, you're not seeing the whole picture. It's what you don't see that will hurt you. So David devises plan A, plan B and plan C, to cover up his sin. Plan A was to bring Bathsheba's husband Uriah home from battle to spend the weekend with his wife, so that the baby would appear to be his. But it didn't work. Plan B, getting him drunk and trying to send him home, didn't work either. Plan C wasn't so tame. It was murder. Tragically, this plan worked. "I'd never do that," you say. You'd be amazed what you'd do in a moment of weakness! The fire of sex is meant for the fireplace of marriage. Once it leaves there, somebody's going to get burned. Bottom line: "Let him who thinks he stands take heed lest he fall" (1Co 10:12 NKJV).

ELEVENTH HOUR GRACE

I wish to give to this last man the same as to you.
MATTHEW 20:14 NKJV

Jesus told the story of a farmer who hired day laborers: Some at 6 a.m., some at 9 a.m., some at 12 noon, some at 3 p.m. and some at 5 p.m., one hour before quitting time. Amazingly, he paid them all the same wage. When the complaints started flying, the farmer said, "I wish to give to this last man the same as to you." You say, "Nobody pays a day's wage to one-hour workers." God does. Deathbed converts and lifelong saints enter heaven by the same gate. They don't enjoy the same reward, but they're saved by the same grace. A last minute confessor receives the same grace as a lifetime servant? It doesn't seem fair. The workers in Jesus' story complained too. So the farmer explained the prerogative of ownership: "Am I not allowed to do what I choose with what belongs to me?" (v. 15 RSV). The thief on the cross proves that when you request grace with your dying breath, God answers your prayer. The Prodigal Son "wasted his possessions" (Lk 15:13 NKJV). The Greek word for "wasted" pictures a farmer throwing handfuls of seed into the ground. Imagine the Prodigal Son spurning his father's kindness, going out and "throwing it all away." But he returned. And when he did "his father saw him and had compassion, and ran and fell on his neck and kissed him" (v. 20 NKJV). The Father was saving the son's place. And He's saving yours too. Eleventh hour grace means that if you're able to read these words and respond, it's not too late.

"I NEVER REGRETTED IT"

I thank my God upon every remembrance of you.
PHILIPPIANS 1:3 NKJV

Paul knew that he couldn't do the job alone, so he didn't even bother to try. In his writings he acknowledged those who worked alongside him: "I thank my God upon every remembrance of you...for your fellowship in the gospel from the first day until now." Andrew Carnegie said: "It marks a big step in your development, when you realize that other people can help you do a better job than you can do by yourself."

A key player in the Billy Graham Association was his childhood friend, Grady Wilson. In 1948 Billy asked Grady to come and work with him. At first Grady said no, but Billy persisted: "God has told me you're to come and work with me. I need an evangelist; somebody who knows me and my ministry, somebody I can trust." Wilson later recalled, "I didn't want to come; I already had a successful ministry of my own holding citywide crusades." But after praying, he made the decision to follow Billy Graham (and God). He set aside his dreams to be part of another man's. That decision made a huge difference not only in his own life, but in the lives of multitudes they reached and won for Christ until Grady Wilson's death.

Sometimes God will ask you to give up your dream to be part of another person's dream. It takes courage and humility to do that. But look at the results. Heaven alone knows the impact Grady Wilson and Billy Graham had together. And what was Wilson's take on it? "I never regretted it!"

GET TO KNOW GOD BETTER

Can you discover the depths of God?

JOB 11:7 NAS

You're on the adventure of a lifetime when you pursue a greater knowledge of God. What you've learned about God so far should give you a hunger to know Him even more. You must never be satisfied with what you know about Him already. Here are four practical benefits of knowing God:

(1) Blessing. The more you know God and obey His will, the more you'll experience His blessing. "If you obey all the decrees and commands I am giving you today, all will be well with you and your children" (Dt 4:40 NLT). *(2) Peace.* "Grace and peace be multiplied to you in the knowledge of God" (2Pe 1:2 NAS). The more you know God, the more at peace you'll be. Yes, struggles and setbacks will come, but even then you'll have a sense of wellbeing because you'll feel His nearness. *(3) Wisdom.* Paul prayed that God would give the Ephesians "a spirit of wisdom and of revelation in the knowledge of Him" (Eph 1:17 NAS). Wisdom is seeing things the right way. Revelation is when God bypasses the limitations of your mind and shows you things you otherwise wouldn't know. Instead of finding a solution to life's problems every now and then, you can walk each day in a "spirit of wisdom and of revelation." *(4) Freedom.* "When you did not know God, you were slaves to those which by nature are no gods" (Gal 4:8 NAS). Without the confidence that comes from knowing God, and your standing before Him, you become a slave to circumstances, emotions, or other people's opinions. Refuse to live that way. Instead, get to know God better.

SIX PRINCIPLES TO LIVE BY

Get understanding.

PROVERBS 4:7 NKJV

Incorporate these six principles into your life: *(1) Don't worry, when you're doing your best.* God accepts no less, but He demands no more. "Trust in the Lord, and do good...and He shall give you the desires of your heart!" (Ps 37:3-4 NKJV). *(2) Don't hurry, when success depends on accuracy.* "Good planning and hard work lead to prosperity, but hasty shortcuts lead to poverty" (Pr 21:5 NLT). *(3) Don't form conclusions until you have all the facts.* Everyone you meet has unmet needs, unhealed wounds and unfulfilled hopes. If you want people to evaluate you by your best qualities rather than your worst, "Do to others as you would like them to do to you" (Lk 6:31 NLT). *(4) Don't believe a thing is impossible without trying it.* When you are in God's will, doing things God's way, sensitive to His timing and willing to persevere, your problems are just a platform for Him to work on your behalf (See Ro 8:28). *(5) Don't waste your time on trivial matters.* In order to put first things first, you must ask yourself, "What is it that only I can do, or do best?" Only when you've answered that question will you know what you should do. *(6) Don't think that good intentions are an acceptable excuse for doing nothing.* Examine your life; are you a "talker" or a "doer?" Get specific about your diet and your devotions, your finances and your family, etc. Write these words on a card and read them regularly: "If it's to be, it's up to me." James writes: "Faith by itself, if it does not have works, is dead" (Jas 2:17 NKJV).

KEEP PREPARING YOURSELF

I have seen [the] son of Jesse...who is skillful.
1 SAMUEL 16:18 NKJV

David didn't suddenly become an expert marksman with a slingshot when Goliath showed up, or a master harpist when King Saul invited him to the palace. He took the long, slow, disciplined route. David had no idea what his future held, he simply found joy and fulfillment in discovering and developing his gifts. Your greatest obstacle to personal growth isn't ignorance, it's the illusion of knowledge. It's in believing you've "arrived." When that happens you're done growing, which means—you're done! Which zone do you live in? *The challenge zone:* "I attempt to do what I haven't done before." *The comfort zone:* "I only do what I already know I can do." *The coasting zone:* "I don't even do what I've done before." Phillips Brooks said: "Sad is the day for any man when he becomes absolutely satisfied with the life he is living, the thoughts he is thinking, and the things he is doing; when there ceases to be forever beating at the doors of his soul a desire to do something larger which he seeks and knows he was meant and intended to do."

David's brothers knew his skills, yet none of them told King Saul about him. Be encouraged; you'll get there without them! "Then one of [Saul's] servants...said, 'Look, I have seen [the] son of Jesse...who is skillful in playing, a mighty man of valor.'" David didn't compete with his brothers or complain about his status as a sheepherder. He just kept developing his relationship with God and sharpening his skills, and when the time was right God promoted him. So, keep preparing yourself.

TOO PERFECT FOR THEIR OWN GOOD (1)

Train up a child in the way he should go.
PROVERBS 22:6

Do you have a child who has to do everything perfectly? They're only happy in school when they get an "A." A "B" depresses them. Driven by their own impossible standards they never feel "good enough." Parent, here are ten traits to help you identify and deal with the perfectionist child: (1) They may over-function in pursuit of perfect results, becoming mislabeled as a young workaholic. (2) They may under-function to avoid the pain of anticipated failure, getting mislabeled as lazy. (3) They may avoid social contact to keep others from discovering their imperfections. (4) When they "ace" an assignment, they can't enjoy their success for worrying about failing their next one. (5) Fearing failure, they hesitate to try new things. (6) They over-focus on their mistakes. (7) They procrastinate, under-achieve, leave work unfinished or quit before completion to evade failing. (8) To prevent criticism from others they'll do almost anything including lie, rationalize, excuse themselves and blame others. (9) They're often anxious and worried, anticipating the worst. (10) They may be subject to physical complaints like frequent headaches, stomach upsets, fatigue, eating problems, etc.

Children don't automatically know how to behave. Without your help their perfectionism can intensify, dominating them and diminishing the quality of their life. Parent, you are called and empowered by God to: "Train up your child in the way [they] should go and when they are older," it'll stick with them. God promises: "If any (parent) lacks wisdom...ask God ...and it will be given" (Jas 1:5 NIV). Talk to God; He knows about parenting!

TOO PERFECT FOR THEIR OWN GOOD (2)

Train up a child in the way he should go.

PROVERBS 22:6

The words "the way he should go" mean: "The way best suited to your child's unique make-up, abilities, and God-given personality." Perfectionism violates these characteristics, encouraging your child to be something they weren't intended to be in order to gain approval. To help your child overcome this: (1) Convince them that they're valuable to God and you because of who they *are,* not because of what they accomplish. (2) Help them to understand that it's impossible to complete every assignment without errors. Train them to think about mistakes as opportunities to experiment, clarify personal values, learn and improve their skills, thinking and decision-making. (3) Share with them your mistakes and poor decisions. Discuss your flaws and how you've grown through them. (4) Explain that perfectionists get "tunnel vision," locking themselves into limited and limiting options for problem-solving. Explain that there's more than one way to solve a problem, organize a project and get things done. Discuss some of these other ways as a means of expanding their perceptions and introducing greater flexibility into their life. (5) Celebrate the effort—not just the result. Praise things unrelated to achievement, such as generosity, honesty and kindness. (6) Reduce their pressure. Do they really need all those advanced courses, or to participate in every extracurricular activity? Perfectionism is "too much of a good thing." It starts early and they don't "grow out of it" naturally. Helping reduce it systematically will improve your child's quality of life.

DISCOVERING WHAT'S IN YOUR CHILD

The father of a righteous man has great joy;
he who has a wise son delights in him.

PROVERBS 23:24 NIV

Dad, read this: "For years I poked and prodded Gordon, my oldest son, to get higher grades. I was always a little disappointed in him because he never quite measured up to my standard of excellence. One day when Gordon was a senior in high school we were invited to an awards assembly. Clearly he was going to be awarded for something, but I couldn't imagine what. Had they invited us to fill seats? I thought we would have to sit here and see every student marching up the aisle, getting applause, while my son sat at the back of the room. Why didn't he try harder? My attitude grew steadily worse. Then the principal came to the microphone and announced: 'For the first time, I am presenting a special award to a young man who's been so exceptional that we couldn't overlook his accomplishments!' He called Gordon to the front, then spent several minutes describing my son's fine character, kindness toward others, trustworthiness, and quiet leadership. 'We've never had a student like Gordon in our school,' he said, 'and there may never be another. We're giving you, Gordon, the first and possibly last Principal's Cup Award for integrity, diligence and decency. Thank you for what you've brought to our school. No one who has really gotten to know you will ever be the same again.' In that moment I realized he was talking to me. I had never really gotten to know my son, much less appreciate him for who he was. And I knew that once I did, I—his father—would never be the same again."

THINKING OF QUITTING? DON'T!

Be steadfast.

1 CORINTHIANS 15:58 NKJV

George Frideric Handel was a musical prodigy. At twenty-one he was a keyboard virtuoso. When he turned to composing he gained immediate fame and soon was appointed Kapellmeister to the Elector of Hanover (later King George I of England). When Handel moved to England his renown grew. By the time he was forty he was world famous. But despite his talent and fame he faced considerable adversity. Rivalry with English composers was fierce. Audiences were fickle; sometimes they didn't turn out for his performances. He was the victim of the changing political winds. Several times he found himself on the verge of bankruptcy. His problems were compounded by failing health. He suffered a stroke which left his right arm limp and damaged the use of four fingers in his right hand. Although he recovered, it left him battling depression. Finally, at fifty-six, Handel decided it was time to retire. Discouraged, miserable and consumed with debt, he felt certain he'd land in a debtor's prison. So on April 8, 1741, he gave what he considered his farewell concert. Disappointed and filled with self-pity, he gave up. But that year something incredible happened. A wealthy friend named Charles Jennings encouraged Handel by visiting him and giving him a libretto based on the life of Christ. The work intrigued Handel so he began writing. Immediately the floodgates of inspiration opened. For three weeks he wrote almost nonstop. Then he spent another two days creating the orchestrations. In twenty-four days he had completed the 260-page manuscript of *Messiah*. Thinking of quitting? Don't! "Be steadfast."

TURN ASIDE AND LISTEN TO GOD

I must turn aside and look.

EXODUS 3:3 NRS

Moses was working his regular job as a shepherd when he walked past a burning bush, just like the ones he'd seen a hundred times before. Only this time the bush was on fire with God's presence. Moses said, "I must turn aside and look." In that moment everything depended on his willingness to interrupt his daily routine and make time for God. He could have said, "I'm busy," and kept on going. But he'd have missed his calling and the reason for his existence. He'd have missed knowing God and doing great things. But he didn't; he "turned aside." God wanted to begin a new nation, and He wanted Moses to lead it. The timing seemed strange. With God, it often does. Forty years ago Moses was young, the product of the finest education system in the world. He had powerful connections and high hopes. But now he was a nobody, a lowly shepherd in a forgotten desert, rejected by his people and a fugitive on the run. "Who am I that I should go to Pharaoh?" (v. 11 NRS), Moses asked God. "Nobody knows me. I don't speak too well. And my track record isn't too good." God said, "I know about your past, and it doesn't matter. Your failure and inadequacies are no longer the ultimate truth about you. You are what you are, but you're not yet what you will be—because I will be with you."

Do you need direction for your life? Slow down, turn aside, listen to God. What He has to say is more important than anything else you'll hear.

LIVING BY "THE FAITH RULE"

These all died in faith.

HEBREWS 11:13 NKJV

The Bible says, "These all died *in* faith, not having received the promises, but having seen them afar off were assured of them." People of faith anticipate what God promised, whether they ever experience its fulfillment or not. "How can I believe in a promise I don't see fulfilled?" you ask. People like Abraham didn't live to see the ultimate fulfillment of God's promise in their lives, yet they died believing it. Trusting God means banking on His Word, even when there's nothing visible to demonstrate that what He says is going to come true. Even when you're on your deathbed and it still hasn't happened, you still trust Him. That's living by faith. The words "in faith" in this Scripture are different from the words used in all the verses that read "by faith." The words "in faith" actually mean "according to faith." These people lived by "the faith rule." Faith was the ruling principle in their lives! So even if they went to their graves without seeing God's promises fulfilled, they exited saying, "God still told the truth." They knew that the fulfillment was coming, and they lived in anticipation of it. That's what God is asking of *you* today. He wants you to live before Him in such a way that you anticipate His promises, even when every circumstance seems opposite to what those promises say. It also means you don't manipulate the circumstances to "help God out" as Sarah did when she produced Ishmael. It means trusting God to do it His way, in His time, and for His glory.

"DOING GOOD"

Do not withhold good.
PROVERBS 3:27 NKJV

Dan Clark recalls when he was a teenager, he and his father once stood in line to buy tickets for the circus. They noticed a poor family immediately in front of them. The parents were holding hands. They had eight children, all probably under the age of twelve. He could tell that the circus was going to be a new adventure for them. The attendant asked how many tickets they wanted. The man proudly responded, "I'd like to buy eight children's tickets and two adult tickets." When the attendant quoted the price, the man's wife let go of his hand and her head drooped. The man leaned a little closer and asked, "How much did you say?" The attendant quoted the price again. The man obviously didn't have the money. He looked crushed. Clark says his father watched all this, put his hand in his pocket, pulled out a twenty-dollar bill and dropped it on the ground. His father then reached down, picked up the bill, tapped the man on the shoulder and said, "Excuse me, I think this must be yours." The man knew exactly what was going on. He looked straight into Clark's father's eyes, took his hand, shook it, and with a tear streaming down his cheek, replied, "Thank you, thank you, sir. This really means a lot to me and my family." Clark and his father went back to their car and drove home. They didn't have enough money to go to the circus that night, but it didn't matter. They'd blessed a whole family, and it was something neither family would ever forget. That's called "doing good."

DEALING WITH STRIFE

Let there be no strife between you and me.
GENESIS 13:8 NKJV

When the grazing land they shared became too small for their flocks, Abraham said to his nephew Lot, "Let there be no strife between you and me...for we are brethren." We learn two important lessons from this story:

(1) Don't wait, take the initiative. Abraham didn't say, "I'm not getting involved in this." No, he realized that left unchecked it had the potential to drive a wedge between them, so he nipped it in the bud. Hindsight may be 20/20, but foresight is what's needed to build lasting relationships. God had just told Abraham, "I will bless you and make your name great" (Ge 12:2 NKJV). But growth and blessing call for wisdom. If God's plan for Abraham was to be fulfilled, this situation had to be dealt with. Nobody enjoys confrontation, but your future peace and prosperity require handling things wisely, before they get out of hand. *(2) Don't worry about getting short-changed, God will make it up to you.* Lot, the younger of the two men, chose the fertile, well-watered plains of Jordan, leaving Abraham with what looked like the short end of the stick. As senior partner, Abraham had the right to pull rank and demand the best land for himself, but he didn't. That's because he realized two things: (a) That he'd outgrown his relationship with Lot; now it was time to exit with grace, not contention. (b) That his goals and values were incompatible with Lot's. What Lot chose went up in smoke; what Abraham chose blessed all mankind. So be a peacemaker, and walk in God's blessing.

MEAN WHAT YOU SAY (1)

Let your 'Yes' be yes, and your 'No,' no.
JAMES 5:12 NIV

Remember when people said what they meant? Maybe you didn't like it, but you understood *what* they meant, and you knew they *meant* it. The word "cool" meant somewhere between warm and cold, and if you said, "wicked good," someone would've asked which one it was. It seems like straightforward speech is going the way of the horse and carriage. The Bible tells us, "Let your 'Yes' be yes, and your 'No,' no." In other words, mean what you say and say what you mean. Failing to do so damages relationships. We avoid saying no, or we say yes when we don't want to, out of the fear of rejection. And what are the results?

(1) We live with stress, anger or resentment over feeling mistreated by others. (2) Our life becomes a classic double-bind where we feel trapped whichever way we go: "If I say no, you'll be mad at me; if I don't, I'll be mad at myself and you!" So we stay stuck in our own pressurized trap. (3) The other person will never know how we really feel, or understand why we act as we do. Unless you say what you feel, you'll never get what you need from others. People don't change, until you change how you interact with them. (4) Your choice to avoid what you fear is what makes you a victim, not other people's words or actions. (5) You become part of the problem, surrendering to others the power God gave *you* to determine your own direction and set your own boundaries. So start saying what you mean, whether it's yes or no!

MEAN WHAT YOU SAY (2)

Let your 'Yes' be yes and your 'No,' no.

JAMES 5:12 NIV

Saying what you mean is just the beginning. Meaning what you say is the next step. When you say it, stick with it. If you don't intend to, don't say it. We train others how to handle us, by how we handle them. By lying down, we train them to walk on us. If we promise to discipline our kids but don't, we're training them to ignore our instructions. If our angry outbursts intimidate others, we're training them to be defensive around us or to avoid us. To break those negative patterns with others, begin doing these four things:

(1) Figure out what *they do* to you that you don't like. Be as clear as possible. "You treat me unfairly," isn't concrete enough. "You leave two-thirds of the workload for me to do," is observable, measurable, and suggests possible solutions. (2) Figure out what *you do,* that invites them to do what they do to you. Complaining to them, or to the boss, is unlikely to produce positive change. Altering *your* contribution to the situation is what invites and motivates others to change. (3) Figure out *how* and *when* to say no, then *act* on it. Instead of doing two-thirds of the workload and resenting it, when you've done your share, stop! Others won't do what they should, if you're doing it for them. (4) Remember, retraining others takes persistence. Having changed your part of the old pattern, *keep* doing your new part until others make the desired adjustment. Mean what you say!

LOVING PEOPLE

Love one another.
JOHN 15:12 NKJV

Loving people is only a vague concept, unless we do these five things: *(1) People are insecure—give them confidence.* Beneath their façade lie memories of a painful past and anxiety over what's coming their way next. Tell them God says, "I will never leave you nor forsake you" (Heb 13:5 NKJV). When nothing else works, God's Word does. *(2) People need to feel special—compliment them.* Do it when they least expect it, and it's clear you seek nothing in return. Mary Kay Ash said, "Everyone has an invisible sign hanging around their neck saying, 'Make me feel important!'" Notice how often God's Word tells us how much He loves us, how special we are, and His plans for us. *(3) People are looking for a better tomorrow—give them hope.* Let them know that when you put God in the center of your life, your future can be better than your past. "As long as he sought the Lord, God made him prosper" (2Ch 26:5 NKJV). *(4) People need to be understood—listen to them.* The trouble is, this takes more time than we're willing to give. We're in too much of a hurry to hand out advice and move on, and it doesn't work. Before people can be "fixed," they must feel understood. *(5) People need role models—be one.* Paul told the Corinthians, "You follow me as I follow Christ" (See 1Co 11:1 NIV). Too often we're unaware of the example we set and the impression we're making. Like it or not, what you do—and don't do—influences others. When you leave this world, what you leave behind is your influence.

STEWARDSHIP (1)

Give an account of your stewardship.

LUKE 16:2 NKJV

The issue of "ownership" is a key point in understanding biblical stewardship. A steward doesn't own the property he manages, so he needs to handle things with an eye to pleasing his boss, the owner. Today that rubs us the wrong way. We think: "My time is my own. My abilities are mine to use in the advancement of my career because I'm the one who worked hard to develop them. This is my stuff, bought and paid for." The Bible says: "What do you have that you did not receive? Now if you did indeed receive it, why do you boast as if you had not received it?" (1Co 4:7 NKJV). Every good thing you have is a gift from God—try to keep that in mind!

Like a wise investor, a good steward does three things: *(1) He looks to the future.* He refuses to be influenced or side-tracked by those who are "blowing" everything they have on immediate pleasures, living just for the moment. *(2) He is disciplined and patient.* He remains steady through the highs and lows of life, understanding that "...in due season we shall reap if we do not lose heart" (Gal 6:9 NKJV). *(3) He takes risks for the benefit of his boss.* Not foolish risks, but prayed-over and carefully thought-out risks. No investor can be totally sure his financial future won't come crashing down if something drastic happens. But here's the difference. When we follow God's plan for our lives, even if we lose some of it on earth, we can still gain much more in heaven.

STEWARDSHIP (2)

The lord of those servants...settled accounts.
MATTHEW 25:19 NKJV

In His famous parable of the talents, Jesus points out two things about our stewardship to God:

(1) "He gave...to each according to his own ability" (v. 15 NKJV). God knows what you can handle and He won't give you more, so don't ask Him to. He knows what He's called you to do. The master didn't burden the one-talent guy with a five-talent responsibility, or vice versa. Now we're not saying that those who have lots of stuff are the best stewards, or that those who have less must be poor stewards. But God knows each of us intimately, and He deals with us according to that knowledge. So you won't have to answer for what God didn't give you, or gave someone else. You're only responsible for yourself. Whatever God's entrusted to you to manage, He's done so knowing you're capable of handling it. *(2) "After a long time the lord of those servants came and settled accounts with them."* It may seem like "a long time," but Jesus is coming again! He hasn't changed His mind or His plan. The first time He came to save, the next time He comes to reign—and reward His stewards. "Who then is that faithful and wise steward, whom his master will make ruler over his household ...Blessed is that servant whom his master will find so doing when he comes" (Lk 12:42-43 NKJV). Don't get weary or sidetracked. Keep your eyes on the prize. Imagine the Master saying to you, "Well done!" That's what you want to hear, isn't it?

STEWARDSHIP (3)

Well done, good and faithful servant.

MATTHEW 25:21 NKJV

In Jesus' parable of the talents, the first two stewards were rewarded for multiplying what was entrusted to them. The first steward said, "I have gained" (v. 20 NKJV). Now, when God entrusts something to us He doesn't sit up in heaven pulling all the strings, controlling how we handle our stewardship. We have a choice. We've the freedom to mess up His affairs, or maximize them. The first two servants did with their master's money what he expected of them. God gives it to us—but we must handle it. God's not going to handle it for us! That's obvious from the fate of the third steward, who said, "Lord, I knew you to be a hard man...And I was afraid, and went and hid your talent in the ground" (vv. 24-25 NKJV). He was like those who say: "God's standards are too high. I'm afraid if I say yes to Him, He'll demand too much of me. I'll just stay here on the sidelines where it's safe." That's bad stewardship and even worse theology. Don't let anyone convince you that you can't do what God expects of you. By His grace, you can. The first two stewards knew their master's expectations; that's what being a good steward is all about. We *know* what God requires of us because He's put it in His Word for us to read. The reason the master's commendation meant something, is because the stewards' work meant something. They had authentic responsibility and they carried it out faithfully. So, where do you rank on the faithfulness charts today? If you're not sure, examine yourself!

STEWARDSHIP (4)

If anyone will not work, neither shall he eat.

2 THESSALONIANS 3:10 NKJV

The story's told of a guy who came to church looking very sad. "What's up?" his pastor asked. "Well, two weeks ago my uncle died and left me $75,000. Then a week ago my aunt died and left me $50,000." His pastor asked, "Then why are you so sad?" The guy answered, "Because nobody died this week." Cute story; only one problem, the Bible says this man ought to "labor, working with his hands...that he may have something to give him who has need" (Eph 4:28 NKJV). The first job God gave Adam, was to take care of the garden and be productive. Even in a perfect environment, Adam had work to do. If you want to be a good steward, taking your master's resources and increasing them, you must engage in productive work. To have "something to give," you need to have "something left over." That's what's wrong with gambling; you can't substitute luck for labor. Now, you're not supposed to help people who don't want to work. Tony Evans writes: "Instead of wondering when he is going to get a slice of a handout pie, a good steward is busy baking pies, enjoying the results, and sharing what he has with others." Some people question investing because it doesn't fit their idea of work. No, God told Adam to plant seeds. Planting seed is an investment made in anticipation of a harvest. Ever since the fall we've been inventing ways to avoid honest, productive labor. Your *job* is part of your stewardship. Are you performing it as if God were your employer? He is!

RECOVERING FROM LOSS

Pour out your heart before Him.

PSALM 62:8 NKJV

Here are five keys to recovering from loss: *(1) Process your grief.* Emotions like fear, anger, worry, depression, resentment, helplessness and grief are normal. It's no good to stuff them or deny they exist. God created us to feel; He doesn't expect us to act happy when we're grieving. "Blessed are those who mourn, for they will be comforted" (Mt 5:4 NIV). Be honest with God. "Pour out your heart before Him," and He will comfort you. *(2) Accept help.* It's a mistake to isolate yourself in the aftermath of a tragedy. We all need the encouragement and the support of others. We're called to carry one another's burdens (See Gal 6:2). *(3) Choose the right response.* When you choose bitterness, you hurt yourself and shut the door on happiness because you can't be happy and bitter at the same time. During some recent California wildfires there were victims who said, "We've lost everything and we're sad, but we'll work together as a family and rebuild." Others said, "My life's over! I can't go on...I'll never recover." You can choose to believe you're on your own, or that God's with you and bounce back. *(4) Know your joy comes from God.* There's no correlation between your circumstances and your joy. Joy comes from within; it's based on whom you trust, not what you see and feel. *(5) Concentrate on what you've got, not on what you've lost.* Make a list of the good things in your life, and thank God for what you still have. It's impossible to be grateful and hopeless at the same time.

LOOK AND LIVE!

Everyone who believes in him will have eternal life.
JOHN 3:15 NLT

When Jesus told Nicodemus, "You must be born again," this Jewish scholar didn't get it. So Jesus explained that in the birthing process, the infant allows the parent to do the work. "There must be more," thought Nicodemus. Using this visiting professor's favorite book, the Torah, Jesus said, "As Moses lifted up the bronze snake on a pole in the wilderness, so the Son of Man must be lifted up, so that everyone who believes in him will have eternal life" (vv. 14-15 NLT). Nicodemus got the point!

When God had heard all the complaining He could put up with, He "sent fiery serpents...and many of the people of Israel died" (Nu 21:6 NKJV). The survivors pleaded with Moses to ask God for mercy. "Then the Lord said to Moses, 'Make a fiery serpent, and set it on a pole; and...everyone who is bitten, when he looks at it, shall live'" (Nu 21:8 NKJV). The snake-bitten Israelites found healing by looking at the pole—and sinners find salvation by looking to Christ. Look and live! The simplicity of it troubles us. We expect a more complicated cure. Moses and his followers might have expected more as well: manufacture an ointment, treat one another, or at least fight back. We say, "God helps those who help themselves." But Jesus says, "Only believe." You believe the chair will hold your weight, so you sit on it. You trust the work of the light switch, so you flip it. You regularly trust power you cannot see to do a work you cannot accomplish. Today, Jesus asks you to do the same.

THE ULTIMATE GUARANTEE

Having believed, you were marked...with a seal.

EPHESIANS 1:13 NIV

Jesus said, "I give them eternal life, and they shall never lose it" (Jn 10:28 AMP). As parents we understand this. When our children fall we pick them up. We correct them, but we don't disown them. They were born with our DNA and will die with it. And God has the same relationship with us. When we believe and become "children of God" He alters our lineage, redefines our spiritual parenthood, and in doing so secures our salvation. To accomplish this, He seals us with His Spirit. "Having believed, you were marked...with a seal, the promised Holy Spirit."

Max Lucado writes: "For a short time in college I worked in a vacuum-cleaner plant. We assembled the appliance from plug to hose. The last step on the assembly line was 'sealing and shipping.' By this point the company had invested hours and dollars in the machine. So they took extra care to protect it. They mummified it in bubble wrap, secured it with Styrofoam, wrapped the box with tough-to-tear tape, stamped the destination on the box, and belted it inside the truck. That machine was secure. But compared to God's care for His saints, the machine [might as well have been] dumped into the back of a pick-up truck. God vacuum-seals us with His strongest force: His Spirit. He sheathes His children in a suit of spiritual armor, encircles us with angels, and indwells us Himself. The Queen of England should enjoy such security." Good news: God has "identified you as his own, guaranteeing that you will be saved on the day of redemption" (Eph 4:30 NLT).

HOW TO HANDLE CRITICISM

I cannot come down.

NEHEMIAH 6:3 NKJV

Nehemiah teaches us three important truths about handling criticism: *(1) Expect it.* When spectators watch a race, where do they focus their attention? On the front runners! Someone said, "Criticism is something you can avoid easily— by saying nothing, doing nothing, and being nothing." But those three options don't work. So Nehemiah answered his critics, "I am doing a great work, so that I cannot come down." Don't step down to the level of your critics. *(2) Evaluate it.* "Sanballat...sent to me, saying, 'Come, let us meet...But they thought to do me harm'" (v. 2 NKJV). When people say, "I'm going to tell you something for your own good," often they've nothing good to tell you. When you're criticized, ask yourself: (a) "Who criticized me?" "Faithful are the wounds of a friend, but the kisses of an enemy are deceitful" (Pr 27:6 NKJV). Has this person earned the right to speak into your life? (b) "Why was this criticism given? Out of a personal hurt, or for my benefit?" Hurting people hurt people; so maintain the right attitude, looking for the grain of truth, making the necessary changes, and taking the high road. *(3) Outlive it.* When Nehemiah's friends told him to run and hide, he replied, "I will not...So the wall was finished...in fifty-two days...when all our enemies heard of it...they perceived that this work was done by our God" (Ne 6:11-16 NKJV). Sometimes you're in more danger from the counsel of your friends than you are from the criticism of your enemies. That's when you must know who you are, what God's called you to do, and outlive the criticism!

GOD LOVES YOU, HE REALLY DOES!

Can anything...separate us from Christ's love?
ROMANS 8:35 NLT

Our limited minds can't comprehend God's love because it comes with no strings attached. He doesn't love us "if," but "in spite of." As a parent you may not approve of your child's behavior, but you always love and accept them. Paul asks, "Can *anything* ever separate us from Christ's love?" Then he answers, "No, nothing!" Doesn't that blow your mind? We have just enough ego to believe there are certain sins God can't get over—like the ones *we* never commit. Do you remember the Pharisee in the temple who prayed, "God, I thank You that I am not like other men—extortioners, unjust, adulterers, or... this tax collector [standing next to me]" (Lk 18:11 NKJV). Understand this: God's standard is perfection, and you couldn't reach it in a thousand lifetimes! Grace is the only hope any of us have.

Our love for God relates to the level of the forgiveness we've received from Him. The Pharisees were shocked that Jesus would allow a woman with a bad reputation to kneel at His feet, bathing them with her tears and drying them with her hair. They thought, "If Jesus was a prophet He'd know what kind of woman this is" (See Lk 7:39). No, it wasn't that Jesus didn't *know,* it was that He didn't *care.* Turning to the woman He said, "Thy sins are forgiven." Then He gives us the bottom line: "To whom little is forgiven, the same loveth little" (Lk 7:47-48). And what should our response to God's love be? "This is love for God: to obey his commands" (1Jn 5:3 NIV).

OVERCOMING YOUR FEAR OF PEOPLE (1)

Be not afraid of their faces.
JEREMIAH 1:8

Do you avoid certain activities and social occasions because of insecurity? If so, you might have "social phobia," the fear of being inadequate, embarrassed or negatively evaluated. Some of us even experience panic attacks that leave us immobilized to the point of dysfunction. Yet it's avoiding such situations rather than facing them, that allows our fears to control us. How great our fear becomes depends on what we say to ourselves when it hits. And what we say to ourselves is largely a function of what psychologists call our "sub-personality type." Here are some common sub-personality types, and ways we can handle them:

"The Worrier." Worriers anticipate the worst, create grandiose images of potential tragedy, and are always hyper-vigilant for any small signs of trouble. Their favorite self-talk expression is, "But what if...?" Learn to replace your worrier self-talk with, "So, what if...By God's grace I can learn to handle this. I can feel anxious and still do it. I don't like it, but I can stand it till it passes. I'll get used to it with practice and God's help." When Jeremiah's fears kicked in and he wanted to run from a public speaking assignment, God said to him: "You must go wherever I send you and say whatever I tell you. And don't be afraid of the people, for I will be with you and will protect you" (vv. 7-8 NLT). Instead of running from it, choose to face it in faith—and watch how God will get you through it!

OVERCOMING YOUR FEAR OF PEOPLE (2)

Be not afraid of their faces.

JEREMIAH 1:8

Another sub-personality type contributing to our fear of people is called *"The Critic."* It's that part of you which constantly judges your own behavior, compares you unfavorably with others, points out your flaws and reminds you you're a failure. Its favorite self-talk expressions are, "You're stupid; can't you ever get it right? Look how capable so-and-so is. How come you can't be like them?" While "the worrier" suffers from anxiety, "the critic" suffers from low self-worth. What's the answer? Learn to replace your critic self-talk with, "They're what God made them; I'm what God made me, and I accept myself as His unique creation. I *make* mistakes, but I'm *not* a mistake. With God's grace, I'm working on being the lovable, capable person God made me."

"The Victim" is another sub-personality type underlying our fears. It's that part of us which feels helpless or hopeless, believes we're inherently inadequate and unworthy, sees insurmountable obstacles in our path, and bemoans the way things are. Its favorite self-talk expressions include, "I can't...It's useless. I'll never be able to. Why even bother?" Replace your victim self-talk with, "I don't have to be perfect now. I'm a new creature in Christ and I'm growing a little more each day. I choose to see the glass half-full rather than half-empty. Since God says I can, I choose to believe I can—and I will—in His time and way." Face your fears. Do what you've been afraid to do. God's promise, "I am with thee" (Jer 1:19), was all Jeremiah needed—and it's all you need too.

DON'T DROP THE BALL

He who lacks these things is shortsighted.
2 PETER 1:9 NKJV

Brian Dyson, former Vice Chairman of Coca-Cola, delivered the commencement address at Georgia Tech in 1996. In it he said: "Imagine life as a game in which you are juggling five balls in the air. You name them—work, family, health, friends and spirit. You will soon understand that one is a rubber ball. If you drop it, it will bounce back. But the other four balls—family, health, friends and spirit—are made of glass. If you drop any of these they will be irrevocably scuffed, marked, nicked, damaged or even shattered. They will never be the same. You must understand that and strive for balance in your life."

Many of the people we admire are out of balance; they can build great churches and companies, but not great relationships. Solomon wrote: "They made me the keeper of the vineyards, but my own vineyard I have not kept" (SS 1:6 NKJV). Pastors who teach the importance of building strong families sometimes raise children who turn out resentful because they got none of Dad's time and attention. And worse, he told them, "We have to make these sacrifices for God and the ministry." In what areas are you out of balance? In your quest not to drop the ball in your public performance, make sure you don't drop it in your personal life—where it counts most. The Bible bottom-lines it: "Add to your faith virtue, to virtue knowledge, to knowledge self-control, to self-control perseverance, to perseverance godliness, to godliness brotherly kindness, and to brotherly kindness love...he who lacks these things is shortsighted" (2Pe 1:5-9 NKJV).

"COME AND SEE"

They came and saw...and remained with Him.

JOHN 1:39 NKJV

For John and Andrew, it wasn't enough to listen to John the Baptist. Most of us would have been content to be around the nation's most famous evangelist. Could there be a better teacher? Yes. And when John and Andrew met Jesus, the One John the Baptist spoke about, they left John and followed Him. Notice the request they made: "Where are You staying?" (v. 38 NKJV). Jesus replied, "'Come and see.' They came and saw...and remained with Him" (v. 39 NKJV). They wanted to know Jesus; to find out what caused His head to turn and His heart to burn and His soul to yearn; to look in His face and follow in His steps. They wanted to know if He could be who John said He was—and if He was, what on earth was He doing? And you can't answer such a question by talking to others, you've got to spend time with "The Man" Himself. Jesus' answer to the disciples, and to you, is, "Come and see." See what?

(1) See how He handles power. Not once did Jesus use His power to impress others or enrich Himself in any way. *(2) See how He handles people.* He didn't see them as interruptions, irritations or obstacles on His path to personal fulfillment. No. "When He saw the multitudes, He was moved with compassion" (Mt 9:36 NKJV). *(3) See how He handles priorities.* "Vast crowds came to hear him...But Jesus often withdrew to the wilderness for prayer" (Lk 5:15-16 NLT). Did He know something we don't? No commitment is harder to keep, or more important, than spending time in prayer each day.

BE PASSIONATE ABOUT IT

So we built the wall.

NEHEMIAH 4:6 NKJV

Nehemiah rebuilt the walls of Jerusalem in less than two months. How did he do it? Passion! He gave up a high-profile job, overcame relentless opposition, and worked passionately. "So we built the wall...for the people had a mind to work." But first we read: "They said to me...'The wall of Jerusalem is also broken down, and its gates are burned with fire'... when I heard these words...I sat down and wept" (Ne 1:3-4 NKJV). Observe:

(1) Passion is your first step to achievement. Your desire, not your IQ or your DNA, determines your destiny. The greater your desire, the greater your potential. *(2) Passion will increase your willpower.* Only when you want something badly enough will you pay the price to achieve it. God despises a lukewarm attitude (See Rev 3:15). An indecisive person gets nowhere with Him (See Jas 1:8). *(3) Passion will change you.* When your desires are in harmony with God's will and you follow them with a passion, you can't help but become a more productive person. *(4) Passion will make the impossible, possible.* Beware of "experts." Sometimes what they present as wisdom is just shortsightedness. In 1895 Lord Kelvin, president of England's Royal Society, said, "Heavier-than-air flying machines are not possible." In 1905 the U.S. President Grover Cleveland said, "Sensible and responsible women do not want to vote." In 1923 Nobel Prize winner in physics Robert Millikan said, "There's no likelihood man can ever tap the power of the atom." Jesus said, "With God all things are possible" (Mk 10:27). When you become passionate about God's purposes, He will show you what's possible.

DIGGING WELLS THAT WON'T HOLD WATER!

My people have...dug...cisterns...
that cannot hold water.

JEREMIAH 2:13 NIV

Do you feel like there's something missing in your life? Are you running from place to place and person to person trying to find it? Until you put God at the center of your life, you'll keep digging "cisterns...that cannot hold water."

We all want to be loved and feel successful, so we look to our *jobs* or to *others* for a sense of fulfillment. But by expecting a person or a paycheck to do what only God can, we keep coming up short. "Cursed is the...one who depends on mere humans...He's like a tumbleweed...rootless and aimless...But blessed is the man who trusts...God...They're like trees... putting down roots near...rivers...calm through droughts, bearing...fruit every season" (Jer 17:5-8 TM). Fulfillment doesn't come from having "the right people" in your life, or more money, prestige and accomplishments. A larger house won't do it; you'll just have more to clean. The latest car won't do it; you'll just end up with bigger payments. A job promotion won't do it; you'll just have more stress and longer hours. Yes, you'll make more money, but after taxes and buying what you need to maintain your new image, you'll be back to square one. At the end of a lifetime spent "striving after [the] wind" (Ecc 2:11 NAS), Solomon said, "Everything...can be put into a few words: Respect and obey [honor and put your trust in] God! This is what life is all about" (Ecc 12:13 CEV). The One you're looking for today has been there all along, and He's ready to meet you at the point of your need. You just have to invite Him in!

WORK ON THE INNER YOU (1)

The inward man is being renewed day by day.
2 CORINTHIANS 4:16 NKJV

Paul writes: "Though our outward man is perishing, yet the inward man is being renewed day by day." There's an outer you—your body, reputation and persona. And there is an inner you—your character, spirit and soul. The outer you is what everybody sees, the inner you is invisible. The outer you can be coerced by other people or forces, the inner you is always free to choose. The outer you is temporary, the inner you is eternal. Like it or not, the outer you is "perishing." From age twenty-five, bones begin to lose calcium and get brittle, skin begins to lose elasticity and shrivel, and age spots begin to multiply. If you're over thirty, you lose thousands of brain cells every day. Weight starts shifting from the poles of your body toward the equator. And everyone in your life who's over thirty wants you to know they understand. They love you, but frankly, they're looking forward to it. You can fight it, but you won't win. You can lavish time and money on the outer you: exercise it, starve it, Botox it, stretch it, lift it, tuck it, tan it and dress it up in Neiman Marcus, yet the truth is, "All are from the dust, and all return to dust" (Ecc 3:20 NKJV). But here's what's important: *You* will never cease to exist. Your spirit—the inner you—is in the process of becoming something either unbelievably good or unimaginably dark. That something is the main thing God sees when He looks at you. It's what matters most to Him. So work on the inner you!

WORK ON THE INNER YOU (2)

The inward man is being renewed day by day.
2 CORINTHIANS 4:16 NKJV

One day God sent the prophet Samuel to find someone to be Israel's next king. Samuel saw a very impressive-looking guy and thought, "This must be the one." But God, who measures with a different yardstick, said, "Man looks at the outward appearance, but the Lord looks at the heart" (1Sa 16:7 NKJV). One of the criticisms Paul lived with, was people saying his looks weren't very impressive (See 2Co 10:10). His body wasn't just aging; it had been whipped, stoned, starved, beaten and locked in a cell. "It doesn't bother me much," he said, "it's what's inside that matters. Something's going on inside of me; it's like the opposite of what's happening outside. Outside I'm dying a little every day. Inside I'm coming to life, changing, getting stronger. Joy keeps bubbling up—even in prison. I keep getting more hopeful, even though I know my body's going to die soon. I keep loving people more, even the people who put me here. It's the strangest thing: I'm dying on the outside, but inside I'm coming to life." Paul had mastered the inner game. His thoughts ran constantly heavenward. As an old man in prison he was more alive than he had ever been. So he wrote: "Who shall separate us from the love of Christ? Shall tribulation, or distress, or persecution, or famine, or nakedness, or peril, or sword?" (Ro 8:35 NKJV). Well, trouble and hardship can win the outer game pretty easily. But there is a *you* in you, that no one can touch. That's the one you must pay attention to, for that's the game you can win!

WORK ON THE INNER YOU (3)

The inward man is being renewed day by day.
2 CORINTHIANS 4:16 NKJV

Be grateful for the outer you. Make peace with it. Rejoice in its strengths. Accept its limitations. Let it work hard. Be happy when it gets promoted. But remember, it's wasting away. The inner you, on the other hand, is capable of a glory you can't even imagine. "Beloved, now we are children of God; and it has not yet been revealed what we *shall* be, but we know that when He is revealed, we shall be like Him, for we shall see Him as He is. And everyone who has this hope in Him purifies himself, just as He is pure" (1Jn 3:2-3 NKJV). Make your biggest investment in the thing that will last.

We have scales and mirrors and tape measures to track the development of our outer selves. But how can we track the well-being of the part of us that will last? This may look a little different for each of us, but here are a few mirrors and scales and tape measures that will help you get started: (1) Self-examination and confession. (2) Friends who love you enough to speak the truth to you. (3) Time to be alone and listen to God. (4) Time spent in the Scriptures, renewing your mind. (5) Examination of your calendar and your checkbook. (6) Questions such as: How easily discouraged do I get these days? How easily irritated am I compared to six months ago? (7) Attention to your thought life. What's your mind drawn toward? Where does envy, blaming, judging or lusting rob you of life and joy? Come on, get serious; work on the inner you!

BEING READY

Be dressed ready for service.

LUKE 12:35 NIV

God can move so quickly that one day it feels like all hell has broken loose in your life, and the next, like you're seated in heavenly places. And in both instances, "It is God which worketh in you" (Php 2:13). The Bible uses words like *straightway, immediately,* and *suddenly* to remind us that when God moves we must be ready to move too. He doesn't announce it with trumpets and a fanfare so you must stay prepared, especially for something you've been waiting for a long time. You may be just a moment away from the answer you've been seeking. That's all the time it takes God to change things—a moment! Don't let discouragement dull your faith or procrastination steal your opportunity.

Referring to His second coming, Jesus said, "Let him which is on the housetop not come down to take any thing out of his house" (Mt 24:17). You've got to decide whether you're going to accept what God has for you now and move forward, or return to your house, because your *unfinished business* can cause you to miss God's best. And so can *waiting for others.* A paralyzed man missed his healing for thirty-eight years because he waited for others to act. He told Jesus, "I have no man to put me into the pool when the water is stirred up" (Jn 5:7 NKJV). For years he sat beside the solution, but others caused him to miss it. Nothing is more important than what God is saying and doing in your life right now: not what's going on in your house, not the actions or opinions of others. What matters is *being ready.*

NEVER STOP GROWING

I press on toward the goal.
PHILIPPIANS 3:14 NIV

Paul writes: "I do not consider myself yet to have taken hold of it. But...I press on toward the goal" (vv. 13-14). It's inspiring when a leader shares with us his successes. But sometimes we're helped more when he shares with us his struggles. In his book *Leadership Gold,* Dr. John Maxwell talks frankly about things he's had to work on in life: "I am impatient, I am unrealistic about the time tasks take and how difficult most processes are. I don't like to give a lot of time or effort to people's emotional concerns. I overestimate the ability of others. I assume too much. I want to delegate responsibility too quickly. I want options—so maybe I drive everyone crazy. I don't care for rules or restrictions. I determine my priorities quickly and expect others to have similar attitudes. I process issues quickly and want to move on—even when other people aren't ready to." We all have areas we must constantly work on. Someone has said that the error of youth is to believe that intelligence is a substitute for experience, while the error of age is to believe that experience is a substitute for intelligence. The truth is, young or old, we must never stop growing. We must be content with what we *have,* but never with what we *are.* Personal growth is like riding a bicycle; we're either moving forward or falling off. So, in what areas of your life are you seeing measurable growth? In what areas do you need to grow? Growth only takes place when you confess your lack of it, commit to it, and continue in it!

"JOSEPH PRINCIPLES"

God has made me forget.

GENESIS 41:51 NKJV

Joseph was thirty when he became governor of Egypt. He was seventeen when he was sold into slavery. For thirteen years he dealt with pain and confusion, maintained his character and his commitment to God, and allowed his trials to make him triumphant. So you can't just throw in the towel, have a pity party, or sit around doing nothing.

Joseph didn't simply forget what happened. Anybody who tells you, "Just forget it," isn't living in the real world. It happened, but God can use it to enrich your life. God gave Joseph two sons: he named them Manasseh, which means "God has made me forget," and Ephraim, which means "God made me fruitful in the land of my afflictions." God gave Joseph new relationships to replace the old ones. One reason why old relationships may be destroying you is that you haven't replaced them with new ones. You're hanging out with the wrong reminders. God helped Joseph to forget the pain of what happened. He still had the memory, but he prospered in spite of it. When you walk with God, the promise before you is always greater than the pain behind you. But here are some "Joseph principles" you need to live by: (1) Don't try to ignore or pretend it never happened. God will give you the grace to handle it, not deny it. (2) Believe that God can "make up to you" the time, the relationships and the opportunities you've lost (See Joel 2:25). (3) List the people who've wronged you, forgive them and release them to God in prayer (See Col 3:13 NLT). (4) Tell God you're ready to start over. And start today!

HOW TO HANDLE TEMPTATION

Submit to God. Resist the devil.
JAMES 4:7 NKJV

When it comes to temptation, remember these seven things: *(1) Never say "never."* You never become so spiritual that you're immune. "No temptation has overtaken you except such as is common to man; but God is faithful, who will not allow you to be tempted beyond what you are able, but with the temptation will also make the way of escape, that you may be able to bear it" (1Co 10:13 NKJV). *(2) Realize you can stumble on the last lap.* Because you haven't blown it yet, doesn't mean you can't. Satan is a master of timing, and he's in no particular hurry. *(3) Acknowledge your basic drives.* St. Augustine said, "There is nothing more powerful in bringing down the spirit of a man than the caresses of a woman." Your flesh is powerful; once indulged it will always want more. *(4) Understand that you are responsible.* Sin is a choice. When you choose to abuse God's grace you pay the price, either now or later. "Do not be deceived…whatever a man sows, that he will also reap" (Gal 6:7 NKJV). *(5) You're not a helpless pawn.* You may not be able to change what happened yesterday, but your choice, empowered by God's grace, will determine what happens today and tomorrow. *(6) If you've sinned, there's hope.* God will forgive you and use you again. Jesus told Peter, "I have prayed for you, that your faith should not fail; and when you have returned to Me, strengthen your brethren" (Lk 22:32 NKJV). *(7) Stay safe by staying close to God.* "Submit to God. Resist the devil and he will flee from you."

IT'S TIME TO FACE REALITY

I will arise and go to my father.
LUKE 15:18 NKJV

Nothing changed for the Prodigal Son until he said, "I will arise and go to my father, and will say…'I have sinned.'" His story ends well; yours can too, but you must:

(1) *Decide to take control of your life before circumstances or other people do.* The solution begins with you. A new partner, a new job or a new house won't cure what's wrong if the cause lies in your own attitudes and actions. You may have 101 excuses for the way things are in your life right now, but what are you willing to do to change them? The prodigal's father didn't pick him up and carry him home; the son had to do the leg work. (2) *Face reality as it is, not as you think it should be or wish it was.* The prodigal had to discover that the rules he rebelled against at home were essential to his happiness, that all the fun he thought was waiting for him out there, wasn't, and that he must acknowledge his mistakes and correct them before he could get his life back on track: "Let the wicked forsake his way, and…return to the Lord" (Isa 55:7 NKJV). God will intervene, but only when you operate on the H.O.W. principle: Honesty, Openness, Willingness. (3) *Act now, while you still can.* The law of evolution says things evolve and improve on their own. No, certain things left unattended and uncorrected get worse, not better. That's true whether it's your health, your marriage, your children, your finances, or your walk with God. So, face reality and take action while you still can.

PAY ATTENTION!

This is the way; walk in it.
ISAIAH 30:21 NIV

James Michener said he had a neighbor whose tree stopped producing apples, so he hammered rusty nails around the trunk. That year he got his greatest crop of apples. He said, "Hammering those nails in was a shock to remind the tree that its job is to grow apples." Unscientific, maybe—but it worked! Michener explained how heart bypass surgery, hip surgery and a bout with vertigo were nails God hammered into the trunk of his life. It got his attention! Realizing he wasn't going to live forever he got busy and in five years authored eleven books—including best sellers.

"No discipline seems pleasant at the time, but...Later...it produces a harvest of righteousness and peace" (Heb 12:11 NIV). Verdell Davis says: "There are things we could and should do something about. For example, the loss of material comforts can move us to simplify our lives. A clinical depression can lead us to seek help, and to healthier ways of living and relating. Losing a job we performed well can allow us to uncover gifts and talents we didn't know we had. The loss of some physical capacity can push us to develop other ways of performing, that enrich all who come our way." Harold Sala adds: "Let's face it, when those rusty nails get hammered in we take notice and our lives become productive. [They're] delivered with the exhortation to get on with the business before us. The Father's love allows the hammer blows to goad us into accomplishing the full measure of His will." So when you get a wake-up call from God saying, "This is the way; walk in it," pay attention!

TO LOVE IS TO LISTEN

The greatest of these is love.
1 CORINTHIANS 13:13 NKJV

Stephen Sample says: "The average person suffers from three delusions: that he's a good driver, that he has a good sense of humor, and that he's a good listener. You may succeed in life without the first two, but you won't without the third." Are you a good listener? Do you think what you have to say is more important than what's being said to you? When people talk, do they get the impression you're not listening? If so, write "LL" on a card, carry it with you and look at it regularly. It means *Listen,* and *Look* at people while you're listening. One study says we hear half of what's being said, listen to half of what we hear, understand half of that, believe half of that, and remember only half of that. Translate that into an eight hour work day and it means: you spend about four hours listening, hear two hours' worth of what's said, listen to an hour of it, understand thirty minutes of it, believe only fifteen minutes' worth, and remember less than eight minutes—of all that was said in eight hours. Wow, it sounds like we all need to work at listening!

You cannot "connect" with someone if they don't feel heard and understood. A deaf ear is the first symptom of a closed mind. If you haven't formed the habit of listening—you aren't going to get the facts you need. And when you don't have all the facts, you're in the dark. Paul writes: "The greatest of these is love." One of the greatest expressions of love—is a commitment to listen!

THOUGHTS ON MARRIAGE

A man shall...be joined to his wife.

GENESIS 2:24 NKJV

God said, "It is not good that man should be alone; I will make him a helper" (v. 18 NKJV). God gave Eve one basic responsibility—to help Adam. As a husband, you bear the primary responsibility for the home. When Eve ate the forbidden fruit, God said, "Adam, where are *you?*" (See Ge 3:9 NKJV). Adam was held responsible for the breakdown.

Here's another thought. Before God gave Adam a wife he gave him a job, and specific instructions to obey (See Ge 2:15-17). Don't mess with a guy who doesn't want to work for a living, or obey God. Furthermore, if he tells you, "I don't need you," run! The whole idea of creating Eve was that Adam *needed* her. Until someone can say, "I'm incomplete without you," they're not ready for marriage. Marriage is a big decision, so allow God to help you make the right one. God "brought her to the man" (v. 22 NKJV). As a single person your options are: live an immoral lifestyle, marry a non-believer, or wait for God to give you the right mate.

And one final thought: "A man shall leave his father and mother and be joined to his wife, and they shall become one flesh." This verse is read at almost every wedding. The problem is, most of us don't think about what we're promising. It means breaking all other ties and giving yourself totally to your mate. Rather than working them into your life, it's building your life around them. The word "cleave" means to stick like glue through bad times and good, and to commit to loving and caring for each other.

YOUR MOUNTAIN IS A MOLEHILL

Who are you, O great mountain?

ZECHARIAH 4:7 NKJV

When the Israelites were building the temple, their enemies became like a mountain standing in their way. If that's *your* situation today, read these words carefully: "This is the word of the Lord to Zerubbabel: 'Not by might nor by power, but by My Spirit,' says the Lord of hosts. 'Who are you, O great mountain? Before Zerubbabel you shall become a plain! And he shall bring forth the capstone with shouts of 'Grace, grace to it!'…'The hands of Zerubbabel have laid the foundation of this temple; his hands shall also finish it…For who has despised the day of small things?'" (vv. 6-10 NKJV). The Amplified Bible reads, "O great mountain…you shall become a plain [a mere molehill]!" Start looking at your situation from the perspective of God's enabling grace. In this passage the Lord tells Zechariah that the problem facing the Israelites only appeared to be a mountain; it was actually a molehill. How would you like your mountain to become a molehill? It will, once you start doing what God says. Instead of obsessing over the problem, focus on the Lord and His power.

In the early stages of anything you should live by the words, "Don't despise the day of small things." In the middle stages you must live by the words, "Let us not grow weary while doing good" (Gal 6:9 NKJV). And in the final stages, "Looking unto Jesus, the author and finisher of our faith" (Heb 12:2 NKJV). If God's told you to do something, it is not only His will that you begin it, but that you finish it.

JESUS IS THE WAY

I am the way.

JOHN 14:6 RSV

Judaism sees salvation as a judgment day decision based on morality. Hindus anticipate multiple reincarnations in the soul's journey through the cosmos. Buddhism guides your life according to the Four Noble Truths and the Noble Eight-fold Path. Muslims earn their way to Allah through the Five Pillars of Faith. Many philosophers deem life after death as hidden and unknown, "a great leap in the dark." Some people clump Christ with Moses, Mohammad, Confucius, and other spiritual leaders. But Jesus declares, "I am the way, and the truth, and the life. No one comes to the Father except through me." Many object, "All roads lead to heaven." But how can they? Buddhists look toward Nirvana, achieved after no less than 547 reincarnations. Christians believe in one life, one death, and an eternity of enjoying God. Humanists don't acknowledge the Creator of life. Jesus claims to be the source of life. Spiritualists read your palms. Christians consult the Bible. Hindus perceive a plural and impersonal God. Christ-followers believe "there is only one God" (1Co 8:4 NLT). Every non-Christian religion says, "You can save you." Jesus says, "My death on the cross saves you." All roads don't lead to London, all ships don't sail to Australia, and all flights don't land in Rome. Every path does not lead to God. Jesus blazed a stand-alone trail void of self-salvation. He cleared a one-of-a-kind passageway uncluttered by human effort. He offers us a unique invitation in which He works and we trust, He dies and we live, He invites and we believe. "The work God wants you to do is this: Believe the One he sent" (Jn 6:29 NCV).

THE SPIRIT-FILLED LIFE

Be filled with the…Spirit.

EPHESIANS 5:18 NKJV

The new birth doesn't automatically eliminate the old nature. We live in bodies that are susceptible to sin, so we must *stay* filled with God's Spirit. Paul says, "Walk by the Spirit, and you will not carry out the desire of the flesh" (Gal 5:16 NAS). Then he gives us a familiar illustration: "Do not be drunk with wine …but be filled with the Spirit." Notice:

First, Paul's talking about yielding control of our life to God's Spirit. When someone's drunk we say they're "under the influence." Second, Paul's statement is a command. *"Be* filled." He didn't say, "If you'd like to," or "It would be nice." No, if you are going to please God then you must be constantly filled with His Spirit. Third, this applies to every believer. Sometimes we look at someone and say, "They love Jesus so much; why can't I be like that?" You can. The difference is the filling of the Spirit, not the fact that they have something you don't. Fourth, you can't fill yourself. Like filling your car, you must regularly pull up to the pump. "Blessed are those who hunger and thirst for righteousness, for they will be filled" (Mt 5:6 NIV). Are you hungry? Are you thirsty? Fifth, it's a continuous action. You can't run your car on a single tank of gas; you've got to keep going back to the source. The Spirit's filling is a dynamic, moment-by-moment experience. Why is it that way? Because we live in a world that depletes us spiritually, and constantly contend with a core of carnality that seeks to defeat us. So, "Be filled with the…Spirit."

BE WILLING TO START SMALL

For who hath despised the day of small things?
ZECHARIAH 4:10

D. L. Moody became a spokesman for God and a changer of nations. But if you'd met him early in life you wouldn't have thought it was possible. Although he was raised in church, he was spiritually ignorant. When he moved to Boston he began attending a Bible-preaching church. In April of 1855, a Sunday school teacher came to the shoe store where he worked and led him to Christ. A month later, when he applied to become a member of that church, it was clear that he knew nothing about the Bible. One of his Sunday school teachers later wrote: "I've never met anyone who seemed less likely to become a Christian of clear and decided views, much less fill any place of public usefulness." So they asked him to take a year of Bible study. During his interview with the membership committee a year later, his answers were only slightly improved. He was barely literate and used atrocious grammar. Nobody on that church committee thought God would ever use him. But they were wrong. And the people who say *you* will never amount to anything for God, are wrong too!

Every oak tree starts as an acorn. Jesus began in a stable but He didn't stay there. David was a shepherd boy with a slingshot but he became Israel's greatest king. Joseph was a prisoner but he became prime minister. Understand this: you are a seed capable of producing a harvest for God. So take all that you have and all that you are, place it into God's hands and be willing to start small.

ARE YOU BEARING FRUIT?

The fruit of the Spirit.
GALATIANS 5:22-23 NKJV

Notice three things about fruit: *First, fruit is visible.* Remember the "show and tell" method of learning in school? James writes: "Show me your faith without your works, and I will show you my faith by my works" (Jas 2:18 NKJV). It's not enough to "talk a good game," you must "live it" before others every day. *Second, fruit reflects the character of the tree on which it grows.* If it's an apple tree it's going to produce apples. The more you submit your life to Christ, the more like Him you'll become. *Third, fruit is always borne for someone else's benefit.* You'll never see fruit chewing on itself, or saying, "I don't want to be picked." Good fruit makes someone hunger and reach for it. The Holy Spirit wants to produce fruit in you so that others can feed off you and be nourished. In contrast, all deeds of the flesh are selfish. The flesh says, "You made me mad. I'm not happy. You have what I want. You are irritating me." But the fruit of the Spirit is Christ-centered and others-centered. Notice, the word "fruit" is singular, even though Paul lists nine different kinds of spiritual fruit: "Love, joy, peace, longsuffering, kindness, goodness, faithfulness, gentleness, self-control." But they all come from the same tree. This tree can produce everything you need for every area of your life. You don't have to go to the Holy Spirit for peace, and some other place for love. Or go to the Holy Spirit for patience, and somebody else for self-control. It's all on the Spirit's tree. So, are you bearing fruit?

HINTS ABOUT HEAVEN

I go to prepare a place for you.

JOHN 14:2 NKJV

When it comes to heaven, the Bible gives us just enough information to whet our appetite but not satisfy our curiosity. Here are three hints about heaven:

(1) "There shall be no more curse" (Rev 22:3 NKJV). Unlike Eden, Satan won't be there to tempt us so we won't stumble. We'll be at our best—forever. Every good New Year's resolution we've ever made will be a reality. (2) "God will wipe away every tear...there shall be no more death, nor sorrow" (Rev 21:4 NKJV). No failing health, grieving hearts or broken homes. The "Uppertaker" will put the undertaker out of business. (3) "His servants shall serve Him" (Rev 22:3 NKJV). What is service, if not productive work? Jesus said those who are faithful over a few things now, will rule over many things then. In the first paradise God gave Adam and Eve responsibilities; will He do less in the next one? "Of the increase of His government and peace there will be no end" (Isa 9:7 NKJV). God's new world will be marked by "increase." Increased planets? Increased colors, music? Seems likely. What does the Creator do but create? Will some of us serve then, in the capacity we serve now? Couldn't earthly assignments hint at heavenly ones? One thing's for sure: you'll love it—never weary, selfish or defeated; clear mind, tireless muscles, unhindered joy. Heaven is a perfect place of perfected people with our perfect Lord. And here's the best part! Jesus promised: "When everything is ready, I will come and get you, so that you will always be with me where I am" (Jn 14:3 NLT).

SERVING GOD OR MONEY

You cannot serve both God and Money.
MATTHEW 6:24 NIV

Let's be honest. For most of us, materialism is God's main rival. But it's possible to get increasingly free of it. Author John Ortberg writes: "Sometimes when I'm speaking, I try a little exercise in dethroning the idol. I ask people to take out their wallet...It looks like a piece of leather. But it's really the temple of the 21st century. Most people in our day believe that their ability to experience happiness is directly associated with the contents of this little container. This is where the god Mammon lives. We give this little piece of leather the power to make us feel secure, successful, and valuable. It's very hard for us to surrender control of this little piece of leather. The real issue: Who's in charge? Are you holding it, or is it holding you? So as a little baby step of surrender, I ask people to hand it to the person next to them. At this point the attention level in the room goes way up. Then I announce that we're going to take an offering. I encourage people to give with the extravagant generosity they have always wanted to exhibit. Wallets fly back to their original owners fast at this point. Then I invite them to declare today, 'Enough day.' What I have now—my home, my job, my possessions, my family, my lifestyle—is enough. I will seek another and better kind of wealth than terminal acquisition." Then he tells the audience, "Circle today on your calendar. From this day on, your race with the Joneses is over. The Joneses win, but so do you!"

WHAT MISTAKES ARE YOU MAKING? (1)

Words of the wise...should be heard.
ECCLESIASTES 9:17 NKJV

It's a mistake not to ask yourself, "What mistakes am I making?" One leader writes: "I gave little thought to what might go wrong. I assumed that the 'right way' would be mistake-free. I did not acknowledge mistakes I made to myself, or others. I was not learning from my mistakes. If I wanted to become a better leader, I would have to stop making the mistake of not asking what mistake I was making." It's not the number of mistakes you make—it's how often you keep making the same mistake. If you want to turn your mistakes to your advantage:

(1) Admit your mistakes. Why don't we? Pride: we've an image to uphold. Insecurity: our self-worth is based on our performance. Stubbornness: we'd rather beat a dead horse than bury it and get a new one. Here's a news flash: people already know about your mistakes. When you admit them they're not surprised, they're relieved. They say, "Phew! He knows. Now we can quit pretending!" *(2) Accept mistakes as the price of progress.* Learn to view failure as a healthy, inevitable part of succeeding. Nothing's perfect in life—including you! So get used to it. *(3) Insist on learning from your mistakes.* When you try to avoid failure at all costs, you never learn, and you end up repeating the same mistakes over and over. Those who are willing to learn from their failures don't have to keep repeating them. Author William Saroyan observed: "We get very little wisdom from success. Learn from science. In science, mistakes always precede the discovery of truth."

WHAT MISTAKES ARE YOU MAKING? (2)

Words of the wise...should be heard.
ECCLESIASTES 9:17 NKJV

Don't be afraid to ask yourself, "What am I missing? What do I not know yet?" Some people expect nothing but trouble; they're pessimistic so they don't look for anything good. But others have a tendency to assume everything is good. Both kinds of thinking can hurt you. Elisabeth Elliot, author of *All That Was Ever Ours,* points out: "All generalizations are false—including this one—yet we keep making generalizations. We create images—graven ones that can't be changed. We dismiss or accept people, products, programs and propaganda according to the labels they come under. We know a little about something, and we treat it like we know everything." Learn to be more discerning! It's easy to make decisions based on what you know, but there are always things you don't know. It's easy to choose a direction based on what you see, but what don't you see? We learn only when we're willing to ask, "What am I missing?" That question causes you, and those around you, to stop and think. It's easy to see what's obvious, but asking tough questions brings to the surface things that aren't obvious. Not asking questions is to assume that a project is potentially perfect and that if it's handled with care, there will be no problems. You learn in life, often painfully, that this simply isn't reality. Two things will stop you dead in your tracks: (a) Overanalyzing to the point that you're paralyzed and afraid to act. (b) Under analyzing and moving ahead before you have sufficient knowledge and the wisdom to implement it.

WHAT MISTAKES ARE YOU MAKING? (3)

Words of the wise...should be heard.
ECCLESIASTES 9:17 NKJV

A sign in a high-pressure sales office brings a smile: "Do you like to travel? Do you want to meet new friends? Do you want to free up your future? All this can be yours if you make one more mistake." Fear of making mistakes keeps us from reaching our highest potential, from seeking honest counsel and feedback, and from speaking out lest we become criticized or abandoned. To be successful you must give the people around you permission to push back. When you don't get input it can be disastrous. In *It's Your Ship,* Michael Abrashoff writes: "The moment I heard about it [the tragic sinking of a Japanese fishing boat off Honolulu by the submarine *USS Greenville*], I was reminded that, as is often the case with accidents, someone senses possible danger but doesn't actually speak up. As the *Greenville* investigation unfolded, I read in a *New York Times* article that the submarine's crew 'respected the Commanding Officer too much to question his judgment.' If that's respect, then I want none of it. You need to have people that can tap you on your shoulder and say, 'Is this the best way?' or 'Slow down,' or 'Think about this,' or 'Is what we are doing worth killing or injuring somebody?' History records countless incidents in which ship captains or organization managers permitted a climate of intimidation to pervade the workplace, silencing subordinates whose warnings could have prevented disaster. Even when the reluctance to speak up stems from admiration for the commanding officer's skill and experience, a climate to question decisions must be created in order to foster double-checking."

WHAT MISTAKES ARE YOU MAKING? (4)

Words of the wise...should be heard.
ECCLESIASTES 9:17 NKJV

One day King Zedekiah said to the prophet Jeremiah, "I will ask you something. Hide nothing from me" (Jer 38:14 NKJV). Zedekiah displayed wisdom we don't display often enough. One author writes: "I changed from someone who avoids potentially bad news to someone who invites it. For many years I've given permission to members of my inner circle to ask me hard questions and give me their opinion when they disagree with me. I don't ever want to make a mistake, then hear a team member say, 'I thought that was going to be a bad decision.' I want people to tell me on the front end, not after it's too late for their advice to help. Pushback before a decision is made is never disloyalty. You need to give them permission to ask hard questions and pushback against your ideas. That decision must be given to others by the leader. Too often leaders would rather have followers who turn a blind eye instead of ones who speak with a blunt tongue. But if all is quiet when decisions are being considered, it probably won't be quiet after it plays out." Sir Francis Bacon observed, "If a person will begin with certainties, he will end in doubts; but if he will be content to begin with doubts, he will end in certainties." Job said, "Men listened to me and waited, and kept silence for my counsel" (Job 29:21 NKJV). You must constantly ask yourself: What is my attitude toward mistakes? Am I owning up to my mistakes? Am I learning from them? Do I get the best input possible?

JUST DO IT!

A doubtful mind will be as unsettled as a wave.

JAMES 1:6 TLB

The Bible says: "A doubtful mind will be as unsettled as a wave...driven and tossed by the wind. People like that should not expect to receive anything from the Lord. They can't make up their minds" (See Jas 1:6-8 TLB) This Scripture applies specifically to asking God for wisdom, then rationalizing and vacillating when He gives you an answer. But the same principle applies to *all* of life. Have you ever seen anything more fickle than a wave? The wind that takes it one direction today, takes it in an entirely different one tomorrow. "How does this apply to me?" you ask: (1) If you've grown up in a family where every decision was made for you. (2) If you've spent your life around people who made reckless decisions that left you feeling "it's too easy to get it wrong and too hard to get it right." (3) If the bad decisions you've made in the past have sabotaged your confidence—then today's devotion is just for you!

James makes the point that *none* of us learn to hear from God without making mistakes. So don't be hard on yourself. Learn from your mistakes, correct the ones you can, and continue being decisive. Don't fall back into a pattern of indecision because you got it wrong a few times. Often you'll only know that you've done the right thing—when you do it! Devote a reasonable amount of time to waiting on God, and when necessary seek the counsel of others. But don't be afraid to act; make a decision and follow through with it. In other words, "Just do it!"

IF WE'RE WILLING TO PAY THE PRICE

As many as I love, I rebuke.

REVELATION 3:19 NKJV

Addressing the end-time church, Jesus said: "You say, 'I am rich...and have need of nothing'—and do not know that you are wretched, miserable, poor, blind, and naked—I counsel you to buy from Me gold refined in the fire, that you may be rich; and white garments, that you may be clothed, that the shame of your nakedness may not be revealed; and anoint your eyes with eye salve, that you may see. As many as I love, I rebuke and chasten. Therefore...repent" (vv. 17-19 NKJV).

Those are strong words! Why would Christ say that to us? Because: (1) Instead of believing God for New Testament results, we say God doesn't do miracles anymore. (2) We've tolerated division in the name of denominational loyalty. (3) We've taught that Christianity is mainly about avoiding things. As a result we've lost our joy, because intimacy with Christ cannot be achieved through performance. (4) Many of our leaders have stopped modeling servant-hood and forgotten that Jesus washed feet and rode on a donkey. (5) Instead of using our financial blessings to reach the world for Christ and care for the poor, we're acquiring and splurging on ourselves. (6) We get upset when somebody uses contemporary methods to reach the younger generation. Instead of engaging the culture we're hiding from it. (7) Instead of "occupy till I come," we'd rather fly away. We read rapture novels when we should be praying for those living on the verge of martyrdom. Why can't we have their kind of faith? We can—if we're willing to pay the price.

BE CAREFUL WHAT YOU COMMIT TO!

Which is the greatest commandment?
MATTHEW 22:36 NIV

When Jesus was asked, "Which is the greatest commandment?" He answered, "Love the Lord…and…Love your neighbor as yourself" (vv. 37-39 NIV). So our greatest commitments should be based on the two greatest commandments. The problem is, we get involved with things that keep us from doing this. The Bible says, "No one serving as a soldier gets involved in civilian affairs—he wants to please his commanding officer" (2Ti 2:4 NIV). In other words, be careful what you commit to. There are three types of commitments: *(1) Dramatic commitments.* Like getting married or buying a home. Unfortunately, we don't consider the hidden costs. When we buy a house we think only of the additional square footage, not the extra hour each day commuting to work or the time taken away from our family. *(2) Routine commitments.* These may look mundane, but don't underestimate their power. Any parent who's signed up their child for a sports league knows the time-consuming potential of the routine commitments. *(3) Unspoken commitments.* These are the commitments we make to ourselves, but often fail to keep. In life, the dramatic commitments receive most of our attention, but the routine ones end up controlling us. Because there are so many of them and because they come on a daily basis and individually look so small, we don't sense the gap growing between what we say matters most to us, and what we're actually *doing* with our lives. So Jesus simplified it: "Love the Lord…and…Love your neighbor." When you measure your life by that yardstick, you've a better chance of living by the right commitments.

TOUGH LOVE

Arise and walk.

MATTHEW 9:5 NKJV

Misguided sympathy is dangerous because: (a) it enables someone to feel sorry for themselves, yet take no action to change things; (b) it digs the hole deeper, so they've less chance of getting out of it; (c) it creates a "learned helplessness" guaranteeing they'll feel even more hopeless. Sometimes tough love is what's needed. Although Jesus had compassion for hurting people, He never merely felt sorry for them. Whenever possible He helped them to help themselves. Before He worked on their behalf, He often asked them to *do* something. And sometimes His instructions seemed radical. For example, He told a crippled man to rise, take up his bed and walk (See Mt 9:6). He told a man who'd received word that his daughter was dead, not to fret (See Mk 5:35-36). He spat on the ground, made mud and rubbed it on a blind man's eyes. Then He instructed him to walk to the pool of Siloam and wash it off (See Jn 9:1-7). How could a crippled man rise, take up his bed and walk? How could a man who had just received the report of his daughter's death be expected to stay calm? How could a blind man even see to get to a certain pool of water? Instead of merely feeling sorry for people, Jesus moved them to action. He helped them to get their minds off their problems, and motivated them to *do* something about them. At times we feel like we're being unkind if we confront people who have problems, when in reality "tough love" is what they need.

HANDLING ABANDONMENT (1)

Jesus...asked, "Are you also going to leave?"
JOHN 6:67 NLT

We say, "What'll I do if they leave and never come back?" It's one of our greatest fears—abandonment! Watch the newborn when Mom leaves the room—terror appears on its tiny face. Our memory records those traumatic moments and replays them later when an important relationship is disintegrating in our hands. Jesus understands how you feel. "Many of his disciples turned away and deserted him" (v. 66 NLT). What was His reaction? Indifference: "Who needs you?" False bravado: "I can get along without you?" Revenge: "I don't get mad, I get even?" No, we hear His intensely human emotions: "Are you also going to leave?" It's all there: the pain of loss, wondering what's going to happen next, anticipating how it will impact us and if we'll be able to get through it.

When you're facing abandonment by someone you love and dread losing, remember: (1) Efforts to keep someone from abandoning you usually don't work. Begging, manipulating, tears and promises often intensify their determination to go. (2) At some point we all experience the heartbreak of losing someone we love, or being disappointed in people. It's why God tells us over and over, "Fear not, I am with you." (3) The pain you feel is legitimate. Those who say, "You shouldn't feel this way," are well-meaning but wrong. Acknowledging pain initiates the feeling-dealing-healing process. You can't heal what you won't feel or deal with. So, embrace your feelings, draw on God's grace, and move through the healing process.

HANDLING ABANDONMENT (2)

Jesus...asked, "Are you also going to leave?"

JOHN 6:67 NLT

When you face abandonment, your greatest enemy is your own anxiety! It pushes you into all the wrong reactions. Learn to manage it or it'll bring about your worst fears. Here are some guidelines to help you: *(1) Stay out of the "pursuer" role.* Most relationships have a "pursuer" and a "distancer." When we feel vulnerable we fall into whichever role is characteristic and act it out. When one distances, the other pursues, and vice versa. The problem is: when you pursue a distancer and they get anxious, distancing more, it increases your anxiety and pushes you to pursue more—the vicious cycle. Though it will feel unnatural, by faith, decide to stop pursuing. You'll decrease the distancer's anxiety and invite them to stop distancing. Letting go is frightening and feels as though it might encourage them to leave. It won't necessarily, but holding on will. Managing your anxiety calls on you to do what you fear, but it will reduce the anxiety level!

(2) Control your anxiety-inducing self-talk. "As he thinks ...so is he" (Pr 23:7 NKJV). Your anxiety is being caused by your thoughts and self-talk, not your partner or circumstances. Saying, "Oh, I'll die if he (or she) leaves me," generates and magnifies your fear. Construct a helpful self-talk list. "If he leaves, it'll hurt, but with the help of God and my family, I'll get through it." Factor God in; He's the changer of hearts and minds. Lean on Him and He will lessen your anxiety and increase your peace and confidence!

HANDLING ABANDONMENT (3)

Jesus...asked, "Are you also going to leave?"

JOHN 6:67 NLT

By managing your anxiety when feeling abandoned, you're taking control where it counts most and brings the greatest benefits. Here are some helpful guidelines:

(1) Always remember that your thoughts are under your control. When anxiety kicks in, your thoughts begin to run amok. At this point you must take charge of your mind, "Casting down imaginations...bringing into captivity every thought" (2Co 10:5). Don't argue, resist or reason with your thoughts. Give them a "stop!" order, breathe deeply and select an encouraging thought from your scriptural self-talk list. Feel your anxiety dropping and give God thanks for victory over your anxiety. *(2) Stay out of the "waiting room!"* By waiting for someone to change or decide to stay, you're putting your life on hold, pending someone else's decision. That's not how God made you to function! "Live purposefully...making the very most of the time [buying up each opportunity]" (Eph 5:15-16 AMP). Fill your days with worthwhile activity, taking initiative wherever possible and directing your time to useful, rewarding purposes, especially ones that glorify God. *(3) Helping others will help heal you.* God's law of reciprocity says you reap when you sow, and receive when you give. It offers you the chance to help yourself by helping others. The Bible says, "The Lord restored Job's losses when he prayed for his friends" (Job 42:10 NKJV). Research consistently shows that acts of kindness toward others improve the emotional state of those doing them. By helping others you actually instruct your body to increase its positive endorphin levels, boosting your own joy, peace and confidence. Watch it work for you, no matter how the relationship goes!

HOW TO HAVE A GOOD DAY

Without Me you can do nothing.

JOHN 15:5 NKJV

When Satan has negative plans for your day—you can change the course of your day by spending time with the Lord, especially when you sense any attitude or behavior in yourself that's not Christ-like. Jesus said, "Without Me you can do nothing." On the other hand, through Him we can do all things (See Php 4:13). Negative feelings are like unwelcome house guests: the worst thing you can do is to invite them in. You may not be able to override them in your own strength, but if you seek God's help He will enable you to walk according to His ways, not by your negative emotions and perspective. "But what if someone offends me?" The Bible says we're not to be oversensitive or easily offended. Actually we are commanded to forgive those who hurt us, not let things fester. Sometimes we want to forgive and do what's right, but we find doing it difficult. More often than not, the right thing is the *hard* thing to do, not the *easy* thing. That's when you need to pray and allow God to talk to you through His Word. Only then will you find the strength to do the right thing.

Remember, you're in a war, and the battle begins the moment your eyes open each morning. To win, you must know how to use the weapons God has placed at your disposal. And you must put on your armor *before* the battle begins (See Eph 6:10-20). Your greatest weapons are prayer, praise, reading God's Word, and Christian fellowship. If you want to have a good day, learn to use them.

TIME—MAKE THE MOST OF IT!

Teach us to number our days.

PSALM 90:12 NKJV

Our days are like identical suitcases, but some people pack more into them than others. That's because they know *what* to pack. Everybody gets twenty-four hours, but not everybody gets the same return on their twenty-four hours. The truth is, you don't manage your time, you manage your life. Time cannot be controlled; it marches on no matter what you do. Nobody—no matter how shrewd—can save minutes from one day to spend in another. No scientist is capable of creating new minutes. With all his wealth, Warren Buffett can't buy additional hours for his day. People talk about trying to "find time," but they need to quit looking; there isn't any extra lying around. Twenty-four hours is the best any of us is going to get. Wise people understand that time is their most precious commodity. As a result, they know where their time goes. They continually analyze how they are using their time and ask themselves, "Am I getting the best use out of my time?" In his book *What to Do Between Birth and Death: The Art of Growing Up,* Charles Spezzano writes: "You don't really pay for things with money, you pay for them with time. We say, 'In five years, I'll have enough money put away for that vacation house we want. Then I'll slow down.' That means the house will cost you five years—one-twelfth of your adult life. Translate the dollar value of the house, car, or anything else into time, and then see if it's still worth it."

GOOD ENOUGH!

I will build you, and you shall be rebuilt.
JEREMIAH 31:4 NKJV

Don't allow anybody but God to tell you what you're worth. That's too much power to give anyone. If people can label you, they can limit you. Until you know how *God* feels about you, you'll know neither your worth as an individual nor your life's purpose. You'll worry about how you look, what others think, and whether or not you're going to succeed in life. But when you believe God's promise, "I have loved you with an everlasting love…I will build you, and you shall be rebuilt" (vv. 3-4 NKJV), you're free to focus on improving and reaching your God-given potential. What life has torn down, God can rebuild.

Today, if you're suffering from lack of self-worth, here's a prayer to help you: "Father, sometimes I think I'm of no use, that I can't do anything right, that nothing I do is ever good enough. But I know that when You look at who I am, and who I can be—You see Jesus. And He is good enough! It's good enough that He shed His precious blood to cover my unworthiness. Good enough that He paid the price for every sin I would ever commit. Good enough that He's working to perfect me each day. Good enough that He sees me as 'righteous' in Christ. Good enough that He's interceding for me at the throne of God right now. Good enough that He's mending the broken areas of my life and making me whole. Good enough that His love for me is everlasting and guaranteed. Thank You, Father, that everything Jesus does is good enough, and that in Him, I am good enough too!"

HOW TO OVERCOME IN TROUBLED TIMES

Let not your heart be troubled.

JOHN 14:27 NKJV

Jesus said, "My peace I give to you...Let not your heart be troubled, neither let it be afraid." Underline the words, "Let not." You can't control what goes on around you, but Jesus said you can control what goes on inside you. How? By doing two things:

(1) Fill your mind with God's Word. Jesus said, "These things I have spoken to you, that in Me you may have peace. In the world you will have tribulation; but be of good cheer, I have overcome the world" (Jn 16:33 NKJV). Rearrange your priorities and take time to read God's Word each day. Process it, apply it to each circumstance, and stand on it in times of difficulty. You'll be amazed at the results!

(2) Pray about the situation, then leave it confidently in God's hands. Here's a prayer to help you do that: "Lord, everything seems to be falling apart around me. Everybody wants a piece of me. There's far too much to do and never enough time to do it. My head is clogged with all kinds of junk and my heart is ready to break. Lord, where are You? I feel like the disciples in the storm, the waves are too big for me. My cry is the same as theirs, 'Somebody go and get Jesus—I'm about to drown out here!' Prince of Peace, I need you. Father, who never slumbers nor sleeps, take charge. Let me find in You a quiet place, a place where I can pillow my head on Your breast, hear Your loving heartbeat and feel secure knowing You'll work things out for me. This I pray, believing, in Jesus' name, amen."

FORGIVE THEM, AND LET IT GO

Forgive whatever grievances you may have.
COLOSSIANS 3:13 NIV

We talk about grudges the way we talk about babies. You can *hold* a grudge, *carry* a grudge, *bear* a grudge, or *nurse* a grudge. The trouble is, when you nurse something you feed it, make it grow, and pretty soon it's full grown. Are you carrying a grudge? Why? It doesn't make sense. Why would you pick up something each day that weighs you down and carry it around with you? "But they hurt me." Yes, but by carrying a grudge you enable them to *keep* hurting you. Don't do that to yourself!

We know we're supposed to forgive other people, but sometimes forgiving feels like we are *giving up* something. One of Lincoln's stories was about a man on his sickbed who had been told by the doctor that he didn't have much time to live. He summoned an old friend named Brown with whom he'd quarreled bitterly. They hadn't spoken for years. The man talked of how he was going to die soon, of how their petty differences looked in the face of death, and asked if they might be reconciled. The scene moved everyone in the room to tears. Brown clasped the dying man's hands, embraced him, and turned to walk out of the room, a shattered man. Suddenly the man on the sickbed, having one final thought, raised himself up on one elbow and spoke for the last time: "But see here, Brown; if I recover, the old grudge still stands." This story makes us smile and think, "How foolish!" But if you are carrying a grudge, are *you* any different?

ARE YOU RUNNING FROM GOD? (1)

Jonah arose to flee to Tarshish.

JONAH 1:3 NKJV

Ninevah was about 550 miles east of Jonah. Tarshish was 2,500 miles west of him. Rather than go 550 miles in God's will, Jonah decided to go 2,500 miles out of it. Ever do that? God says, "Go here," but you go there. The bad news is, you not only have to come back the 2,500 miles you went in the wrong direction, but the 550 miles God told you to go in the first place. Furthermore, whenever you run from God, you get to pay the fare. "He...found a ship going to Tarshish; so he paid the fare" (v. 3 NKJV). The good thing about going to Ninevah is, God will provide the fare. The bad thing about going to Tarshish is, you get to pick up the tab. Many of us are paying a high price for our Tarshish trip, when, if we had done it God's way, He'd have picked up the tab. And notice something else: when you disobey God you not only mess yourself up, but also those around you. Those poor sailors on the ship didn't ask for Jonah's mess, but they got it. Are you messing up the lives of others because of your rebellion? Think about it; if the wind, the sea and the whale had to obey God, what were Jonah's chances of escaping? Jonah didn't rebound until he got swallowed, and some of us are not going to do the right thing until we are swallowed too—until God permits circumstances so adverse that running *to* Him, instead of *from* Him, is the only thing left. Is God saying something to you today?

ARE YOU RUNNING FROM GOD? (2)

The word...came to Jonah the second time.
JONAH 3:1 NKJV

Jonah did some serious praying in the whale's belly; he repented of his prejudice and learned to love people he despised. It was there he became willing to preach things people don't like to hear. And you'll notice something else. God didn't intervene until he repented. Most of us want God to move before we've moved. No, Jonah acted, then God responded; He commanded the fish and it vomited Jonah up onto dry land, whereupon the runaway prophet asked for directions to Ninevah. Sometimes because of our rebellious spirit we don't get it right until the next marriage. Sometimes because of our rebellious spirit we don't get it right until we're fifty. Sometimes because of our rebellious spirit we don't overcome our addiction until later, although we could have overcome it sooner. Like Jonah we have to go to the bottom. But whatever it takes, God will do it. You can go to Ninevah yourself, or God can take you there. But it's easier to obey the first time.

Jonah's story proves that the Lord is a God of second chances. "The word of the Lord came to Jonah the second time." Good news: Even though you've run from God, made "shipwreck" of your life and feel like you're drowning, God will redeem and restore you if you'll turn to Him. He will give you a second chance in your marriage, your ministry or your vocation. But there's one condition—God is not going to change *His* mind to accommodate what you want, so you need to change *your* mind and attitude and do what He says, okay?

CORRECT YOUR CHILD

A father corrects a child in whom he delights.

PROVERBS 3:12 NLT

You're destroying your child's motivation and self-esteem when you allow them to think they don't have to work for anything because it's "owed" to them. The story's told of a telemarketer who phoned a house, saying, "I'd like to talk to the person who makes the final purchasing decisions for the family." The woman replied, "I'm sorry, that person is still at kindergarten and won't be home for another hour." Cute story, but not so cute when it's reality. Parent, love your child, provide them with opportunity and a secure home environment, but teach them to be responsible. This sounds like a no-brainer; so why don't we do it?

(1) Misguided love. We say, "My kids shouldn't have to struggle like I did." Your children interpret that kind of indulgence as lack of interest—you taking the easy way out. As a result their demands increase because what they're really saying is, "I don't really want more stuff, I want you!" *(2) Low expectations.* As a parent you owe your children a chance to excel in life. Don't rob them of the fulfillment that comes from working hard to improve their grades, clean their room and earn their way. *(3) Guilt.* We all feel bad about not spending enough time with our kids, or having failed them. One sixteen-year-old told her dad that he "owed" her a car. And she got it! Why? Because her parents were divorced and Dad felt bad about "letting her down." Don't try to buy your child's affection; you'll only end up paying later. God corrects His children—you need to correct yours!

MAKING THE TOUGH CALLS

The Lord is on my side; I will not fear.
PSALM 118:6 NKJV

All the heroes of the Bible were flawed. And dispositionally, they were as different as chalk and cheese. But they'd one thing in common: they were willing to make the tough calls. Observe: *(1) Tough calls demand risk.* When the Soviet Union overran and annexed Latvia in 1940, the U.S. Vice Consul in Riga was concerned that the American Red Cross supplies in that city would be looted. To guard against it he requested permission from the State Department in Washington, D.C. to place an American flag above the Red Cross to deter anyone from taking the supplies. "No precedent exists for such action," the Secretary of State's Office cabled back. When the Vice Consul received the message he climbed up and personally nailed the American flag to the pole, then he cabled the State Department: "As of this date, I have established precedent." *(2) Tough calls require character.* Chuck Swindoll writes: "Courage is not limited to the battlefield or the Indianapolis 500 or bravely catching a thief in your house. The real tests of courage are much quieter. They are the inner tests, like remaining faithful when nobody's looking, like enduring pain when the room is empty, like standing alone when you're misunderstood." Whether you lead a family, a business or a church, the temptation to complain comes easy. Thank God for the tough times. They're the reason you're there—to be the leader. If everything was going well you wouldn't be needed. When the tough calls must be made, your confidence can be found in these words: "The Lord is on my side; I will not fear."

IN SPITE OF FAMILY AND FRIENDS

For this purpose I have been sent.

LUKE 4:43 NKJV

After going home to a cool reception Jesus said, "A prophet is honored everywhere except in his own home town" (Mk 6:4 TLB). In other places He was considered a hero, but not here. "His family...thought he was out of his mind" (Mk 3:21 NCV). So how did Jesus handle His family?

It's worth noting that He didn't try to control their behavior, nor did He let their behavior control His. He loved them, but He didn't demand that they always agree with Him. He didn't sulk or retaliate when they insulted Him. And He didn't make it His mission in life to try and please them. If your family is making it difficult for you to serve the Lord, observe three things about Jesus: (1) He recognized that His spiritual family could provide what His physical family didn't. That's why we need the support and stability that comes from the fellowship in a local church. (2) He didn't let the difficult dynamic of family overshadow His call from God. Your family may not understand or agree, but you can't let that keep you from doing what God's called you to do. (3) He refused to let the opinion of the crowd dictate His direction. The whole town of Capernaum "tried to keep Him from leaving them" (Lk 4:42 NKJV). But He resisted the undertow of people by anchoring to the rock of His purpose: to build God's kingdom, not His own. Imagine the whole town wanting you to stay, and you leave anyway. Could all those people be wrong? Yes! Jesus followed the will of God. And you must too.

GOD WILL TELL YOU WHAT TO SAY

Don't worry about what to say.

MATTHEW 10:19 TLB

Jesus said: "Don't worry about how to respond or what to say. God will give you the right words at the right time. For it is not you who will be speaking—it will be the Spirit of your Father speaking through you" (vv. 19-20 NLT). Does that mean we should not prepare ourselves? No, it just means we should stop trying to figure out in advance everything we need to say and do in every situation we face. You'll wear yourself out trying to prepare for every circumstance you're likely to run into in the future. Jesus told His disciples to entrust their lives fully to God and depend on His indwelling Holy Spirit to guide, protect and equip them when the situation arose. The same goes for us. For example, when we have to make hard decisions or solve complicated problems or confront difficult people, God's Spirit will decide the proper *time* and the best *approach*. He will also give us the right *words* to say. Until then, we don't need to bother ourselves with it. If we will listen to what the Lord is telling us here in this passage, not only will we have more peace, but we will also enjoy more success. When we do have to speak, what comes out of our mouths will be spiritual wisdom from God and not something we have come up with out of our own carnal mind. Your responsibility is not to know the future, it's to trust in God who holds the future, and be confident that you're safe in His hands.

LEARNING TO PRAY

The Spirit...makes intercession for us.
ROMANS 8:26 NKJV

Prayer isn't natural to us. Our natural inclination is to depend on ourselves. Some of us haven't learned how to pray. Others don't pray enough to be comfortable with it. Still others don't understand enough of God's Word to pray biblically and get results. Whatever the case, we've no excuse not to pray. The Holy Spirit who lives within us can clarify, correct and change our prayer so that by the time it reaches God it's all sorted out. The Bible says: "The Spirit also helps in our weaknesses. For we do not know what we should pray for as we ought, but the Spirit Himself makes intercession for us...Now He who searches the hearts knows what the mind of the Spirit is, because He makes intercession for the saints according to the will of God. And we know that all things work together for good to those who love God, to those who are the called according to His purpose" (vv. 26-28 NKJV). Who do "all things work together for good" for? Just anybody and everybody who believes? No, those who "love God." And more importantly, those who have learned to allow the Holy Spirit within them to pray, because what *He* asks for will *always* be in line with God's will.

Learning to pray is like learning a foreign language. The best way to learn it is to hang out in an environment where the language is spoken. So if you want to learn to pray you must: (a) take the time to do it; (b) spend time with those who know how to do it; (c) allow the Holy Spirit to lead and guide you.

DO WHAT YOU'RE CALLED TO DO

Having then gifts...let us use them.
ROMANS 12:6 NKJV

In *Growing Strong in the Seasons of Life,* Dr. Charles Swindoll writes: "Once upon a time, the animals decided that they should do something meaningful to meet the problems of the new world. So they organized a school. They adopted an activity curriculum of running, climbing, swimming, and flying. To make it easier to administer, all the animals took all the subjects. The duck was excellent at swimming. In fact, he was better than his instructor was! However, he made only passing grades in flying, and was very poor in running. Since he was so slow in running, he had to drop swimming and stay after school to practice running. This caused his webbed feet to be badly worn so he became only average in swimming. But 'average' was quite acceptable, therefore nobody worried about it—except the duck. The rabbit stayed at the top of his class in running, but developed a nervous twitch in his leg muscles because he had so much make-up work to do in swimming. The squirrel was excellent in climbing, but he encountered constant frustration in flying class because his teacher made him start from the ground up instead of from the treetop down...so he only got a 'C' in climbing and a 'D' in running. The eagle was a problem child and was severely disciplined for being a nonconformist. In climbing classes, he beat all the others to the top, but insisted on using his own way of getting there!"

"Having then gifts...let us use them." When God has gifted and graced you to do something, give yourself to it and let the rest go.

TAKE A LEAP OF FAITH (1)

You give them something to eat.

MATTHEW 14:16 NKJV

Lee Brown noticed a little girl begging in her neighborhood. Later she searched, but couldn't find her at the local school. That day Brown decided to make a difference for other kids by adopting a first-grade class in one of the city's lowest-performing schools, pledging to pay for any student wanting to attend college. Brown wasn't wealthy. She was a cotton-picker-turned-real estate agent making $45,000 a year and raising two kids—but she honored that pledge. She's personally contributed $10,000 every year, in addition to raising donations from others. Brown's leap of faith rescued students who'd otherwise end up on the streets.

It takes courage to make a difference, especially when you can't see a way to do it. When he was in Africa, David Livingstone received a letter saying, "We want to send helpers. Have you found a good road into your area yet?" Livingstone wrote back, "If they only want to come when there's a good road, don't send them. I want people who'll come when there's no road!" Surrounded by 5,000 hungry people, Jesus told His disciples, "You give them something to eat." It seemed impossible, but when they obeyed they witnessed a miracle. One writer says: "Christ will lead you into seemingly impossible situations …don't avoid them. That's where you'll experience God… If you attempt only things you know are possible with the resources you possess…you'll receive the credit and God will have no part in it…Have you received a word that awaits your next step of faith? Proceed, no matter how incredible it seems. You'll experience the joy of seeing God perform a miracle, and so will those around you."

TAKE A LEAP OF FAITH (2)

Faith is...the conviction of things not seen.
HEBREWS 11:1 NAS

One day two caterpillars were plodding up a hill when they noticed a butterfly dipping and weaving overhead. Turning to his buddy, one said, "You'd never get me up in one of those things!" Raise your sights, take a leap of faith! "Faith is...the conviction of things not seen."

Glynnis Whitwer says: "God calls us to obedience without showing us the end result...There are days I'm tired of getting called out of my comfort zone...I've been known to whine and ask if I can serve God from the safety of my recliner. But that's not God's way. He doesn't want me limited by my desire for security and control...Something inside is revealed when we're pressured from without...[it] shines light on the truth about our faith...To grow, faith must be stretched, and that's uncomfortable...Unlike some, I haven't learned to trust God the easy way...by reading a book...listening to a sermon...or hearing how my friend trusts Him. I'm learning by stepping out into the adventure of obedience and discovering that He's trustworthy. This happened when my husband and I started tithing (after I resisted for years), and watched God cover our needs and more...When I obeyed His command to write a book (although I didn't know what I'd write about), and watched God open doors of opportunity...When we said yes to adoption, and are watching the blossoming of two little girls with hope and a future...Obeying when God hasn't revealed the steps... or the final destination is challenging. But when we walk by faith He gets the glory, because we know we couldn't have done it." So, take a leap of faith.

"LIFE TO THE FULL"

I have come that they may have life...to the full.
JOHN 10:10 NIV

At a street meeting, a young Salvation Army drummer was testifying about his past. "Before I became a Christian I used to drink and gamble, but I don't do that anymore. I used to swear and womanize, but I don't do that anymore either. Come to think of it...all I do now is stand on the same old street corner and beat the same old drum!" Ever felt like that? You get up, go to work, come home, eat dinner, watch TV, drop into bed, get up next day and do it all again? Like Solomon, sometimes you can feel like "Everything is meaningless" (Ecc 12:8 NLT). But it doesn't have to be that way.

Francis Schaeffer said, "Man has a purpose—to be in a relationship with God...when he forgets his purpose he forgets who he is and what life means." There's more to life than beating the same old drum day after day. Jesus came that you "might have life to the full," and the first step is acknowledging that He died to show you the way back to God. Step two is recognizing you *need* a personal relationship with Him. Step three is using the Bible as a blueprint for purpose and fulfillment. It's the only book that answers the important questions, "Who am I?" and "Why am I here?" You're not "a mistake" as one woman said after discovering her mother had tried to abort her. In God's eyes you have great value, and today He offers you "life to the full."

HIT THE DELETE BUTTON

Forgiving one another…as God…has forgiven you.
EPHESIANS 4:32 NLT

I magine living in a society where adulterers wear a scarlet letter and thieves wear a ball and chain. Imagine being identified only by your past. "They probably deserved it," you say. Really? Jesus said if you look at a member of the opposite sex with lust, you've committed adultery in your heart (See Mt 5:28). Ouch! Then He went on to say that the standard of judgment you impose on others is the standard by which you'll be judged (See Mt 7:1-2). Can you live with that? Now, God's not soft on sin. His love won't let you off. "The Lord disciplines those he loves" (Heb 12:6 NIV). But His love won't let you go. "Nothing will ever be able to separate us from the love of God" (Ro 8:39 TLB).

We're not too familiar with a scarlet letter or a ball and chain, but we are familiar with a computer. And when someone hurts or upsets us, God says, "Forgive, and hit the delete button!" Otherwise you'll be corrupted with a virus that controls the way you think, act and talk. Worst of all, it'll keep you chained to the memories. "But forgiving is hard," you say. Sure it is. That's why Jesus said, "Pray for those who mistreat you" (See Mt 5:44). *Forgiving* someone begins with *praying* for them. "But I need to try and understand why they did it." Smart people do stupid stuff. Good people do bad stuff. And misguided people don't know what they're doing. That's why Jesus prayed, "Father, forgive them; for they know not what they do" (Lk 23:34). You may understand someday, or you may never understand. Either way, for your own sake forgive, hit the delete button and move on!

THE PROMISE OF LONG LIFE

*That by his death he might…free those who…
were held in slavery by their fear of death.*

HEBREWS 2:14-15 NIV

If a parent died when you were young, you may be living with the unspoken fear that you won't live longer than they did. The Bible addresses this: "Only by dying could he break…the power of death…[and] set free all who have lived their lives as slaves to the fear of dying" (vv. 14-15 NLT). Observe: *(1) When your work on earth is done, God promotes you to a home in heaven.* Imagine your dream home, then add the words: "far better" (Php 1:23). And who is the architect, builder and designer of this home? Jesus: "I go to prepare a place for you" (Jn 14:2). *(2) By disobeying God you can shorten your life; by honoring Him you can lengthen it.* King Hezekiah proved this. Fighting illness and facing death he cried out to God: "Remember, O Lord, how I have walked before you faithfully and with wholehearted devotion and have done what is good in your eyes (2Ki 20:3 NIV). God answered, "I have heard your prayer and seen your tears; I will heal you…I will add fifteen years to your life" (vv. 5-6 NIV). You say, "Can God still heal today?" Absolutely! James writes: "Is any sick among you? Let him call for the elders of the church; and let them pray over him, anointing him with oil in the name of the Lord: And the prayer of faith shall save the sick, and the Lord shall raise him up" (Jas 5:14-15). *(3) If you're worried about dying, stand on God's Word.* "With long life will I satisfy him and show him my salvation" (Ps 91:16 NIV).

COME AS YOU ARE

Follow me, and I will make you...
MATTHEW 4:19

Understand this: Jesus doesn't invite us to follow Him because *we* believe in Him. He invites us to follow Him because *He* believes in us! He says, "Follow me and I will make you." He knows what we can become when His grace touches our lives. Matthew, a Jew, collected taxes for the Romans who enslaved his people. In their eyes he was lower than scum. Yet Jesus called him and he ended up writing the first book in the New Testament. When Nathaniel was invited to meet Jesus he was downright skeptical. "Can...any good thing come out of Nazareth? Philip saith unto him, Come and see" (Jn 1:46). Even after three years of exposure to His miracles and messages, they still had doubts. Check how often He says to them, "O ye of little faith...why do you not believe?...If only you believed you would see." Knowing they were anxious about what would happen when He left them and went back to heaven, Jesus said, "I will pray the Father, and he shall give you another Comforter [the Holy Spirit], that he may abide with you for ever" (Jn 14:16). The Greek word for comforter is *paracletos,* which means "one who comes alongside to help." There will never be a day when you won't need God's help!

So, come as you are. Come with your self-righteous or sordid past. Come with your halo or your hang-ups. Come, even though you wonder if He can do what He promises. Let His power and presence rub off on you. What do you have to lose? You've tried your way and it didn't work; now try His way. Come. You won't be disappointed!

BE FAITHFUL TO THE SCRIPTURES

All Scripture is God-breathed.
2 TIMOTHY 3:16 NIV

The first lie ever recorded was the one Satan told Eve when he said that God didn't really mean what He said. And he's still peddling the same line. You hear it in comments like: *(a) "If you're sincere, it doesn't matter what you believe."* What if you're sincerely wrong? If your car brakes don't work your sincerity won't stop you; telephone poles and buildings will. *(b) "We must be careful not to offend anyone."* What if people don't want to hear the truth or live according to it? Should we soften or edit the Scriptures based on what we think they can handle? If you love someone, wouldn't you interrupt their sleep to keep them from burning up with the house? *(c) "There is truth in the Bible, but not all the Bible is true."* Paul writes that "All Scripture is God-breathed." And Isaiah says, "If they speak not according to this word, it is because there is no light in them" (Isa 8:20). Twelve inches must make one foot, otherwise we're all open to each other's interpretations and subject to each other's value judgments—and somebody's going to get the short end of the stick.

Now, when we become arrogant in presenting the truth, the cause of Christ suffers and spiritually hungry people are turned off. We who have received grace and mercy must show it. But let's not compromise what God's Word says. Interestingly, when polled recently, the majority of today's young people (16-29) said, "Give it to me straight. And if you don't live it, don't give it!" How refreshing! Bottom line: God's Word is wholly, solely, fully, completely and altogether true. So be faithful to the Scriptures!

DISCOVERING YOURSELF

It's in Christ that we find out who we are.
EPHESIANS 1:11 TM

One day a boy climbing in the mountains found an eagle's nest with an egg in it. When he got home he put it under a hen along with her other eggs. When the eagle hatched he thought he was a chicken. He learned chicken behavior and scratched in the chicken yard with his "siblings." He didn't know any better. Sometimes he felt strange stirrings within himself but he didn't know what to do with them, so he ignored or suppressed them. After all, if he was a chicken he should behave like a chicken. One day an eagle flew over the chicken yard and the eagle looked up and saw him. In that moment he realized he wanted to be like that eagle, to fly high, to go to the mountain peaks he saw in the distance. As he spread his wings he suddenly understood that he *was* like that eagle. Though he'd never flown before, he possessed the instinct and capabilities. At first he flew unsteadily, then with greater power and control. Finally as he soared he knew he'd discovered his true self—the creature God made him to be.

Phillips Brooks remarked, "When you discover you've been leading only half a life, the other half is going to haunt you until you develop it." Self-discovery is what Paul had in mind when he wrote, "It's in Christ that we find out who we are and what we are living for." You were made *by* God and *for* God. Until you understand that, your life won't make sense. It's "in Christ" that we discover our purpose, our significance and our destiny. In other words, we discover our true selves!

KNOWING AND DOING GOD'S WILL

I am sending you.
JOHN 20:21 NIV ✓

Gladys Aylward was just a simple woman who did what she believed God called her to do. In 1920 she sailed to China where she opened a home for orphaned children who'd been left to starve or wander the streets until the government placed them in wretched warehouses. She'd read the Scripture: "If you spend yourselves in behalf of the hungry and satisfy the needs of the oppressed...The Lord will guide you always; he will satisfy your needs" (Isa 58:10-11 NIV). When the Japanese invaded China Gladys was forced to flee. She ended up on the island of Formosa with over a hundred children to care for. In the face of extreme difficulty and danger she devoted her life to becoming a mother to each of them. Years later when she was publicly honored, she explained her amazing work like this: "I did not choose this. I was led into it by God. I'm not really more interested in children than I am in other people. But God gave me to understand that this is what He wanted me to do— so I did it!"

Jesus said, "As the Father has sent me, I am sending you" (Jn 20:21 NIV). The mission Jesus had while on earth is now *our* mission. "All of us must quickly carry out the tasks assigned us by the one who sent me, for there is little time left" (Jn 9:4 TLB). William James said, "The best use of life is to spend it for something that outlasts it." Only the kingdom of God is going to last; everything else will eventually perish. To fulfill your kingdom-purpose here on earth is to have lived well, and lived successfully!

ARE YOU A GOSSIP? MEND YOUR WAYS!

A word out of your mouth...
can accomplish nearly anything—or destroy it!
JAMES 3:5 TM

There's a saying that goes, "The deepest wounds in life come not from swords but words." If you don't believe it look at the walking wounded; they're all around you! Are you yourself still struggling with the hurtful words of an insensitive parent, a schoolteacher, a marriage partner, or a boss? Or worse, a Christian who thinks God's Word on the subject of gossip doesn't apply to *them?* God takes the sin (yes, it's a sin!) of gossip so seriously that He devotes an entire chapter of the Bible to it. If we were to read James chapter three regularly we might show more consideration before opening our mouths. The Bible says: "A word out of your mouth may seem of no account, but it can accomplish nearly anything—or destroy it! It only takes a spark, remember, to set off a forest fire"!

One day a woman came to her pastor with a troubled conscience. She had "sliced and diced" just about everybody in church. "How can I make things right?" she asked. He said, "Take a box of feathers and drop one on the doorstep of each person you've criticized." After doing so she came back and said, "Is that all?" "No," he said. "Now go, pick up all of them and bring them back to me." A week or so later, the woman returned without a single one: "The wind blew them all away," she said. After a long silence the pastor said, "That's how it is with words; they're easily spoken, but you can never take them back again." Are you a gossip? Mend your ways!

A WORD TO LEADERS (1)

Joshua ordered the officers of the people.

JOSHUA 1:10 NIV

Before Israel entered the Promised Land God gave two important instructions to their leaders:

(1) "Cross over ahead of your brothers" (v. 14 NIV). If God has called you to lead, step up to the plate and swing the bat. Believe in yourself and your mission! Accomplishment is more than just working harder and smarter; it's about believing the right thing. Someone called it the "sure enough" syndrome. If you expect to fail, sure enough you will. If you expect to succeed, sure enough you will. Personal breakthroughs begin with a change in your beliefs. What you believe deep down determines what you expect, and what you expect determines how you will act. In the long run, a belief is more than just an idea you possess, it's an idea that possesses you!

(2) "Be strong and courageous" (v. 6 NIV). Your life will expand or shrink in proportion to the measure of courage you display. If you're willing to take risks you'll go further than those who timidly follow the safe and predictable path. Orison Swett Marden writes: "The moment you resolve to take hold of life with all your might and make the most of yourself at any cost, to sacrifice all lesser ambitions to your one great aim, to cut loose from everything that interferes with that aim, to stand alone, firm in your purpose whatever happens, you set in motion the forces implanted within you for your own development. Live up to your resolve, work at what God meant you to work at for the perfecting of His plan, and you will be invincible. No power on earth can hold you back from success."

A WORD TO LEADERS (2)

Joshua ordered the officers of the people.

JOSHUA 1:10 NIV

God said to Israel's leaders when entering the Promised Land: "Help your brothers" (v. 14 NIV). "How long do I have to keep investing in this person?" you ask. Want a *Bible* answer? "Until they too have taken possession of the land that ...God is giving them" (v. 15 NIV). It's not an occasional act of assistance; it's a lifestyle of serving. At the end of every day we should each ask ourselves, "Did I do a good job today? Was I an asset and not just an expense?" Author Richard L. Evans remarked: "It's priceless to find a person who will take responsibility, who will finish and follow through to the final detail—to know when someone has accepted an assignment that it will be effectively, conscientiously completed." And Paul raises the bar for followers of Christ! "Whatever you do or say, do it as a representative of the Lord Jesus" (Col 3:17 NLT).

People who take advantage of others inevitably fail. Dr. John Maxwell writes: "If you desire to succeed, live by these four simple words: *add value to others*. That philosophy will take you far. All talented people have a choice to make: to do their own thing and get all the credit, or do the team thing and share it. My observation is that not only do talented people accomplish more when working with others, but they are also more fulfilled than those who go it alone." So here's the deal: you are only qualified to enjoy the privileges and benefits of leadership when you're willing to: (a) go first and (b) put others first. God says, "After that, you may go back and occupy your own land" (Jos 1:15 NIV).

"GOOD TO THE LAST DROP!"

So here I am today, eighty-five years old!
JOSHUA 14:10 NIV

When the Canadian sprinter Donovan Bailey ran the 100 meters in 9.84 seconds he was hailed as the world's fastest man. But it could all have ended very differently, because with so many wins to his credit Bailey had problems accepting instructions and committing to the rigorous training necessary to meet the challenge. After his big win experts who critiqued videos of the race made an interesting discovery: Bailey never once lost momentum. In fact, he was *still* accelerating as he crossed the finish line.

Isaiah says, "He gives strength to the weary and increases the power of the weak" (Isa 40:29 NIV). *Live fully until the day God calls you home!* Caleb did; listen: "So here I am today, eighty-five years old! I am still as strong today as the day Moses sent me out; I'm just as vigorous to go out to battle now as I was then…give me this hill country that the Lord promised me that day…Then Joshua blessed Caleb…and gave him Hebron as his inheritance…because he followed the Lord…wholeheartedly" (Jos 14:10-14 NIV). Christian author Alma Barkman writes: "I've already covered half the miles in this 'race…set before us' (Heb12:1). Sprinting is out of the question. Jogging is risky. Even a brisk walk leaves me puffing…at my stage of the game I just want to enjoy life. But my Coach won't allow me to coast. Growing older means I've more time and resources to exercise the gifts God's given me. Instead of slowing down, I want to be accelerating when I cross the finish line." Or as the folks at Maxwell House Coffee used to say: "Good to the last drop!"

IT'S ALL PART OF HIS PLAN

In everything God works for the good
of those who love him...because that was his plan.

ROMANS 8:28 NCV

When you're in a situation where you've got more questions than answers, it takes faith to accept that "in everything God works for the good of those who love him." What you consider wasted experiences can become confidence-builders and priceless sources of insight—when you make up your mind to learn from them! If you don't, they'll keep happening until you do. The Israelites went in circles for forty years before they finally wised up. Don't let that happen to you.

When you get too comfortable God stirs things up. The mother eagle teaches her little ones to fly by making their nest so uncomfortable that they're forced out of it. Next they are pushed off a cliff edge. Can you imagine their thoughts: "It's my mother doing this?" *Who* and *where* you are at this moment in time has been divinely appointed. God in His wisdom knows that you need the challenge of certain situations to mature and stretch you. The job you dread going to every day is developing your skills, endurance and sense of responsibility. Those people who rub you the wrong way are actually making you more like Jesus! Paul says, God "understands...and knows what is best for us at all times" (Eph 1:8 TLB). So instead of asking Him to change things, thank Him for the experience and the lessons you're learning. And if you can't figure out what those lessons are, ask Him. James says, "If...you need wisdom ...ask God" (Jas 1:5 CEV). When you do, you'll discover—it's all part of His plan!

THE MARTYR ATTITUDE!

God's gift to us is...happiness.
ECCLESIASTES 3:13 CEV

People with a "martyr attitude" do things out of a sense of duty, not joy. They feel guilty about enjoying life. They tend to begrudge happiness to those around them. They resent it when others don't do things for them, yet they won't ask for help in case they create a sense of obligation. The fact is, "martyrs" don't value themselves so they think nobody else does. That's not how God wants you to live. The Bible says there's a time to work...to play...to laugh, and enjoy life, because "God's gift to us is...happiness." Jesus said, "I came to give life ...in all its fullness" (Jn 10:10 NCV). You need fun and relaxation. They're not unspiritual! Without them you become unbalanced and you open yourself to stress-related illness, mood swings and compulsive behaviors. You find yourself constantly vulnerable, driven and unable to relax.

Refuse to take on a false sense of responsibility. Don't neglect or deny your own legitimate needs. Yes, you're called to help others, but it's not wrong to do things for yourself, to receive from God, and those He sends to bless you. If somebody compliments you, accept it graciously. If they attempt to belittle you, ignore it and move on. One counselor writes: "When you find yourself trying to prove how much you've been hurt, or trying to 'top' someone else's pain, stop and figure out what's going on. The reward is learning to stop the pain and move into joy, peace and fulfillment." David said, "In Your presence is fullness of joy" (Ps 16:11 AMP). So begin to spend more time with God. You only get to make the journey once, so enjoy it and make it count.

WEEDS GROWING IN THE WHEAT!

An enemy did this.
MATTHEW 13:28 NIV

Matthew, chapter thirteen, verses twenty-four through thirty is an eye-opening parable. Jesus warned that while we are planting wheat (God's Word), the enemy is planting weeds (error). And it's happening in the same field! Why? *(1) Because we've fallen asleep.* "While everyone was sleeping, his enemy... sowed weeds among the wheat" (v. 25 NIV). Wake up! Dynamic personalities and big crowds don't guarantee truth is being taught. Paul warns the Ephesian church: "After I leave, savage wolves will come in among you and will not spare the flock" (Ac 20:29 NIV). *(2) Because the sowers look and sound alike.* Who are these people sowing bad seed? Paul answers: "From your own number men will arise and distort the truth" (v. 30 NIV). Note, they started out right but went wrong. You say, "Should we pull up the weeds?" No. Jesus said: "While you are pulling the weeds, you may root up the wheat with them. Let both grow together until the harvest. At that time I will tell the harvesters: First collect the weeds and tie them in bundles to be burned; then gather the wheat and bring it into my barn" (Mt 13:29-30 NIV). There are many "voices" speaking today and you need *discernment* as to the spirit that's at work in them. Think it's no big deal? One degree off course may seem harmless enough, but stay on that trajectory and you'll end up far from where God wants you to be, then realize, "An enemy did this." Protect yourself by living in God's Word, stay filled with the Holy Spirit which will "guide you into all truth" (Jn 16:13) and surround yourself with those of "like precious faith" (2Pe 1:1).

KNOWING GOD BETTER

The Spirit will take from what is mine
and make it known to you.

JOHN 16:15 NIV

Spiritual *activities* can never replace spiritual *intimacy*. A lot of us go to church with the wrong focus. We want to know what the pastor's subject is. What we should be thinking is: "Lord, whatever the preacher says today, I want You to speak to me personally so I'll know what Your will is for my situation." When God's Word starts coming alive for you in ways that change you and take you in a direction you would never have discovered for yourself, you're on the same wavelength as the Holy Spirit, whose job is to clarify and reveal God's purpose for your life. Living on this wavelength puts you in a world apart from others, even many professing Christians.

Paul said in First Corinthians, chapter two, verse fourteen, that the "natural man" (NAS) can't grasp anything from God because his spirit is dead. He says the things of God are "foolishness" to such a person. So a mature believer is worlds removed from the understanding of the spiritually dull or dead person. The truth is, even church-goers don't understand the mature believer. Paul said such a person "is appraised [properly understood and evaluated] by no one" (1Co 2:15 NAS). Folks can't figure mature believers out because they have "the mind of Christ" (v. 16 NIV). This kind of intimacy with God is rare today, even though the mind of Christ is God's will for, and is available to each of us. Spiritually mature believers have a passion to pursue and know God, and they aren't satisfied until they are in an intimate relationship with Him. So make your goal—knowing God better.

HOW'S YOUR ATTITUDE?

The Lord is the judge of our motives.
PROVERBS 16:2 CEV

Solomon said, "We may think we know what is right, but the Lord is the judge of our motives." Writer Isabel Wolseley says: "I'm a placid, get-along-with-everybody person. But that changed when my friend and I had a disagreement. I told her I was right, and why, and others commended me for having been right. The trouble is, I didn't feel any better...I felt worse. 'Lord,' I prayed, 'You know I was right, so why do I feel so terrible?' I stewed for several days then I sensed His answer: 'Yes, you were right, but your attitude was wrong!' I won a little victory in a difference of opinion, but I'd lost in the realm of friendship. I asked my friend to forgive me. She did, and our relationship was restored. This happened several years ago, and know what? I can't even remember what the argument was about. It seemed so all-absorbing at the time. Not now."

Don't let your need to "always be right" rob you of opportunities to show grace and allow God to deal with others. To the hard-headed amongst us James writes: "Be quick to hear [and] slow to speak" (Jas 1:19 NAS). You must *earn* the right to speak into someone's life, and that takes time. It also means trying to *understand* what they're going through, otherwise they'll tune you out. Ask yourself, "What's my goal? To win the argument? To look good and sound smart?" That's a guaranteed formula for damaging relationships. Paul writes: "Let the Spirit renew your thoughts and attitudes" (Eph 4:23 NLT). Bottom line: when you pay attention to the Holy Spirit He will tell you when you need an attitude adjustment.

SPEAK TO THEIR SPIRIT! (1)

Henceforth know we no man after the flesh.
2 CORINTHIANS 5:16

We've all heard the stories of people in a coma, incapable of response, yet fully aware of what was going on around them. One patient tells of feeling trapped inside his body, listening in despair as his loved ones gave up on him and doctors talked about pulling the plug. There's an important survival principle here. When you speak to someone battling adversity or serious illness, speak life to their *spirit*. Speak to the part of them that's capable of rising up in faith and responding. "Faith cometh by hearing, and hearing by the word of God" (Ro 10:17). How does faith come? By hearing what *God* thinks, what *God* says and what *God* can do when others have given up.

You say, "But the situation looks hopeless." Maybe, but until God has been heard from, the last word hasn't been spoken. God told the prophet Ezekiel to go and stand in a valley full of dead bones (that's about as bad as it gets!) and say, "This is what the Sovereign Lord says to these bones: I will make breath enter you, and you will come to life" (Eze 37:5 NIV). Now, you can't hold on to a loved one when God in His sovereign wisdom decides it's time to take them home. But until then, speak words of life to their spirit. And speak them to yourself too. Faith does not deny the reality of the circumstances—it just refuses to be intimidated, limited or ruled by them. That's why Paul writes, "Henceforth know we no man after the flesh." So speak life to their spirit—and to your own spirit too!

SPEAK TO THEIR SPIRIT! (2)

Henceforth know we no man after the flesh.

2 CORINTHIANS 5:16

When God speaks to us He often does it through people. The trouble is, our spiritual ears are not developed and attuned to His voice. In some cases we have become doubting and cynical. What a loss! Your fear of "getting it wrong" will rob you of vital input only God can give you. Jacob woke up one morning after having an encounter with God the night before and said, "Surely the Lord is in this place, and I was not aware of it" (Ge 28:16 NIV). You need to wake up spiritually and: (a) desire above all else to hear from God; (b) eliminate mental clutter, slow down and take the time to understand what He's saying; (c) believe that God will actually speak to you. If you don't, you'll be at the mercy of your own best thinking, or worse, the influence of others just like you. Self-sufficiency is the enemy of hearing from God! As long as you can do it without God, you won't reach for God. Seven times in two chapters of the Book of Revelation God says, "He that has an ear [a spiritually developed one] let him hear what the spirit says." Until you hear from God you're working with severely limited information and you'll keep making mistakes, costly ones. Hearing from God must become a priority so great, you adjust your schedule and your attitudes to it every day. Paul writes: "Henceforth know we no man after the flesh." Stop shutting out the people God wants to speak to you through because they are flawed. God doesn't speak to you through their flesh; He speaks through their spirit—to *your* spirit!

PRESS THROUGH!

If God is for us, who can be against us?
ROMANS 8:31 NIV

To reach your God-ordained destiny you must do these seven things: *(1) Refuse to give in to wrong thoughts.* Guard your mind. Make it a walled city that refuses to allow negative thoughts and harmful influences to penetrate. *(2) Resist any temptation toward introspection.* Only the Holy Spirit has the right to search the hearts and minds of men. When the Lord is ready to reveal an area of your life that needs correction, He will. *(3) Fight, using God's Word.* Let the Rhema Word, the God-breathed Word found in Scripture, be your strength in times of difficulty and testing. In the wilderness temptation, Jesus used Scripture to put Satan to flight. And the weapon of God's Word still works today. *(4) Listen to the still small voice of God within.* God doesn't play hide-and-seek with His will. Discipline yourself to spend unhurried time with Him and you'll thrive. *(5) Shift to a higher level of faith.* Before killing Goliath, David had to kill a lion and a bear. Today we are contending with issues that require us to move to a new level of faith. *(6) Get into proper alignment.* God's aligning His people— putting together those who'll stand as one in the day of battle. It's imperative to know who you can go to war with. You only discover such people in times of testing. Treasure them; they're "covenant relationships." *(7) Ask God to give you understanding about the place you are in.* Knowing you are in preparation for your destiny will keep you from pulling back, vacillating or throwing in the sponge. The word for you today is—press through and seize your God-given destiny!

A CONSCIENCE—GROUNDED IN GOD'S WORD

Holding on to faith and a good conscience.

1 TIMOTHY 1:19 NIV

Paul writes to Timothy: "My son, I give you this instruction in keeping with the prophecies once made about you, so that by following them you may fight the good fight, holding on to faith and a good conscience. Some have rejected these and so have shipwrecked their faith. Among them are Hymenaeus and Alexander" (vv. 18-20 NIV). What do we know about Hymenaeus and Alexander? Not much. But what we do know is sobering. Having failed to develop, protect, and live by a conscience grounded in God's Word, they ended up spiritually shipwrecked. What a picture. A fine sea-going vessel lies shattered on the rocks because it got off course. The saying, "Let conscience be your guide," needs one more phrase added: "As long as your conscience is grounded in God's Word." When we want to do our own thing and go our own way, we tend to justify it by saying, "If it feels so right how can it be wrong?" Understand this: if God's Word says something is wrong—it's wrong, no matter how right it feels! Your conscience must line up with the unchanging truth of Scripture. When the ultimate arbiter of your choices and actions is "feelings," the winds of temptation, compromise and comfort will sweep you off course and you'll end up shipwrecked. The apostle John gives us an all-important reason for keeping our conscience in good repair: "If we don't feel guilty, we can come to God with bold confidence. And we will receive from him whatever we ask because we *obey* him and do the things that please him" (1Jn 3:21-22 NLT).

DO YOU HAVE A VISION? (1)

Slowly, steadily, surely, the time approaches
when the vision will be fulfilled.

HABAKKUK 2:3 TLB

In the early stages of pregnancy a baby is easier to lose. The same applies to your God-given vision; you need to protect it. The Enemy tried to destroy Moses and Jesus before they reached their second birthday. Why? He feared their future— and he fears yours too! Furthermore, when a prospective mother is not "showing," she has to go on the word of her physician. Getting the idea? There are certain things you need to do in order to "deliver" what God has promised. When your doctor says, "No smoking, drinking or eating certain foods, etc.," he's thinking about your future. "But others can do these things," you say. Yes, but they're not carrying within them what you are. The call to give birth to a vision means daring to be different, even radical: it means disconnecting from relationships that can hurt you, staying out of certain places, and reordering your priorities according to your God-given destiny, not popular consent. If you think fulfilling a vision is easy, check the price tag! Like childbirth, it's hard, it's lonely, it's sleepless, it's appetite-changing, it's schedule-altering. It involves pain and leaves stretch marks. So before you give lip service to, or play around with God's purpose for your life, ask yourself, "Am I ready to carry this thing full term?" Visions aren't for the immature, the impatient or the faint of heart. And you can't downsize them when things get tough.

Esther's vision meant putting her life on the line and saying, "If I perish, I perish" (Est 4:16). Did she perish? No, but she had to be willing to. Are you?

DO YOU HAVE A VISION? (2)

*Slowly, steadily, surely, the time approaches
when the vision will be fulfilled.*

HABAKKUK 2:3 TLB

Many people wear themselves out trying to fulfill a vision God didn't give them. So where did their vision come from? (a) The most dominant influences in their life. (b) Their need to "prove" something to someone. (c) Their unresolved issues: trying to win a parent's love, or to demonstrate they're as talented as their brother, sister, peer, or in some cases the pastor of the bigger church across town.

Abraham learned this lesson the hard way. God promised him a son. But he got impatient, worried about getting old, took bad advice and ended up fathering Ishmael. Be careful; all your praying, planning and pushing won't turn the wrong road into the right road! Furthermore, God won't empower you to do what He put into somebody else's heart to do. That's why it's foolish to compare yourself with others. God didn't promise to give you what He gave them. You're unique. So is His plan for your life. People who make this mistake end up with a sense of failure and frustration because they're constantly measuring themselves by somebody else's assignment. If you're not "graced" to do it, you'll wear out yourself (and everybody else). Identify the origin of your vision!

Even when your vision is of God you'll experience disappointment, discouragement and delays. The truth is, the greater your vision the greater the attack that will come against you. But when you know deep down that your vision is of God, you'll be able to persevere through the hard times, and you'll have the assurance of the Psalmist, "The Lord will work out his plans for my life" (Ps 138:8 NLT).

DO YOU HAVE A VISION? (3)

*Slowly, steadily, surely, the time approaches
when the vision will be fulfilled.*

HABAKKUK 2:3 TLB

When God gives you a *vision*—He also gives you the *provision* needed to fulfill it! Often He'll use something you already possess even though you don't know it, or think it's not equal to the challenge. Faced with feeding five thousand hungry people, the disciples felt totally inadequate. But Jesus said, "How many loaves do you have...Go and see" (Mk 6:38 NIV). God will open your spiritual eyes to see what you already have—or is within your reach. And when you recognize it, give it to Him. After He blesses it, it will be more than enough. The key to your success is found in the words "go and see."

Stop procrastinating, making excuses, feeling sorry for yourself, "talking down" to yourself, or being intimidated by those who say you don't have what it takes. Listen to God! He has provided *everything* required to get you where you need to go. Paul writes: "Now glory be to God who by his mighty power at work within us is able to do far more than we could ever dare to ask or even dream of—infinitely beyond our highest prayers, desires, thoughts, or hopes" (Eph 3:20 TLB). Notice the words "far more" and "his mighty power at work within us." Look in the mirror and announce, "I am full of resources. God has given me everything I need to fulfill His plan for my life." This is not hype, pride, or mind-over-matter. It's *faith* speaking, it's *faith* connecting with God, it's *faith* tapping into the resources needed to do what God has called you to do!

"I KNEW YOU WHEN..."

Isn't this the carpenter?

MARK 6:3 NIV

Be careful around those who love to say, "I knew you when..." in an attempt to *label* or *limit* you. When David volunteered to fight Goliath his faith was an embarrassment to his big brother Eliab, an officer in King Saul's army. Eliab was thinking, "If my little brother wins everybody will ask, 'How come *you* didn't go out and fight him?'" Understand this: your decision to step out and follow God will put pressure on others. And the first place you'll feel it will be amongst those closest to you, especially if your calling sets you apart, and takes you to a higher level. The Bible records that Eliab "burned with anger at [David] and asked, 'Why have you come down here? And with whom did you leave those few sheep in the desert? I know how conceited you are and how wicked your heart is'" (1Sa 17:28 NIV). Before David could overcome Goliath he had to overcome the thoughts and opinions of those around him. And you will too!

Look at the life of Jesus. When He went back to His hometown they said: "What's this wisdom that has been given him, that he even does miracles! Isn't this the carpenter? Isn't this Mary's son...And they took offence at him. Jesus said to them, 'Only in his hometown, among his relatives and in his own house is a prophet without honor.' He could not do any miracles there, except lay his hands on a few sick people and heal them. And he was amazed at their lack of faith" (Mk 6:2-6 NIV). Bottom line: be careful around those "who knew you when."

"GIVE GOD THE REINS"

*Trust in the Lord with all your heart
and lean not on your own understanding.*

PROVERBS 3:5 NIV

Cliff Schimmels says: "When I was young my dad had a team of horses. One day he said to me, 'Son, would you like to drive?' So I took the reins. I was in control. I was driving. But the plodding bothered me, it was too slow. So I clucked the horses along and they began to trot. Then Babe and Blue came up with a better idea. They decided that if they ran we would get home faster. Soon they were running as fast as I've ever seen horses run. As the prairie-dog holes whizzed by I concluded that we were in a dangerous situation, so I tried my best to slow down the runaway team. I tugged on the reins until my hands cramped. I cried and pleaded, but nothing worked. Old Babe and Blue just kept running. I glanced over at my dad and he was just sitting there, watching the world go by. By now I was frantic. My hands were cut from the reins, tears streaming down my face, frozen from the winter cold. Finally in desperation I turned to my dad and said, 'Here, take the reins, I don't want to drive anymore.' Now that I'm older and people call me grandpa, I re-enact that scene at least once a day."

Regardless of how old we get or how capable we think we are, there's always that moment when the only way out is to turn to our heavenly Father and say, "Here, take the reins, I don't want to drive any more." And He *will*, but you've got to give them to Him!

THE GIFT OF REPENTANCE

I gave her time to repent.

REVELATION 2:21 NLT

When God tells you to repent, He gives you *time* and *grace* to do it. If you don't, there are consequences. "I gave her time to repent, but she [would] not…Therefore…[she] will suffer greatly" (vv. 21-22 NLT). This Scripture is an arrow to the heart of that stubborn sin you want to keep holding on to. Sin is always a choice. If you choose to keep sinning you can reach a place where your ability to say "no" is so weakened, you become enslaved to what you've chosen. As long as you prefer the rewards your sin brings, you won't seek deliverance from it. The Greek word for repentance is *metanoia;* it means "to change, to turn around and go the other way." One counselor writes: "I kept trying not to commit a particular sin, praying about it over and over, only to do it again. Finally I got mad at God and cried out, 'Why don't you help me with this?' He answered, 'Because you aren't disgusted with it yet. You're still enjoying it.' I protested, 'I do not. I hate it.' God replied, 'If you hated it enough you'd quit it.' In that moment I realized that I enjoyed the rewards of my sin more than the rewards of obedience. I also discovered something else; I couldn't hate sin enough by the power of my own fleshly will to come to true repentance. I stood helpless in corruption. Repentance is a gift of love which comes from God. And until that love is allowed to work in us, touching and exposing those carefully guarded areas, we cannot change." So today ask God for the *gift* of repentance.

BEFORE YOU DIE—LIVE!

Do not boast about tomorrow,
for you do not know what a day may bring forth.
PROVERBS 27:1 NIV

In *The Finishing Touch* Chuck Swindoll writes: "The plane was headed for New York—a routine, normally very boring flight. But this time it proved to be otherwise. As they were on their descent pattern the pilot realized that the landing gear was not engaging. He messed around with the controls, trying again and again to get the gear to lock in place…without success. He then asked ground control for instructions. As the plane circled the landing field and emergency crews coated the runway with foam, fire trucks and other emergency vehicles moved into position. Meanwhile the passengers were told how to maneuver in that calm, unemotional voice pilots do so well. Flight attendants glided about the cabin with an air of cool reserve. Passengers were told to place their heads between their knees and grab their ankles just before impact. There were tears, panic and cries of despair. Then when the landing was only minutes away the pilot suddenly announced over the intercom, 'We are beginning our final descent. At this moment, in accordance with international aviation code established at Geneva, it is my obligation to inform you that if you believe in God you should commence prayer.' Scouts' honor…that's exactly what he said."

So what's the message? "Do not boast about tomorrow, for you do not know what a day may bring forth." Live each day in the light of eternity. Seize the moment and wring every drop out of it. Love and enjoy the people who matter. Take another step toward your goals and the fulfillment of God's plan for your life. In other words, before you die—live!

REJECTION-PROOFED

*Our Father loves us, for he calls us his children,
and that is what we are!*

1 JOHN 3:1 NLT

Ever wonder how anybody could find you lovable? For many of us the question becomes a self-fulfilling prophecy. The fear of rejection is so intense that we protect ourselves by: *(a) Vowing never to let anybody get close enough to hurt us again.* Sounds good in theory, but by closing others out we close ourselves in, and all our relationships suffer. *(b) Putting on our best "game face."* I'm tough! Who needs other people anyway? As a result nobody meets our needs. *(c) Pushing others away.* When we feel rejected we imagine we're being attacked even when we're not. So we put on our boxing gloves and come out swinging. *(d) Trying to buy rejection-protection by doing favors for people.* Or by putting up with abusive relationships because we think it's what we deserve and it may be our last chance at love. *(e) Practicing perfectionism.* Give it up! God already loves you unconditionally, and human standards vary so much that you'll never make everybody happy however you try.

As long as you keep trading with a diminished sense of worth, you'll keep attracting the wrong people. So listen up. "Our Father loves us, for he calls us his children, and that is what we are." And "that's only the beginning...when Christ is ...revealed, we'll...become like him" (v. 2 TM). If your self-worth comes from any opinion other than God's, you'll always be vulnerable. Your critics will diminish you; trying and failing will keep you from rising again. Worst of all, you'll never discover or be discovered for the unique and wonderful person God made you to be.

OVERCOMING PROCRASTINATION!

Find out and do whatever the Lord wants you to.

EPHESIANS 5:17 TLB

To overcome procrastination you must: *(1) Take responsibility for your life.* No matter how hard you wish, the tooth fairy isn't going to come while you're sleeping and replace failure with success. Great souls have wills, feeble souls have wishes. You need to *do* something! *(2) Examine your excuses.* An excuse puts the blame on something other than you, which means the solution is beyond your reach. Excuses are like exit signs on the road of progress; they take us off track. It's easier to move from failure to success, than from excuses to success. So examine your excuses and eliminate them. *(3) Focus on the benefits of completing a task.* To get you over the hump, focus on what you'll "get out of it" when you get it done. Will it bring you benefit? Clear the way for something else you'd like to do? Be a milestone in your personal development or the completion of something bigger? Will it help to clear the decks for you emotionally? Admiral William Halsey said, "Problems become smaller if you confront them. Touch a thistle timidly and it pricks you, grasp it boldly and its spines crumble." *(4) Ask for help.* Columbus didn't discover the New World on his own, he needed a crew. Speaking of the church, Paul writes: "Each part ...helps the other parts grow" (Eph 4:16 NLT). There's no way to value the assistance others can give you when it comes to breaking old habits and beginning new ones. Yes, it means taking a risk because you will be vulnerable in sharing your hopes and fears. But the risk is worth taking.

BECOMING UNSELFISH

Let us fix our eyes on Jesus.

HEBREWS 12:2 NIV

The Bible says: "Let us fix our eyes on Jesus, the author and perfecter of our faith, who for the joy set before him endured the cross, scorning its shame, and sat down at the right hand of the throne of God." Now we might be tempted to think that Jesus is just the *finish line,* and that we should keep our eyes on Him as a runner would focus on the tape. No, this Scripture is urging us to think of Jesus as our *example.* As the starter and finisher of our faith He not only designed the course of the race, He ran it perfectly and completely. The Greek term which is translated, "Fix our eyes on Jesus," means to look exclusively at something and study it intently while looking away from all distractions.

As great athletes study the films of champions to discover their techniques, we are encouraged to go to the film vault and peer intently at one scene after another as we study Christ. In other words, "Look exclusively and thoughtfully at the one who not only designed the course, but ran it flawlessly. And run exactly as He ran." As He lived, you are to live. As He decided, you are to decide. As He obeyed, you are to obey. As He pleased the Father, you are to please the Father. As He surrendered, you are to surrender. Do you want to be like Christ? Begin thinking *less* about yourself. Work toward becoming unselfish. For one full day, let go of anything that serves your own interest to the exclusion of others. On that same day, fix your attention on Jesus by surrendering in complete selflessness.

TRUSTING GOD IN THE DARK

You do not realize now what I am doing,
but later you will.

JOHN 13:7 NIV

Mary and Martha were upset that Jesus didn't come until their brother Lazarus was dead. "Lord...if you had been here, my brother would not have died" (Jn 11:21 & 32 NIV). But instead of giving them reasons, Jesus replied, "Did I not tell you...if you believed, you would see [God glorified in this?]" (v. 40 NIV). When God asked Abraham to sacrifice his son Isaac he didn't understand, but *later* he witnessed God's faithfulness when Isaac was restored to him. Moses didn't understand why he had to spend forty years in the wilderness, but *later* when God called him to lead Israel to freedom, he got it. Joseph didn't know why his brothers mistreated him or why he was imprisoned unfairly, but *later* he saw God's hand in everything. His father questioned why Joseph had been taken away from him, but *later,* looking into the face of the man who had been made governor and who'd saved the lives of the nation, God's purposes became clear.

Just like your children don't always think your decisions make sense, we don't understand God's ways. That's why Jesus said to Mary and Martha, "You do not realize now what I am doing, but *later* you will." God doesn't expect you to understand, but He does expect you to trust Him. In spite of his boils, bankruptcy and bereavement Job said, "When he has tested me, I will come forth" (Job 23:10 NIV). Is God testing you in this situation? If He is, what are you learning? Is the experience making you *bitter,* or making you *better* by causing you to draw closer to Him?

SEEING YOUR TRIALS THE RIGHT WAY

Blessed is a man who perseveres under trial.

JAMES 1:12 NAS

Too many of us view our trials the way we watch television. Some televisions have a second channel in the corner of your screen that enables you to divide your focus and watch two programs at once. A lot of us try to superimpose our human viewpoint on the screen of God's will for our lives. God gives us a divine perspective, then we open up a second screen, a human one, and try to figure it all out. Don't waste your trials by trying to fit them into your limited vision and understanding or you'll end up frustrated. It's much better to trust God, rest in His wisdom and take Him at His word.

A spiritual perspective on your trials will keep you from buckling under the weight of them when times are hard. When you begin to look at your trials from God's perspective, your spirit is renewed and you're enabled to press on and receive what God has waiting for you. James writes: "Blessed is a man who perseveres under trial; for once he has been approved, he will receive the crown of life." Now the Crown of Life is not just something you receive in Heaven, you can enjoy it today. And who's it for? Those who "persevere." When God gives you this Crown, He's saying, "You've passed another of life's tests, now you're ready for a new level of blessing." Remember the wonderful feeling you had when you passed some of your hardest tests in school? Don't get discouraged. God is up to something good. Keep going—don't stop until you receive the Crown of Life.

WORTH-SHIP

The Father seeketh such to worship him.

JOHN 4:23

Jesus revealed some of His greatest insights on worship to a flawed woman with five failed marriages and a live-in boyfriend. No wonder His disciples were "shocked to find him talking to [her]" (v. 27 NLT). So what is Jesus teaching us about worship?

(1) That anybody can do it! True worship has nothing to do with your religious denomination (Jews and Gentiles), and cannot be limited to a physical location (Mount Gerizim or the temple in Jerusalem). Once you've made Him Lord of your life, Jesus accepts your worship. You're in! *(2) That God is actually looking for people who will do it.* Here's a stop-you-in-your-tracks thought: God created you to do the only thing He cannot do for Himself—worship! "Thou art worthy, O Lord, to receive glory and honour and power: for thou hast created all things, and for thy pleasure they are and were created" (Rev 4:11). We were actually created to worship God! *(3) That there's no "only" way to do it.* According to *Vine's Complete Expository Dictionary of Old and New Testament Words,* "The worship of God is nowhere defined in Scripture." That's because it's such a powerful outpouring of our hearts toward the Lord and represents such love, gratitude and devotion that it cannot be put into words; nor can it be defined by a song, a shout, or silence. Jesus said, "True worshipers will worship the Father in spirit and truth" (Jn 4:23 NIV). True worship comes from the depths of your *spirit* and is based on the *truth* of God's Word. To understand worship, think: worth-ship! How much do you value the Lord? We never get tired of talking about what we value most!

DON'T CROSS THE LINE

You become the slave of whatever you choose to obey.
ROMANS 6:16 NLT

Set clear boundaries for yourself–and keep them! Wisdom says: *(1) Don't cross the line.* The first time you do you tell yourself, "Just this once." But what you don't know is, you've opened a door you may not be able to close. *(2) It's easier to cross it the second time.* The man who slips downstairs while his wife's sleeping to watch pornography on his computer soon discovers that, like an addict, he has to increase the dosage. Before long, he is driven to seek ever higher states of arousal. Paul writes: "Don't you realize that you become the slave of whatever you choose to obey?" *(3) Eventually the line gets blurred.* You keep commuting between what's right and what's wrong, thinking, "I can quit any time I want," and Satan whispers, "Gotcha!" *(4) Finally the line disappears.* Like the Prodigal Son, you lose everything. Spiritually, you lose your confidence before God. Personally, you lose your sense of self-worth. Publicly, you lose respect and influence with others.

And "good" things can hurt you too. A work ethic is a good thing, but lack of balance can make you neglect your family and lose your marriage. Rest and relaxation are good things, but too much time "vegging out" in front of the TV will stunt your spiritual growth. Caution and thoughtfulness are good things, but too much of them will clip the wings of your faith and keep you from rising to fulfill your God-given destiny. So draw a clear line for yourself—and stay on the right side of it!

STAY FOCUSED (1)

Let's keep focused...
those of us who want everything God has for us.
PHILIPPIANS 3:15 TM

You become effective by being selective. It's human nature to get distracted. We're like gyroscopes, spinning around at a frantic pace but not getting anywhere. Without a clear purpose you keep changing directions, jobs, relationships, churches, etc., hoping each change will settle the confusion or fill the emptiness in your heart. You think, "This time it will be different," but it doesn't solve your real problem—lack of focus.

The power of focusing can be seen in light. With a magnifying glass the rays of the sun can set paper on fire. But when light is focused even more as a laser beam, it can cut through steel. *Nothing is as potent as a focused life.* The men and women who make the greatest difference in life are the most focused. For instance, the apostle Paul said, "I am bringing all my energies to bear on this one thing" (v. 13 TLB). Paul's obsession was to make Christ known. So if you want your life to have impact, focus it! Stop dabbling. Stop trying to do it all. Do less. Turn away from even good activities and do only that which matters most. Never confuse activity with productivity. Poet William Matthews wrote: "One well-cultivated talent, deepened and enlarged, is worth a hundred shallow faculties. The first law of success in this day when so many things are clamoring for attention is concentration—to bend our energies to one point, and to go directly to that point, looking neither to the right nor to the left." Does focus come easily or naturally? No, it's a discipline that must be practiced every day.

STAY FOCUSED (2)

Do not swerve to the right or the left.

PROVERBS 4:27 NIV

Focus does three things for you: *(1) It keeps you on target.* We find ourselves pulled in a dozen different directions, spending much of our time and energy on things we don't really care about. Author Don Marquis put it this way: "Ours is a world where people don't know what they want, and are willing to go through hell to get it." The Bible says, "Let your eyes look straight ahead…Do not swerve to the right or the left" (vv. 25-27 NIV). *(2) It increases your energy.* Attempting everything, like attempting nothing, will suck the life out of you. Focus gives you energy. Admiral Richard Byrd, the polar explorer, said, "Few men come anywhere near exhausting the resources dwelling within them. There are deep wells of strength that are never used." One of the reasons those wells go untapped is lack of focus. The mind doesn't reach toward achievement until it has clear objectives. *(3) It lifts you.* It's been said that "the world stands aside to let anyone pass, who knows where he or she is going." In a sea of mediocrity, just knowing what you want to do and making an effort to pursue it distinguishes you from almost everybody else. Henry David Thoreau asked, "Do you ever hear of a man who had striven all his life faithfully and singly toward an object, and in no measure obtained it? If a man constantly aspires, is he not elevated?" Just by striving to become better than you are, you become elevated—even if you don't accomplish what you desire, and even if others don't step aside for you. By trusting God and aiming higher, you move to a higher level.

STAY FOCUSED (3)

Acknowledge him, and he shall direct thy paths.

PROVERBS 3:6

When it comes to staying focused, keep in mind: *(1) Focused people always look for a better way.* What got you where you are, won't necessarily get you where you need to be. A family who moved into a new neighborhood got a late start one morning. As a result their six-year-old missed her school bus. Though it would make him late for work her father agreed to take her to school if she gave him directions. After twenty minutes of going in circles they finally arrived at the school, which turned out to be only a few blocks away from where they lived. Steaming, her dad asked why she drove him all over the place when the school was so close to home. "We went the way the school bus does," she said. "That's the only way I know." *(2) Focused people concentrate a little harder and a little longer.* Hall of Fame baseball player Hank Aaron says, "What separates a superstar from the average ballplayer is that he concentrates just a little bit longer." Focused thinking is the ability to remove distractions and mental clutter so that you can concentrate with clarity. *(3) Focused people make commitments, not excuses.* A sign on the desk of an officer at the Pentagon read: "The secrecy of my job does not permit me to know what I'm doing." It's a cute joke, but not so cute when it's true. When you don't know what you're doing, you become frustrated and end up failing. That's why praying and getting direction from God are critical for your life. "In all thy ways acknowledge him, and he shall direct thy paths."

STAY FOCUSED (4)

Forgetting the past.

PHILIPPIANS 3:13 NLT

Notice: *(1) Focused people don't live in the past.* Too many of us *yearn* for the past and get stuck in it. Instead we should *learn* from the past and let go of it. Elbert Hubbard wrote: "A retentive memory may be a good thing, but the ability to forget is a token of greatness. Successful people forget. They're running a race. They can't afford to look behind. Their eye is on the finish line. They're too big to let little things disturb them. If anyone does them wrong, they consider the source and keep cool. It's only the small people who cherish revenge. Be a good forgetter...success demands it." *(2) Focused people don't think about the difficulties, but the rewards.* If you dwell on the difficulties too long you'll start to develop self-pity instead of self-discipline. As a result you'll accomplish less and less. By focusing on results you'll stay encouraged. Make Christ your example. "He was willing to die a shameful death on the cross because of the joy he knew would be his afterwards" (Heb 12:2 TLB). *(3) Focused people choose their friends carefully.* Here are five types of people you'll encounter: (a) Refreshers—who strengthen your faith and energize you. (b) Refiners—who sharpen you and clarify your vision. (c) Reflectors—who mirror your energy, neither adding to nor subtracting from it. (d) Reducers—who try to diminish your goals and efforts to their comfort level. (e) Rejecters—who don't understand you or what God's called you to do. So, remain focused and you'll stay grounded; the praise of others is less likely to go to your head, and the negative impact of your critics will be minimized.

STAY FOCUSED (5)

That special gift...you were given...
keep that dusted off and in use.

1 TIMOTHY 4:14 TM

Paul told Timothy to focus on his strengths. "That special gift...you were given...keep that dusted off and in use." Focused people don't hide their weaknesses or excuse them; instead they focus on their strengths! There's a story about a couple who decided to build a farm. Then they began to argue. The wife wanted to build the house first. The husband wanted to build the barn first to house the animals. They went back and forth until finally the man said, "Look, we have to build the barn first—because the barn will enable us to build the house, the garage, the silo, the kids' swing set, and everything else!" When you focus on putting first things first, everything else is more likely to fall into place.

Anthony Campolo says, "What you commit yourself to, will change what you are and make you into a completely different person. The future conditions you, not the past. What you commit yourself to become, determines what you are—more than anything that ever happened to you yesterday. Therefore, I ask you, 'What are your commitments? Where are you going? What are you going to be? Show me somebody who hasn't decided, and I'll show you somebody who has no identity, no personality, no direction.'" Focusing on weaknesses instead of strengths is like having a handful of coins, a few made of gold, the rest of tarnished copper, and setting aside the gold coins to spend your time shining the copper ones in hopes of making them more valuable. No matter how long you spend, they'll never be worth what the gold ones are. So, stay focused on your God-given strengths!

LEARNING TO HEAR GOD'S VOICE

His sheep follow him because they know his voice.

JOHN 10:4 NIV

One evening a friend visiting Peter Lord's home told him he could hear no fewer than eighteen different kinds of crickets in his garden. Peter was amazed—he'd lived there for years and never heard *one*. The difference was, this man was a professor of entomology and he had learned to distinguish over two hundred different cricket calls with his natural ear. Imagine learning to listen to crickets! Looking back, Peter wrote: "I suddenly understood that a person must *want* to hear, and *learn* to hear, and there were many sounds I was *not* hearing." Think what you've been missing all these years because you haven't wanted or learned to hear the voice of God speaking to you.

God often speaks to us through others. But the very gifts He speaks to us through can weaken our desire to hear from God for *ourselves*. The children of Israel said to Moses, "We want you to hear from God for us" (See Ex 20:18-19). The problem is, when you only hear from God through secondary sources it's easier not to make any real commitment, or to obey what you've heard. But when you know God is speaking to you personally you must make a clear-cut decision. Jesus said, "His sheep follow him because they know his voice." Examine the "heroes" in your Bible. They were all flawed! So what gave them the strength to accomplish such great things? They knew God's voice! Nothing, absolutely nothing in your life, is more important than learning to know God's voice when He speaks to you!

OVERCOMING YOUR PRIDE

Do not be wise in your own eyes.
PROVERBS 3:7 NIV

To overcome your pride you must: *(1) Recognize your pride.* Benjamin Franklin observed: "Not one of our natural passions is harder to subdue than pride. Even if I could conceive that I had completely overcome it, I should probably be proud of my humility." In *The Indispensable Man,* Saxon White Kessinger writes: "Sometime when you feel that your going would leave an unfillable hole, just follow these simple instructions, and see how they humble your soul. Take a bucket and fill it with water, put your hand in it up to the wrist; pull it out and the hole that's remaining, is the measure of how you'll be missed." It's humbling how quickly the hole we think we're leaving, disappears or gets filled in by others. *(2) Express gratitude often.* Paul writes: "No matter what happens, always be thankful" (1Th 5:18 TLB). Oprah Winfrey suggests, "Keep a gratitude journal. Every night list five things that happened this day that you are grateful for. It will change your life. If you concentrate on what you don't have, you'll never have enough. If you focus on what you have, you will always see that the universe is abundant and you'll have more." Selfish people never think they get as much as they deserve. Continually expressing gratitude helps to break that kind of pride. *(3) Learn to laugh at yourself.* The Chinese proverb says, "Blessed are they that laugh at themselves for they shall never cease to be entertained." People who have the problem of pride rarely laugh at themselves. Engaging in humor at your own expense shows that pride isn't the problem, and that if it is, it's one you're determined to deal with!

SHUKHOV'S STANDARD

Then you will understand what is right and just and fair.
PROVERBS 2:9 NIV

It's not easy to maintain a strong work ethic when you feel overworked, underpaid and under-appreciated. But that's the point at which your character is tested—and developed. Having a work ethic means: (a) doing what you don't feel like doing, in order to achieve the results you want; (b) paying a higher price than others for something worthwhile; (c) standing up for your principles when someone's trying to knock you down.

In his first novel, author and Nobel prizewinner Alexander Solzhenitsyn wrote about Ivan Denisovich Shukhov, a political prisoner in a Siberian labor camp. Shukhov is forced to build a wall in weather 20 degrees below zero. As it gets darker and colder the foreman gives the order to hurry the job by throwing leftover mortar over the wall instead of using it, so they could be finished for the day. "But Shukhov wasn't made that way," wrote Solzhenitsyn, telling how the man resisted the order, determined to finish the job right. "Eight years in a prison camp couldn't change his nature. He worried about everything he could make use of, about every scrap of work he could do—nothing must be wasted without good reason. The foreman yells at him and then hurries away. But Shukhov—and if the guards had put the dogs on him it would have made no difference—ran to the back and looked about. 'Not bad.' Then he ran and gave the wall a good look-over, to the left, to the right, his eye as accurate as a carpenter's level, straight and even. Only then did Shukhov stop working." So, measured by Shukhov's standard, how's *your* work ethic?

FORGIVENESS (1)

Forgive—only then will your heavenly Father...
wipe your slate clean.
MARK 11:25 TM

How heavy is a glass of water? That depends on how long you have to *carry* it. A minute is no problem, and after an hour your arm might ache. But after twenty-four hours you'll probably be in bad shape! In each instance the glass weighs exactly the same, but the longer you carry it the heavier it feels. And it's the same with a grudge; it can get so heavy it stops you from living. People will hurt you; that's the reality of sharing this planet with others. Sometimes it's intentional, other times they've no idea they upset you, far less broken your heart. Does that mean you should go around pretending nothing's wrong? No, the first step is to confront your feelings. And when the hurt is deep, it's even harder to forgive. That's when you need to pray, "Lord, change my heart and heal me." Jesus said, "Pray for those who mistreat you" (Lk 6:28 NIV). When you do that something unexpected happens; your heart softens and you start seeing them through God's eyes instead of your raw emotions. Jesus said, "If you have anything against someone, forgive—only then will your heavenly Father...wipe your slate clean." When you sow unforgiveness you reap unforgiveness—even from God!

Isaac is a prime example of practicing forgiveness. During a drought he dug wells that his enemies moved in and claimed. But instead of retaliating, he moved on and dug new ones. As a result God filled Isaac's empty wells and promised to bless him, and his children too! (See Ge 26:22-23). And He will fill the emptiness in *your* life, when you forgive those who have hurt you.

FORGIVENESS (2)

People insulted Christ, but…
He let God…take care of him.

1 PETER 2:23 NCV

A little boy who'd been rude to his mom started sneaking off upstairs. "Where you going, young man?" she asked. "To my room to talk to God," he replied. "Isn't there something you want to tell *me* first?" she said. "Nope," he said, "You'll just get mad. God will forgive me and forget about it." Long after you think you've forgiven somebody you can still be harboring hard feelings. Here are some clues that you've still got work to do: you get angry thinking about what happened; you give the offender the cold shoulder; you rehearse the incident mentally and in conversation; you seize every opportunity to remind the offender of what they did. Refusing to forgive and forget is just another way of justifying an unforgiving attitude. The Bible says there are two things God won't share: (1) His glory (See Isa 42:8); (2) His right to settle old scores. He said, "Vengeance is mine; I will repay" (Ro 12:19). Don't usurp His authority by trying to get even; take your hands off the situation and let Him work it out. When "People insulted Christ…he did not insult them in return…He let God…who judges rightly, take care of him." A grudge shackles you to the offender, and you become the hostage! Dwelling on something your parents did, or on how an associate took credit for your work, or on what someone said about you, makes *you*, not them, miserable. You walk around in turmoil and they don't even know you're upset! Why give somebody that kind of control over your life? What's important is what happens *in* you, not *to* you. So forgive, forget, and move on!

FORGIVENESS (3)

[I]...could never have made it apart from...mercy.
1 TIMOTHY 1:15-17 TM

If you're finding it hard to forgive yourself for something you've done in the past, it may be that you're reaping what you have sown. And it's particularly hard (but not impossible) to keep from feeling bad when you've condemned somebody else for doing the same thing. Here's a scriptural truth you need to understand, accept and live by: as long as you're alive you will have to keep forgiving—yourself and others!

When guilt and condemnation tell you your sins are too big for God's forgiveness, remember what Paul said: "Jesus... came...to save sinners. I'm proof—Public Sinner Number One ...someone who could never have made it apart from sheer mercy...evidence of his endless patience." Before his conversion Paul persecuted the church, killing and torturing believers. It's how he made his living! And if he could learn to forgive himself, you can too! In fact, when you don't you're implying that your transgressions are beyond the scope of God's grace to forgive and Jesus' blood to cleanse. And that's a bigger sin—pride! Plus, when somebody always has "issues" with other people, they may be *looking* for somebody to offend them; that way they can point out how bad the other person is and feel better about themselves. Pride and a judgmental attitude feed off each other the way humility feeds off forgiveness. God said, "I, even I, am the one who wipes out your transgressions for My own sake. And I will not remember your sins" (Isa 43:25 NAS). When you adopt a humble attitude and work on forgiving yourself the way God has, it's a lot easier to overlook other people's mistakes. Give it a try; you'll be amazed!

BE PATIENT, IT'LL HAPPEN IN GOD'S TIME!

Rest in the Lord, and wait patiently for him.

PSALM 37:7

The old saying, "You can't always have what you want," isn't necessarily true. When you "Delight yourself in the Lord... he will give you the desires of your heart" (v. 4 NIV). But usually He makes you wait. Dennis Wholey says: "Waiting is an art... If you can wait two years, you can achieve something you couldn't achieve today however hard you worked, however much money you threw at it, however many times you banged your head against the wall." There are things you can't have today that you'll be able to have in the future. So it doesn't make sense to drive yourself crazy and put your life on hold struggling to accomplish something *now*, that'll be easy when the time is right.

James says, "Don't try to get out of anything prematurely. Let it do its work so you become mature" (Jas 1:4 TM). God allows certain things to take place in our lives to teach us important principles like: (a) developing new skills and ways of thinking; (b) showing grace and controlling our responses; (c) maintaining our faith when times get tough. Paul writes: "Patience...[is...the power to endure whatever comes, with good temper]" (Col 3:12 AMP). "Be glad for all God is planning ...Be patient in trouble, and prayerful always" (Ro 12:12 TLB). When you spend time in God's waiting room, He's developing qualities in you that simply can't be developed any other way. When He's finished you'll come out stronger and wiser. And you'll have the maturity to handle what He has in mind for you. So don't let the Enemy rattle you or engineer circumstances that put you into overdrive. "Rest in the Lord, and wait patiently for him."

THE OVERCOMING SPIRIT!

Their weakness was turned to strength.

HEBREWS 11:34 NLT

A grindstone can make a diamond shine, or reduce solid rock to dust. It depends what you're made of. Charles Steinmetz, one of the founders of General Electric, was made of the right stuff. Crippled from birth, he was so short in stature that he looked like a dwarf. His mother died before he was one year old. His father was poor but he determined that young Charles would have an education. Charles couldn't run and play games like normal boys, so he made up his mind to devote himself to science. He set this goal: "I will make discoveries that help other people." When Steinmetz immigrated to the United States he couldn't speak a word of English. His face was swollen from the cold he'd endured on the boat passage. His sight was defective. His clothes were shabby. The port authorities were tempted to return him to Switzerland. But he stayed and found a job that paid $12 a week. There he showed amazing abilities. The infant company, General Electric, quickly realized his incredible potential. His career was marked by unparalleled research and development. When he died in 1923 one writer said, "He had the mind of an angel and the soul of a seer." What did Charles Steinmetz have? The overcoming spirit! Do *you* have it?

If what you're doing doesn't produce resistance, it's not worth doing. The winners in your Bible are described this way: "Their weakness was turned to strength. They became strong in battle." What turns weakness into strength? Faith that refuses to back up, back down, or settle for less than what God has promised.

RESPONDING LIKE JESUS!

Pray for those who persecute you.

MATTHEW 5:44 NIV

A soldier made it his practice to end each day with Bible reading and prayer. As the others gathered in the barracks and retired for the night, he'd kneel by his bunk. Some of them saw this and began to mock him. But one night the abuse went beyond words. As he bowed in prayer one soldier threw his boots and hit him in the face. The others jeered, looking for a fight, but there was no retaliation. Next morning when the boot-thrower woke up he couldn't believe what he saw. There at the foot of his bed were his boots—polished and returned. Imagine shining the boots that kick you! That calls for a new level of grace. It means deciding what your response will be, *before* the offence comes! Some of the guys in the barracks were "leaders," motivated by pride and insensitivity. That's how darkness responds to light. Others were "followers." They weren't necessarily bad, just weak and afraid to be different.

Why did Jesus pray from the cross, "Father, forgive them for they know not what they do"? Because He understood that people who have been raised a particular way, who are driven by certain forces, who wrestle with unresolved issues and fears, who are programmed with an unregenerate mindset, need God. And He saw it as an opportunity to put God on display. This requires more than Sunday-go-to-meeting religion. It calls for a Christ-like, example-setting, love-displaying response that makes others sit up and take notice. Your "rights" and your wounded ego are not the issue—the One you represent is!

WILDERNESS ATTITUDES!

We who...believed are able to enter...God's rest.

HEBREWS 4:3 NCV

After spending half their lives in the wilderness, the Israelites blamed it on their enemies. But it was their own *attitude!* Because God "was angry...they were not allowed to enter... God's rest, because they did not believe" (Heb 3:17-19 NCV). Their doubting, complaining and blame-shifting kept them stuck in the wilderness, and it'll do the same to you. It starts with feeling sorry for yourself and thinking, "If only I'd been born into a different family, had a better paying job, a more spiritual mate, etc., this wouldn't be happening." And from there it spirals downward into a full-blown pity party where everybody else is responsible for your problems. The truth is, 99 percent of the time the solution begins with a change of attitude—in you!

Another wilderness attitude that'll keep you stuck, is insisting on doing everything *your* way! Stubbornness will keep you stumbling around in the wilderness, seeing the Promised Land but never reaching it. Offering a sacrifice to God before going into battle was the way to victory. Only one problem: Samuel the prophet was the only one qualified to offer such a sacrifice. But pride and stubbornness made King Saul think he could. As a result he lost his life and Israel went down in defeat. Samuel told Saul, "You have rejected the word of the Lord, and the Lord has rejected you" (See 1Sa 15:26 NKJV). Understand this: you don't have to do anything to earn God's love, but you must *obey* Him in order to walk in His blessings. So, what has God told you to do? If you want victory in your battles and success in your endeavors, start doing it!

WHEN YOU'RE ON OVERLOAD (1)

When I was...beside myself, you calmed me down.
PSALM 94:19 TM

Before a violin can produce music, stress must be put on the strings. But pull them too tightly and they'll snap. The same's true of you. Enough stress gets the juices flowing and helps you do what needs to be done, but beyond that you snap. Someone quipped, "You know you're on overload when you've no time to cook a TV dinner, the cat's on tranquilizers, and family reunions have to be mediated by law enforcement!" Seriously, before it gets to that point, do two things:

(1) Ask for help: During Hurricane Katrina eight dolphins were swept out of their aquarium into the sea, but because they stuck together they were rescued. If one had tried to go it alone he'd have perished. When you're alone too much you lose perspective. If the Enemy can isolate you, he can influence you. God designed His family to stay connected. Or as Paul says, "So that all the members care for each other" (1Co 12:25 NLT).

(2) Get real with God: Under stress the surge of negative emotions can be overwhelming, and unless you unburden your soul before God you'll explode at the wrong people. The Psalmist addresses this: "Cast your cares on the Lord and he will sustain you" (Ps 55:22 NIV). "Pour out your heart before Him; God is a refuge for us" (Ps 62:8 NKJV). It's no mere coincidence that many of the Psalms start out with the Psalmist crying out to God for help, and end up with him rejoicing because he vented his pent-up frustrations.

WHEN YOU'RE ON OVERLOAD (2)

I'm awake all night.

PSALM 77:4 TM

You can't escape stress, but you can learn to cope with it by taking control of your life in small but important ways. Here are two:

(1) Think about someone other than yourself. David was so frazzled that he was awake all night. Ever been there? That's when you need to "Let...praises shape your worries into prayers, letting God know your concerns. Before you know it, a sense of God's wholeness, everything coming together for good, will come and settle you down" (Php 4:6 TM). Elijah was depressed and suicidal when God showed him how to help himself. How? By leaving the cave he was hiding in, and going out and ministering to others. Focusing on something other than yourself gives you perspective. Paul says [The] "God of all healing counsel...comes alongside...when we go through hard times...and...brings us alongside someone else...going through hard times so...we can be there for that person...as God was there for us" (2Co 1:3-4 TM). Do you need help? Reach out to others. It's in "connecting" that we are made whole!

(2) Don't get bitter. Life is 10 percent what happens to you, and 90 percent how you respond to it. Archbishop Fulton Sheen said, "Nothing creates more deep-seated anxiety, than the false assumption that life should be free from anxieties." When somebody you trust betrays or disappoints you, or you're struggling financially after tithing faithfully for years, it's easy to feel hard-done-by. But "Don't...become bitter" (Heb 12:15 CEV); it destroys relationships and cuts you off from God's presence. The answer is learning to "thank God no matter what happens. This is the way God wants you...to live" (1Th 5:18 TM).

WHEN YOU'RE ON OVERLOAD (3)

Don't get worked up.

MATTHEW 6:34 TM

Everything that can go wrong, has! Your teenager pierced his nose, the dog threw up on the carpet, the toilet's overflowing, and the car's leaking fluid. No wonder you're stressed! When life gets overwhelming remember:

(1) God's still looking out for you. When things look bad, remind yourself that God's bigger than your problem: "Don't get worked up about what may or may not happen tomorrow. God will help you deal with whatever hard things come up when the time comes." *(2) Don't think about quitting!* Every time you reach the breaking point it's a test. You have before you a series of choices that will add up to either quitting, or persevering through to victory. Paul was flogged, thrown in jail, shipwrecked and run out of town, but he refused to give in to circumstances and in the end he was able to say, "I have fought the good fight...finished the race, and...remained faithful" (2Ti 4:7 NLT). *(3) If it doesn't have your name on it, don't pick it up!* Stress comes from micro-managing others and assuming responsibilities that aren't yours. Establish healthy boundaries. If you're not sure what's appropriate, ask God to show you how much to get involved in the lives of friends and family. *(4) Your breaking point can be the start of a breakthrough.* Ever heard the expression "hitting the wall"? Runners use it when they're exhausted and feel like giving up. But seasoned athletes know if they push through the pain they'll get their second wind and experience a "runner's high" that'll carry them over the finish line. So keep going—by God's grace you'll make it!

MAKING A LASTING DIFFERENCE

*I will make every effort to see that after my departure
you will always be able to remember these things.*
2 PETER 1:15 NIV

Some of us think we deserve respect simply because of our
position. No, respect must be earned—daily. General J.
Lawton Collins asserted: "No matter how brilliant a man may
be he will never engender confidence in his subordinates and
associates if he lacks honesty and moral courage." Ultimately,
all the skills in the world won't save you if your character is
flawed. Author Stephen Covey writes: "If I try to use human
influence strategies and tactics to get other people to do what I
want...and my character is fundamentally flawed...in the long
run I cannot be successful. My duplicity will breed distrust, and
everything I do will be perceived as manipulative." It makes no
difference how good the rhetoric is or even how good the intentions are; if there is little or no trust, there is no foundation
for permanent success. Character can be built, but only slowly.
If you want to know how long it will take you to get to the top,
consult a calendar. If you want to know how long it will take
you to fall to the bottom, try a stopwatch. Dreams become shattered, possibilities are lost, organizations crumble and people
are hurt when a person doesn't have character protecting his
talent. Character provides the opportunity for longevity in any
career, any relationship, and any worthwhile goal. Author and
Pastor J. R. Miller wrote: "The only thing that walks back from
the grave with the mourners and refuses to be buried, is the
character of a man." *What a man is, survives him, and that—
makes a lasting difference!*

WHY DOES IT TAKE SO LONG?

Practice these things. Devote your life to them.

1 TIMOTHY 4:15 GWT

Why does change take so long? Because: *(1) We are slow learners*. How often have you failed and thought, "Not again! I thought I knew better." The history of Israel illustrates how quickly we forget the lessons God teaches us and revert to old attitudes and patterns of behavior. That's why "We must pay more careful attention, therefore, to what we have heard, so that we do not drift away" (Heb 2:1 NIV). *(2) We have a lot to unlearn*. We go to a counselor with a problem that took years to develop and say, "Fix me. I've got an hour." Whoa! Your problems didn't develop overnight and they won't disappear overnight. There's no pill, prayer or principle that will instantly undo the damage of many years. It requires the hard work of removal and replacement. The Bible calls this "Taking off the old self, and putting on the new self" (See Eph 4:22-23 NIV). We still have old patterns, practices and predispositions that need to be dealt with. *(3) Growth is painful*. Every change involves a loss of some kind. We must let go of our old ways in order to experience the new life Christ promised. And we fear these losses, even if our old ways are self-defeating, because, like a pair of worn-out shoes, they are comfortable and familiar. *(4) Habits take time to develop*. Your character is the sum total of your habits. And there is only one way to develop the habits of Christ-like character: you must practice them over and over! There are no *instant* habits. That's why Paul urged Timothy to "Practice these things. Devote your life to them."

LEARN TO WALK AWAY!

Get some rest.

MARK 6:31 NIV

One of the hardest things to do is "take a break" without feeling guilty and selfish; or worse, feeling like a failure because everything on your "to do" list didn't get done. Here's a news flash: there will *always* be more to do! One of your biggest challenges will be learning the difference between setting high standards for yourself—and setting unrealistic, impossible ones.

We claw our way to success then discover we don't like the pressures that go with it. So what should we do? Learn to walk away! Jesus did. "The apostles gathered around Jesus and reported to him all they had done...Then, because so many people were coming and going that they did not even have a chance to eat, he said to them, 'Come with me by yourselves to a quiet place and get some rest.' So they went away by themselves in a boat to a solitary place" (vv. 30-32 NIV). Jesus understood that if you don't take a break—you'll break! So: (a) Make a list of the things that only *you* can do, then delegate the rest or let them go. (b) Learn to take small steps and celebrate small accomplishments for that's what life is made of. (c) Don't allow the stuff that's still undone, to undo you. (d) Strive for balance; don't become addicted to what you enjoy. (e) Don't allow overachievers to put you into overdrive. You're in for the long haul. You win when you pace yourself. (f) Take time for the people who matter, otherwise you'll lose them. Busyness is a destroyer of relationships. All the success in the world won't compensate for the joy and treasure of your family and your loved ones!

HAVING A STEADFAST PURPOSE!

You will keep in perfect peace him
whose mind is steadfast.

ISAIAH 26:3 NIV

Knowing your purpose gives meaning to your life. This is why people try dubious methods like astrology and psychics to discover it. When your life has a steadfast purpose you can bear almost anything. Without it, nothing is bearable. Isaiah complained, "I have labored to no purpose; I have spent my strength in vain and for nothing" (Isa 49:4 NIV). Job lamented, "I give up; I am tired of living. Leave me alone. My life makes no sense" (Job 7:16 GNT). Dr. Bernie Siegel found that he could predict which of his cancer patients were most likely to survive by asking, "Do you want to live to be 100?" Those with a deep sense of purpose who answered "yes" were the ones.

Having a steadfast purpose simplifies life. It defines what you *do* and what you *don't* do. It becomes the standard you use to evaluate which activities are essential and which aren't. Without purpose you've no real foundation on which to base your decisions, allocate your time and use your resources. You tend to make choices based on circumstances, pressures, and your mood at that moment. When you don't know your purpose you try to do too much, and that causes stress and conflict. It's *impossible* to do everything people want you to do; you have just enough time to do God's will. If you can't get it all done, you're trying to do more than God intended. A steadfast purpose makes your lifestyle simpler and your schedule saner. And it leads to peace of mind: "You will keep in perfect peace him whose mind is steadfast."

SEEING YOURSELF AS GOD DOES (1)

We were like grasshoppers in our own sight.

NUMBERS 13:33 NKJV

When Moses sent twelve spies to check out the Promised Land, ten came back saying, "We saw…giants…and we were like grasshoppers *in our own sight."* Israel had repeatedly witnessed God's power; why now were they intimidated? It's a perception problem called low self-esteem, and it's how the Enemy prevents you from winning. The Israelites quickly forgot their Red Sea deliverance and instead remembered Egypt where they'd lived as slaves. Be careful. Hard times can make you think you don't deserve to be blessed! Anytime you have something of value, the Enemy will attack you. In the Old Testament we read: "When the Philistines heard…David had been anointed king…they went up in full force to search for him" (2Sa 5:17 NIV). Until you claim your rightful place in Christ, Satan will tell you that you *deserve* to be mistreated. So steep yourself in God's Word till it becomes such a part of you that you stop doubting yourself. God made you in His image, redeemed you, indwells you, and that makes you valuable!

A man in the prairie observed an eagle fatally wounded by gunshot. He writes: "With his eyes gleaming…he slowly turned his head, giving one last…longing look towards the sky. He'd often swept those starry spaces with his wonderful wings…the sky was the home of his heart. There he'd displayed his strength a thousand times…played with the lightning and raced the wind. Now far from home, the eagle lay dying, because—just once—he forgot and flew too low…My soul is that eagle. This isn't its home. It must never lose its skyward look."

SEEING YOURSELF AS GOD DOES (2)

We...are being transformed into his likeness.

2 CORINTHIANS 3:18 NIV

A man who was feeling depressed went to see a psychiatrist. After sharing his problems he expected some profound words of wisdom that would make him feel better. "Well," the psychiatrist exclaimed, "I've diagnosed your problem. It's low self-esteem—and it's very common among losers!" When you view yourself negatively you tend to gravitate toward people who talk down to you. But when you know that God loves you and "plans...to give you a future and a hope" (Jer 29:11 NLT), your entire outlook changes. With God you can't lose. Even if you stumble and fall He'll help you to get back up, learn from the experience and move on. When you look at yourself you tend to see somebody who makes mistakes and falls short, right? But when you begin to look at yourself in the mirror of God's Word, you see someone "being transformed into his likeness."

Ever gone to a garage sale or an antique show looking for a bargain? To the untrained eye much of the stuff looks like rubbish; it may even have been gathering dust and mildew in somebody's attic. But the experienced eye sees treasure in disguise, items that just need to be cleaned, polished and restored in order to become valuable again. Well, *God's* the expert with a trained eye. When the Enemy tells you you're worthless, God looks inside you and sees hidden treasure. When you put Him on the throne of your life He'll enable you to overcome your past, resist temptation, break through your self-imposed limitations, and start accepting that in *His* eyes you have great worth.

KEEP TREADING AND TRUSTING!

Every place that the sole of your foot shall tread upon,
that have I given unto you.

JOSHUA 1:3

You'll notice a common thread throughout the Bible. When we really need Him, God shows up and does for us what we can't do. The rest of the time, which is most of the time, He strengthens us and says "keep treading and trusting." There's no magic carpet. To achieve anything worthwhile you have to walk it out in faith, step by challenging step.

The Book of Job has forty-two chapters. In the first forty-one, Job lived through the loss of his health, his wealth and his family. With friends like Job had, he didn't need any enemies. His doubts were relentless. Over and over he questioned God but got only silence for an answer. He persevered through tough days and sleepless nights believing, "When He has tried me, I shall come forth as gold" (Job 23:10 NAS). Notice: (1) It takes fire to produce gold. (2) Only the refiner knows the degree of heat and amount of time required. (3) To rush the process is to produce something of lesser value.

God told Israel that every place the soles of their feet trod, He would give to them. C. V. White says: "The man who succeeds never waits for the crowd. He strikes out for himself. It takes nerve, it takes a lot of grit, but the man who succeeds has both. Nothing important was ever done but the greater number consulted previously doubted the possibility. Success is the accomplishment of that which people think can't be done." Complacency, fatigue, criticism and discouragement are hurdles you must constantly overcome. So, keep "treading and trusting!"

DANGER POINTS!

If the master of the house had known what hour
the thief would come, he would have watched.

MATTHEW 24:43 NKJV

Here are three danger points at which the Enemy will attack you: *(1) Weariness.* In Old Testament times the "birthright" meant you inherited twice as much of your father's estate. Normally Esau wouldn't have considered selling his birthright, but he did in a state of exhaustion. Weariness can cause you to lose perspective and make decisions based on what's convenient, rather than what's good for you in the long term. Remember the H.A.L.T. sign: when you're Hungry, Angry, Lonely or Tired —you're vulnerable, and you'll make bad decisions. *(2) Excitement.* King Herod was seduced by a dancing girl, threw caution to the wind and said, "Whatever you ask me, I will give you" (Mk 6:23 NKJV). She asked for the head of John the Baptist. And since he was king, Herod couldn't go back on his word. That moment of indulgence cost Herod his kingdom and his life. Be careful where you go looking for excitement, and how you react when you find it. It can cost you the game! *(3) Discouragement.* In a moment of discouragement Peter did what he swore he'd never do: denied his Lord. Discouragement can make you say things you don't mean and do things that are out of character. Jude writes: "Carefully build yourselves up in this most holy faith by praying in the Holy Spirit, staying right at the center of God's love" (Jude v. 20 TM). Esau's weariness, Herod's excitement, and Peter's discouragement are what Jesus had in mind when He said, "If the master of the house had known what hour the thief would come, he would have watched."

BEGIN TO SIMPLIFY YOUR LIFE!

Watch how I do it…learn to live.

MATTHEW 11:29-30 TM

A recent report says, *"We can have it all."* By working longer, playing harder and multitasking, it's possible to squeeze thirty-one hours into twenty-four. But it'll cost you! The average office worker is bombarded daily with 220 messages via email, memo, phone, and other interruptions. One in three managers gets sick because of information overload. If technology is saving us all this time and energy, how come we're so frazzled? When the checkout line doesn't move fast enough or we can't find a parking space, we have a meltdown. Madison Avenue and Wall Street won't tell you this, but success brings more opportunities for the Enemy to run you into the ground. That's no way to live, and it certainly isn't what God intended for you.

Jesus said: "Are you tired? Worn out?…Come to me… recover your life. I'll show you how…work with me—watch how I do it…learn to live freely and lightly" (vv. 28-30 TM). Sounds good, doesn't it, but it calls for detoxing your thinking and reprogramming it. One author writes: "The Lord cannot relieve the pressure, while you're in the wrong place at the wrong time doing the wrong thing with the wrong people. If you climb the corporate ladder and neglect your family, His hands are tied because your priorities are out of order. When you're in God's will you can work hard, but travel light! He'll carry your burdens and take the weight. Simplifying your life may mean working fewer hours, scheduling downtime and investing more into your loved ones. Our gifts, assignments, personalities and situations are all different, but these principles hold true for everyone." So, begin to simplify your life!

WHO ARE YOU? (1)

He fashions…hearts individually.

PSALM 33:15 NKJV

The likelihood of anyone else in history having the same genetic make-up as you is zero. You're not just another brick in the wall or another nail in the carpenter's toolbox. God "personally formed and made" you (Isa 43:7 TM). You're the only "you" He created, so if you fail to be who you are His kingdom won't benefit from your unique contribution. You're *not* your parents (which is good news for some of us!) or your Uncle Joe or Aunt Molly or somebody else you've been trying to please or model yourself after. It's okay to learn from others, but always be what God called you to be. The Bible says: "Don't compare yourself…take responsibility for doing the…best you can with your…life" (Gal 6:4-5 TM).

The question is: *Who* are you? Before you answer it, you must ask yourself this: "What are my strengths?" Do you enjoy working with computers, or cars, or animals? Maybe you're an adept people-manager, or you like fixing things, or you're good with finances. Paul says, "God…has made us what we are" (Eph 2:10 TLB). Are there certain jobs that come easily to you and you wonder why others can't do them? If so, that says something about your particular strengths and your God-given assignment in life. God said of Bezalel the builder: "I have filled him with…wisdom…He is a master craftsman, expert in working with gold, silver, and bronze. He is skilled in engraving… mounting gemstones…carving wood" (Ex 31:3-5 NLT). Once you've identified what makes your eyes sparkle and your pulse race—go for it! "Fix your eyes on what lies before you…Don't get sidetracked" (Pr 4:25-27 NLT).

WHO ARE YOU? (2)

God...shaped each person in turn.
PSALM 33:13-15 TM

Paul writes concerning the family of God: "Each one of you is a separate and necessary part" (1Co 12:27 TLB). But in order to determine where you fit in, it helps to know yourself. For example, *what kind of working environment brings out the best in you?* Do you thrive on routine? Are you motivated by other people's needs? Do you enjoy tackling challenges that discourage others? The Bible says, "God...shaped each person in turn," which means you're not supposed to be a carbon copy. *And how about your relationships?* Do you enjoy being part of a team, or do you function better alone? If you only come to life around people, you'll probably be miserable sitting in front of a computer all day. *What lights your fire?* In the movie *Chariots of Fire*, Eric Liddell described his zeal for running in these words: "God made me to be fast, and when I run I feel His pleasure." What makes you feel like that? There's a story about a man who was asked if he could play the violin. "I don't know, I've never tried!" he replied. When you think about it, it's a wise enough answer, because until you've tried something how do you know whether or not you'd be any good at it? For instance, a frog may be a great swimmer but it's a lousy flier. Some of us whose heroes are "birds" walk around feeling bad about ourselves because we can't fly. You're not supposed to! God's Word says, "Be content with who you are" (1Pe 5:6 TM). Stop flapping around out there and give yourself permission to be the person God made you to be!

SURVIVING A SLUMP

The best...I can do is escape to Philistine country.
1 SAMUEL 27:1 TM

In a slump you lose your rhythm, feel sluggish and unfocused, and revert to old habits that didn't work *then* and don't work *now*. It happened to David. On the run from Saul and leading a makeshift army, he started thinking, "Sooner or later, Saul's going to get me. The best...I can do is escape to Philistine country." David knew better! In past crises he "enquired of the Lord," and consulted trusted advisors. This time he was guided by his fears and ended up defecting to enemy territory. And for a while it felt good. Getting wasted, cheating on your mate, filling your mind with porn may seem enjoyable *temporarily,* but: "There's a way of life that looks harmless...look again—it leads straight to hell...people appear to be having a good time, but all that...will end in heartbreak" (Pr 14:12-13 TM). Eventually even the Philistines rejected David and said, "He's not going into battle with us. He'd switch sides in the middle of the fight!" (1Sa 29:4 TM). Be careful; the decisions you make when you're down can have long-lasting ramifications. Rejected by the Philistines, overrun by the Amalekites, with no country of his own and no family to come home to, we learn from David to: *(1) Seek wise counselors*. It's the last thing you'll feel like doing because misery loves company. But when you "Refuse good advice...your plans fail" (Pr 15:22 TM). In fact, "The more wise counsel you follow, the better" (Pr 11:14 TM). *(2) Stop listening to your fears and listen to God*. Standing among the ruins of his life, "David found strength in the Lord" (1Sa 30:6 NIV), and you will too.

ALWAYS DO THE RIGHT THING

He guides me along right paths.

PSALM 23:3 NLT

George Washington said, "Few men have enough virtue to withstand the highest bidder." Yet that's what we must do to develop the kind of character that will sustain us. It's not easy to do the right thing when: (a) it will cost you; (b) the wrong thing is more expedient; (c) no one but you will know. It's in those moments that your character becomes strong. Dr. Martin Luther King, Jr. said, "Cowardice asks: is it safe? Consensus asks: is it popular? Character asks: is it right?"

During the final play-off of the U.S. Open, Bobby Jones' ball ended up in the rough just off the fairway. As he set up to play his shot, he accidentally moved his ball. He immediately turned to the marshals and announced a foul. The marshals hadn't seen the ball move; neither had anyone in the gallery. So they left it up to Jones whether to take the penalty stroke. He did. Later when someone commended him for his integrity, Jones replied, "Do you commend a bank robber for not robbing a bank? No, you don't. This is how the game of golf should be played at all times." Jones lost the match that day—by one stroke, but he maintained his integrity. His character was so well-known that the United States Golf Association's sportsmanship award came to be named *The Bob Jones Award*. So do the right thing, and keep doing it. Even if it doesn't help you move ahead in the short-term, it will protect and serve you well over the long-term. Or as the Psalmist put it, "He guides me along right paths, bringing honor to his name."

DEALING WITH STRONG HOLDS,
IMAGINATIONS, AND THOUGHTS

Pulling down...strong holds; Casting down
imaginations...bringing into captivity every thought.
2 CORINTHIANS 10:4-5

Paul writes: "Pulling down...strong holds; Casting down imaginations... bringing into captivity every thought to the obedience of Christ." What are you to pull down? *Strong holds:* areas of your life that are held in the grip of the enemy. What are you to cast down? *Imaginations:* always fearing the worst instead of believing God for the best. What are you to take captive? *Thoughts:* thinking that doesn't line up with God's Word or submit to the rule of Christ in your life.

Recognize that you are in a war. Old issues and thought patterns will constantly try to reestablish control over you. Don't let them. And be careful who your friends are. If they can barely stay afloat themselves, how can they lift you? So long as these old issues reign in your life, Christ's seat is taken. If they are on the throne, Christ is still on the cross. Put Christ on the throne and your past on the cross!

In the Old Testament a priest could not come into God's presence if he had touched anything dead (See Lev 22:3-4). That means if you are going to walk with God you must bury your old lifestyle. Don't even "touch" those old dead issues any more. It also means forgiving those who hurt you, including yourself, then moving on. The issue is not *whether* you remember but *how* you remember. God is able to take the sting out of the memory and still leave the sweet taste of victory intact. No longer will you be handicapped or hindered by what you've been through; instead you'll be enriched by it!

THE POWER OF PASSION (1)

*[My] life is worth nothing unless
I use it for doing the work assigned me.*

ACTS 20:24 TLB

Paul found God's purpose for his life, and from it came his incredible passion. Notice: *(a) Passion energizes you!* A passionate person with limited ability will outperform a passive person with great ability, because passionate people act with boundless enthusiasm! *(b) Passion overcomes fear.* What makes people take risks, go the extra mile and do whatever it takes to achieve their goals? Passion. As long as the passion is there it doesn't matter how often they fail, or if others are against them. They don't stop until they succeed. *(c) Passion drives you until you find what you're looking for.* Solomon writes: "If you... search for [wisdom] as for hidden treasure, then you will...find the knowledge of God" (Pr 2:4-5 NIV). There's a story about Socrates in which a proud young man supposedly asked, "Oh great Socrates, I came to you for knowledge." Socrates led him down to the sea into waist-deep water. "Tell me again what you want," he said. "Knowledge." Socrates pushed him down under the water, holding him there for thirty seconds. "Now, what do you want?" The young man sputtered, "Wisdom, oh great Socrates." Again the philosopher pushed him under. When he let him up again he asked, "What do you want?" "Knowledge, oh wise and..." he managed to spit out before Socrates held him under again, this time even longer. "What do you want?" repeated Socrates. The younger man coughed and gasped. "Air!" he shouted, "I want air!" Socrates replied, "When you want knowledge as much as you want air, you'll get knowledge." Then the old man returned to the shore. Bottom line: be passionate!

THE POWER OF PASSION (2)

Fan into flame the gift of God, which is in you.
2 TIMOTHY 1:6 NIV

The keys to a successful life are knowing who you are (your calling), and what you're supposed to do (your destiny). Without these you're like an octopus on roller-skates: lots of movement but no real direction. Another key is having the spiritual and emotional fuel to get there. There are two kinds of people: *(1) Those with low flame.* When you don't like what you're doing you become like Eddie, whose grandmother was an opera lover. When Eddie turned eight she took him to a performance of Wagner—in German. The next day he wrote her a note: "Dear Granny, thanks for the birthday present. It's what I always wanted, but not very much. Love, Eddie." It's difficult to achieve when you don't have much desire to do so. The old saying is true: "Find something you like to do so much that you'd gladly do it for nothing, and if you learn to do it well, someday people will be happy to pay you for it." *(2) Those with no flame.* Some people say they feel burned out. The truth is, many of them were never on fire in the first place. Norman Cousins said, "Death isn't the greatest loss in life. The greatest loss is what dies inside us while we live." If you're not careful you could end up like the man whose tombstone read, "Died at thirty. Buried at sixty." Don't let that happen to you. When you find your God-given purpose, with it comes your passion. Will you have to fan that flame? Yes, regularly! But it will energize you and carry you to your destination.

THE POWER OF PASSION (3)

I must be about my Father's business.

LUKE 2:49

Examine the life of Christ. As a boy of twelve He told His parents, "I must be about my Father's business." Later He announced to His disciples, "We must do the work of him who sent me" (Jn 9:4 NIV). Note the word "must." Jesus knew what He was called to do and He refused to allow anything to stand in the way of doing it. When you prioritize your life according to your God-given passion, you risk being misunderstood and criticized by those who don't understand you, or are driven by a different set of priorities. But ask yourself, "Would I rather live with the pain of risk, or the pain of regret?"

Dr. John Maxwell writes: "In the early 1970s I realized that my talents would be maximized and my potential realized only if I matched my passion with my priorities. I was spending too much of my time doing tasks for which I possessed neither talent nor passion. I had to make a change—to align what I felt strongly about with what I was doing. It made a huge difference in my life. It didn't eliminate my troubles or remove my obstacles, but it empowered me to face them with greater energy and enthusiasm. For more than thirty years I have worked to maintain that alignment of priorities and passion. As I have, I've kept these words near to keep me on track: *There are many things that will catch my eye, but there are only a few that catch my heart. It is those I consider to pursue.*" If your priorities are not aligned with your passion, start making some changes right away!

THE POWER OF PASSION (4)

His word is in my heart like a fire.

JEREMIAH 20:9 NIV

If you've ever built a fire you know that its tendency is to go out. You must feed and protect it. Not everyone will help you do that. There are two kinds of people you'll meet in life: *fire lighters* and *fire extinguishers*. The first group will inspire you, encourage you and go out of their way to help you. The second group will throw cold water on you. How can you tell the difference? Fire extinguishers use phrases like: "It's not in the budget...that's not practical...we've tried that before and it didn't work...if it ain't broke don't fix it...who will do all the extra work?...we don't have enough experience, talent, education, etc....who do you think you are?" If you've heard one or more of these excuses coming from the people around you, pray for them, love them, but don't let them influence you. Fire extinguishers focus on what's wrong rather than on what's right. They find the cloud that comes with every silver lining. They doubt. They resist change. They keep you from reaching higher by trying to put out the fire of your passion. Sometimes they do this deliberately, other times unknowingly. Handle them with care! Instead, spend more time with fire lighters who view you not as you are, but as you could be; who fuel your faith and ignite your passion.

It's estimated that there are about 200 million Christians in the Chinese church today. One of the *fire lighters* who helped start it was Hudson Taylor. And he's the man who said, "The sun has not once risen in China in forty years, without finding me on my knees in prayer." *That's passion!*

MASTERING YOURSELF

Everything is permissible for me—but.
1 CORINTHIANS 6:12 NIV

Let your flesh know who's in charge. Look for ways to say no to yourself every day. If you do, you'll be able to do it when it really counts. We're not just talking about cardinal sins, but zeroing in on the undisciplined areas of our lives that we excuse, rationalize, or postpone dealing with. Paul writes: "Everything is permissible for me—but not everything is beneficial. Everything is permissible for me—but I will not be mastered by anything." Paul measures his actions by this yardstick: "Is it beneficial? Does it have the potential to control me?"

How long are you going to keep telling yourself, "I know I need to change, and I will—tomorrow"? You have the *right* to consume chocolate cake and ice cream at bedtime every night. It's "permissible," but not "beneficial," especially if you want unblocked arteries, sugar-free blood, a trim waistline, the ability to run a marathon, or maybe just to keep up with your grandkids. You have the *right* to spend your time and money as you please, but you don't have the right to complain when the law of diminishing returns kicks in and you finish up in the poorhouse. You have the *right* to fill your mind with any kind of garbage you choose. But understand this, constant exposure to the wrong things will weaken your character, rob you of self-respect and eventually enslave you.

When it comes to replacing bad habits with good ones, only one person is going to make it happen—you. Your character is the sum total of your everyday choices. Day by day, what you think, what you choose and what you do, is who you become.

ARE YOU SEARCHING FOR CONTENTMENT?

My people have...forsaken...the...living water,
and...dug...broken cisterns.
JEREMIAH 2:13 NIV

It's easy to be content when things in life are going your way. But how often does *that* happen? The Bible says we are to practice being "happy at any time in everything" (Php 4:12 NCV), because if you put your life on hold waiting for what you want to happen, you may be waiting a long time! Epicurus said, "Don't spoil what you have, by desiring what you don't have. Remember that what you now have, was the thing you once hoped for."

Three things constantly feed our discontentment: *(1) Greed.* When you dwell on what you don't have, you're not enjoying what God's already given you. Be satisfied! Setting goals is good, but stop focusing so hard on the end result and learn to rejoice in the Lord while you're on your way. *(2) Fear.* It wants you to run from something that's not chasing you. It's the enemy's way of: (a) robbing you of peace and stability; (b) tormenting you with the "what if's"; (c) keeping you from trusting God. The Psalmist said, "In God I trust; I will not be afraid. What can mortal man do to me?" (Ps 56:4 NIV). *(3) Seeking satisfaction in the wrong places.* God said, "My people have... forsaken...the...living water, and...dug...broken cisterns that cannot hold water." It's said that we spend our first fifty years searching for security, and the rest of our lives looking for significance. But we don't have to. The hymn writer wrote: "Now none but Christ can satisfy; no other name for me. There's love, life, and lasting joy, Lord Jesus found in Thee!" Are you searching for contentment? Try Jesus!

GROWING IN GRACE (1)

We do not...compare ourselves.
2 CORINTHIANS 10:12 NIV

Chuck Swindoll writes: "When others don't share your viewpoint, do you find ways to signal your disapproval? How about if somebody drives a newer car, lives in a nicer house, wears their hair a certain way and buys clothes *you* would never wear? What if they're divorced, or a single parent, or (God forbid!) in a relationship you don't approve of? Can you 'live in harmony' with them, or do you pull out your 'comparison rule book'? The Bible says we shouldn't 'compare ourselves ...Each of us is an original.' Comparing is wrong because it leads to criticism, competition, control, and covetousness. It's an indicator that you're insecure and that grace is a foreign concept to you. Grace means freeing others to be themselves and losing the legalist attitude that requires them to conform to your standards." Paul addresses this: "Who are you to judge the servant of another? To his own master he stands or falls; and he will stand, for the Lord is able to make him stand" (Ro 14:4 NAS). Note the words, "who are you to judge?" Back off; stop trying to do God's job!

Gladys Hunt writes: "Acceptance means you're valuable just as you are...You aren't forced into someone else's idea... You can talk about how you feel...and why...and if someone really cares...you can try out ideas without being shot down... You can even express heretical thoughts and discuss them with intelligent questioning. You feel safe. No one will pronounce judgment ...even though they don't agree with you. It doesn't mean you'll never be corrected...it simply means it's safe to be you." When you can say that, and mean it, you're growing in grace!

GROWING IN GRACE (2)

Let us not judge.
ROMANS 14:13 NKJV

A close second to *comparing* is *controlling*. Often controllers are steeped in "religiosity." Their *modus operandi* is manipulation, hints and veiled threats. They're not big on grace because they "think [they] know it all" (Ro 12:16 TLB). Do you see any of these traits in yourself? Think how much happier you'd be if you weren't trying to control people and outcomes. Dennis Leonard writes: "Give your loved ones the dignity of making their own mistakes and learning from them. If you're always getting into someone else's business, you're not only going to burn out, you're hindering God from working in their lives...They belong to Him not you!"

Dealing with controversy over Jewish food laws, Paul writes: "Those who feel free to eat anything must not look down on those who don't. And those who don't...must not condemn those who do, for God has accepted them" (Ro 14:3 NLT). Because you don't feel at liberty to do something, don't condemn those who do. Having strong opinions doesn't sanction you to impose them on others. Even good things can be abused. William Barclay talks about "making a tyranny of the Sabbath, surrounding it with a jungle of rules, regulations and prohibitions." Ask yourself if your attitude is likely to cause peace or strife. Growing in grace means building "each other up" (v. 19 NLT), not flaunting your liberty before those who don't share your convictions. Paul says, "Let each [man] be fully convinced in his own mind" (v. 5 NKJV). There are times when you need to humbly and prayerfully "press on, regardless."

GREAT RELATIONSHIPS

There is a friend who sticks closer than a brother.

PROVERBS 18:24 NIV

Building great relationships takes time and energy. And you only discover how valuable such relationships are when they're tested. One author writes: "Contouring your heart to beat with another requires extensive whittling, to trim away self-centeredness. It's like riding the bus; if you're going to have company you must be willing to scoot over to accommodate other people and the baggage they bring. Your actions in doing this express the importance of the other person. One relationship becomes more valuable than others because of its ability to survive and endure realignments."

The qualities we value most in a friend are twofold: (1) The assurance that they won't bail out when the road gets rocky. (2) The knowledge that our imperfections and scars won't change their level of commitment. Solomon said, "A man of many companions may come to ruin, but there is a friend who sticks closer than a brother." It's about quality, not quantity. That's why heart connections can be so much stronger than blood connections. Don't be too quick to discount someone's good qualities because they made a mistake, disappointed you or did something without thinking. You wouldn't haul your car to the junkyard because it had a faulty battery or a flat tire! Love means risk, but the payoffs outweigh the investment. Behind every success story you'll find people who once felt so discouraged they wanted to quit, who fell and needed lifting when someone stepped in, picked them up and helped them to keep going. Life is not built on acquisitions and accomplishments, it's built on relationships. So keep yours in good shape!

EQUIPPING PEOPLE TO SERVE

He...gave gifts...to equip God's people...
and build up the church.

EPHESIANS 4:8-12 NLT

A s a leader you must keep before you at all times the philosophy, plan and purpose behind what you're called to accomplish, and make it clear to the people who work with you. Three of the most common problems in any organization, including the church, are: (1) Putting someone in the wrong slot and leaving them there because there's no one else to do the job. (2) Not understanding someone's gifting and not providing adequate training, direction and information to promote teamwork. (3) Leaders who don't know how to communicate their vision clearly. When any one of these areas is out of whack, we spend our time and energy troubleshooting, putting out fires and running in forty directions. As a result, leaders get discouraged and workers quit.

But the church doesn't have to be like that. Paul outlined the Master Plan for church growth by reminding us that God "gave [these] gifts...to the church: the apostles, the prophets, the evangelists, and the pastors and teachers...to equip God's people to do his work and build up the church." *Why did God assign leaders?* To equip people. *Why do people need to be equipped?* To serve. *Why is service so important?* To build up the body of Christ. That's it! And it's essential to developing a strong, healthy church whose mission is to feed God's sheep and reach the lost with the gospel. That's why as a leader, *everything* you do should be directly related to equipping people to serve. Do that, and you'll be less frustrated, your people more fulfilled, and your church more fruitful!

DO YOU WANT TO CHANGE?

Let God transform you.
ROMANS 12:2 GNT

Change only takes place when you: *(1) Decide to change.* *The Daily Mail* newspaper once invited readers to answer the question, "What's wrong with the world?" G. K. Chesterton supposedly sent the following reply: "Dear Sir, I am." Face it, if you could kick the person responsible for most of your troubles, you wouldn't be able to sit down for a week. Discipleship—the process of becoming like Christ—begins with a decision. Jesus calls to us, and we respond. "'Follow me and be my disciple,' Jesus said to him. So Matthew got up and followed him" (Mt 9:9 NLT). And notice, he took his pen with him! That's all you need to get started: a decision! *(2) Change the way you think.* "Let God transform you into a new person by changing the way you think" (Ro 12:2 NLT). Change starts in your mind. The way you think determines the way you feel, and the way you feel influences the way you act. So wash your mind, feed your mind, and program your mind with God's Word. *(3) Take a small step every day.* Most of us want overnight change. No, change comes slowly. To be successful we must start with small things and do them every day. St. Francis de Sales said: "Have patience with all things, but chiefly have patience with yourself. Do not lose courage in considering your own imperfections, but instantly start remedying them—every day begin the task anew." You say, "But I fall so far short." We all do. Don't be discouraged: "God who began the good work within you will keep right on helping you grow in his grace until his task within you is finally finished" (Php 1:6 TLB).

GREAT EXPECTATIONS

*This day the Lord will hand you over to me,
and I'll strike you down.*

1 SAMUEL 17:46 NIV

It's not the size of the dog in the fight; it's the size of the fight in the dog. David didn't have the rank, equipment or training, but he had the winning attitude. So great was his level of expectation that he "ran quickly toward the battle line to meet [Goliath]" (v. 48 NIV). While Saul and his soldiers were hiding, David was running to meet the challenge. How's that for great expectations? Now we're not talking about faith in our own ability, but in "him who is able to do immeasurably more than all we ask or imagine, according to his power that is at work within us" (Eph 3:20 NIV).

Martin Seligman, Professor of Psychology at the University of Pennsylvania, did some research on a major life insurance company and found that sales people who expected to succeed sold *twice* as much as those who didn't. Researchers have discovered that there's a greater correlation between self-confidence and achievement than there is between IQ and achievement. Know what? The God who lives within you is limited by one thing only: your inability or unwillingness to believe in yourself. The more you believe in yourself, the more you'll be able to accomplish. And if you *keep* believing and expecting, you'll someday find yourself doing what you once considered impossible. Why? Because "with God all things are possible" (Mt 19:26). It's said that if Michelangelo had consulted his doubts or his critics, he'd have painted the floor of the Sistine Chapel instead of the ceiling, and his work wouldn't be around for us to admire. The truth is, great results begin with great expectations!

KEEP PRACTICING

In a race all the runners run, but only one gets the prize...
Run...as to get the prize.

1 CORINTHIANS 9:24 NIV

In a *Peanuts* cartoon, Charlie Brown laments to his friend Linus, "Life is just too much for me. I've been confused from the day I was born. I think the trouble is, we're thrown into life too fast. We're not really prepared." "What do you want," Linus asks, "a chance to warm up first?" You may not get a chance to warm up before entering life, but you can warm up by practicing what's important to you once life has begun. It's during these warm-ups that you grow. If you commit yourself to practice you discover: *(1) Your performance can always be improved.* Author Harvey Mackay says: "A good leader understands that almost anything that has been done in a particular way for a given amount of time, can be done better. Every single performance can be improved." *(2) The sharpening process is better in the right environment.* Improvement always requires some degree of risk and failure. So find a place where growth and experimentation are encouraged. *(3) You must be willing to start with small things.* When you first start to practice your gains will be small. But they will grow. In the Olympics, the difference between the gold medalist and other contestants is often just hundredths of a second. *(4) There's a price to pay to reach the next level.* Sidney Howard remarked, "One half of knowing what you want, is knowing what you must give up before you get it." Too many of us regard practice as an essentially negative experience, but it doesn't have to be if you think of it in terms of discovery and development. So, keep practicing!

THE VERSE AT THE CENTER OF THE BIBLE

*It is better to trust in the Lord than
to put confidence in man.*

PSALM 118:8

Psalm 117 is the shortest chapter in the Bible. Psalm 119 is the longest. Psalm 118 is at the center of the Bible. There are 594 chapters in the Bible before Psalm 118, and 594 chapters after Psalm 118—1,188 chapters. This number can be split 118-8, or Psalm 118:8. Now we know that the chapter divisions in the Bible are not part of original Scripture, but isn't it interesting how this little word-exercise worked out? Or was God in the center of it all? And if He was, shouldn't the central verse of the Bible contain its central theme? It does: "It is better to trust in the Lord than to put confidence in man."

In Psalm 118 the Psalmist recalls seven reasons why God is worthy to be trusted: (a) "I called upon the Lord in distress: the Lord answered me, and set me in a large place" (v. 5). (b) "The Lord is on my side; I will not fear: what can man do unto me?" (v. 6). (c) "The Lord taketh my part with them that help me: therefore shall I see my desire upon them that hate me" (v. 7). (d) "I shall not die, but live, and declare the works of the Lord" (v. 17). (e) "The Lord hath chastened me sore: but he hath not given me over unto death" (v. 18). (f) "This is the day which the Lord hath made; we will rejoice and be glad in it" (v. 24). (g) "Oh, give thanks to the Lord, for He is good! For His mercy endures forever" (v. 29 NKJV).

YOU'LL GET THROUGH THIS STORM

It is I; do not be afraid.

MARK 6:50 NKJV

Are you in a storm today? Then read these words: "The boat was in the middle of the sea; and He was alone on the land. Then He saw them straining at rowing, for the wind was against them. Now about the fourth watch of the night He came to them, walking on the sea, and would have passed them by. And when they saw Him walking on the sea, they supposed it was a ghost, and cried out...But immediately He talked with them and said to them...'It is I; do not be afraid.' Then He went up into the boat to them, and the wind ceased" (Mk 6:47-51 NKJV). There are four lessons here for us:

(1) It's when we feel most separated from God that He's teaching us the most. Dave Dravecky said: "Looking back...I have learned that the wilderness is part of the landscape of faith, and every bit as essential as the mountaintop. On the mountaintop we are overwhelmed by God's presence. In the wilderness we are overwhelmed by His absence. Both places should bring us to our knees; the one, in utter awe; the other, in utter dependence." (2) God doesn't show up early. Usually He comes in the worst part of the storm when you think you can't take any more—but He will always be on time. (3) God takes us through different storms, revealing more of Himself to us in each one. Otherwise, there are aspects of His character and divine strategies we'd never understand. (4) God's presence alone should be enough for us in any storm. That moment when God shows up and says, "It is I," should calm our every fear.

HOW TO DEFEAT YOUR GIANT

The battle is the Lord's.

1 SAMUEL 17:47 NKJV

One day a soldier charged with fleeing from the enemy was brought before Alexander the Great. Alexander the Great asked him, "What's your name?" Dropping his head, he replied, "Alexander." Alexander the Great grabbed him by the shoulders and said, "Soldier, change your conduct or change your name!" You have been called to live a life worthy of the One whose name you carry. Regardless of whether the giant you face is addiction, resentment, fear, lust, pride, envy or anger, you must realize:

(1) You're not unique. Your temptations "are no different from what others experience" (1Co 10:13 NLT). Goliath wasn't always a giant; he was fed and nurtured until he became one. Our giants are usually little sins we overlook and indulge until they assume a life of their own and come back to haunt us. *(2) You can't do it alone.* Your giant will defeat you anytime you tackle him in your own strength. David told Goliath, "This is the Lord's battle, and he will give you to us" (1Sa 17:47 NLT). You need divine help to overcome old habits and establish new behaviors. So, declare with Paul, "Christ...gives me strength" (Php 4:13 NLT). *(3) You must confront your giant head-on.* The Bible says, "As Goliath moved closer to attack, David quickly ran...to meet him" (1Sa 17:48 NLT). Don't run away, don't try to negotiate, don't compromise and don't excuse. Force your giant out into the light and don't let him back into your life. Establish boundaries and make yourself accountable. Stay out of the wrong company. Above all, don't look at God in the light of your giant, look at your giant in the light of God.

WAIT NO LONGER, SPEAK!

Anxiety in the heart of man causes depression,
but a good word makes it glad.

PROVERBS 12:25 NKJV

Few things are as powerful as the right words spoken at the right time. By the same token, words withheld when their season of opportunity is gone are a heavy burden to live with. Looking back, one relationship expert offers these moving words:

"I remember when I took your new car on the road and wrecked it. I thought you'd be livid and come down hard on me, but you didn't. I remember when we went to the beach and you didn't want to go because you said it was going to rain. We went and it rained. I was sure you'd rub it in and say, 'I told you so!' But you didn't. Then there was the time when I spilled blueberry juice down the front of your new white tux. I knew you'd be upset and blame me. But you didn't. And remember that formal evening? I was mistaken and told you it was casual. You wore blue jeans and felt like a fish out of water. I was sure you would storm out in anger and leave me standing there. But you didn't. I wanted to tell you how much I loved you and how much I appreciated you for all those things when you returned from Vietnam. But you didn't."

Solomon said, "There is...a *time* to speak" (Ecc 3:1&7). But it's a limited time, and when it's over it's gone. Don't spend your future regretting and carrying inside you the unspoken words someone needed to hear. "Pleasant words are a honeycomb, sweet to the soul and healing to the bones" (Pr 16:24 NIV). Wait no longer, speak!

BROKENNESS (1)

The sacrifices of God are a broken spirit.
PSALM 51:17 NIV

A world that celebrates success doesn't see value in broken things. But God brings beauty out of brokenness. For a plant to rise from the soil the seed must be broken. For a baby chick to experience larger life the shell must be broken. Even a thoroughbred horse must be broken; it must learn to respond to the tug of the rein and the sound of the master's voice. Getting the idea? After a humbling encounter with Christ on the Damascus Road, Paul reevaluates all the religious activity he once boasted about and calls it "dung" (Php 3:8). And you don't brag about dung, you're repulsed by it.

Brokenness is the work of God by which He strips us of self-sufficiency so that the character of Christ may shine through us. Now don't misunderstand; being broken doesn't necessarily mean experiencing some tragedy. Many people suffer tragedy without drawing closer to God or even acknowledging Him. Indeed, the same sunshine that melts the butter hardens the clay. The issue in brokenness is not so much our circumstances, but our *response*. What is God trying to teach us? True brokenness is when He strips us of self-sufficiency to the extent that we've no strength left to fix ourselves. When God blocks every exit we try to take and we come to see that He alone is our answer, we make a life-changing discovery. "And what's that?" you ask. When God is all you have—God is all you need! Bottom line: God's power is reserved for those who have given up trying to do it in their own strength or to accomplish it for their own ends!

BROKENNESS (2)

The sacrifices of God are a broken spirit.
PSALM 51:17 NIV

Paul writes: "Now may...God...sanctify you entirely; and may your spirit and soul and body be preserved complete, without blame at the coming of our Lord" (1Th 5:23 NAS). This word "sanctify" means to be "set apart," to be used exclusively for God's purposes. Paul describes it as "the high calling of God" (Php 3:14). And it happens from the *inside out!* Notice, our fleshly body comes last in order of transformation for a very simple reason. The problem with a thief isn't his hands, it's in his mind or spirit, which tells him stealing is okay. His mind tells his hands what to do. So if you transform his spirit his hands will follow suit. Otherwise you can handcuff him and take him off to jail, but he's still a thief inside. Too many of us want to get victory over bodily sins without being truly transformed within. But God starts with our spirit because that's the part of our being that makes us conscious of God; that "connects" with Him. When God sets us free in our spirit, then our emotions and our body begin to fall in line.

If you're a parent you know how differently your children respond to discipline. One child will collapse in tears, whereas another will stand up and defy you. God will do whatever it takes, for as long as it takes, to break us of our self-sufficiency so that the life of Jesus can be demonstrated through us. And *we* determine how long the process takes, by our submission or resistance. Paul prayed, "Lord, what do You want me to do?" (Ac 9:6 NKJV). Today, make that your prayer!

BROKENNESS (3)

The sacrifices of God are a broken spirit.

PSALM 51:17 NIV

Sometimes God allows us to hit the bottom in order to discover that He's the rock at the bottom. Gideon faced an army of 135,000 troops with just 32,000 men. And 22,000 of them left the battlefield and went home when he offered them the chance. Do the math. Gideon's thinking, "There's no way we can win!" Then God explains: "The people who are with you are too many for Me to give Midian into their hands, for Israel would become boastful, saying, 'My own power has delivered me'" (Jdg 7:2 NAS). There it is again, the age-old battle of ego that we all fight daily. It's why the Lord's Prayer ends with: "Thine is the kingdom, and the power, and the glory, for ever. Amen" (Mt 6:13). Where does our power come from? God! Who should the glory for our accomplishments go to? God! How long does this arrangement last? Forever!

God had to break Jacob of self-sufficiency so the "Israel" within him could come out. Sometimes God has to take you down before He can raise you up. Moses was called the meekest man on earth. But it took forty years of living as a shepherd in the wilderness to detox him of pride and get him submitted to God. Only then was he ready to stand before Pharaoh and perform miracles that demonstrated God's power—and vindicated Moses!

Brokenness doesn't mean being a wimp, suffering from an inferiority complex or having a case of low self-esteem. No, brokenness means praying, "Lord, if this job is going to get done, and done right, *You're* going to have to do it through me. So my trust is in You."

BROKENNESS (4)

The sacrifices of God are a broken spirit.

PSALM 51:17 NIV

We don't always know the reason for our trials, but God revealed to Paul the reason for his "thorn in the flesh." It was to keep him from being "exalted" (See 2Co 12:7). Success can be intoxicating, and intoxicated people aren't known for being too bright or trustworthy!

What happens when you get a thorn in your flesh? It hurts. And you'll let everything else go while you focus on removing it. Three times Paul prayed for God to remove the thorn, but God had another plan. You see, God is at His strongest in us when we are at our weakest. When Paul discovered that God's power in his life was tied to the thorn that afflicted him, he responded, "I am content with weaknesses, insults, hardships, persecutions, and calamities...for whenever I am weak, then I am strong" (2Co 12:10 NRS). In other words, "If it's for my good, bring it on, Lord!" If you've a thorny person in your life from whom you've prayed to be delivered and it hasn't happened, maybe God wants you to experience His grace and power through dealing with that person. But you won't experience this until you move from pain to praise. The Bible speaks about "the sacrifice of praise to God" (Heb 13:15). A sacrifice means that something has to die on somebody's altar. So if you want to experience God's grace and power in your life, you must be willing to die to self-interest, ego, and independence. There's nothing wrong with asking God to remove your thorn. But when your prayer for deliverance turns to praise, you're on your way to power, because God is giving you grace.

ARE YOU A GOOD LISTENER?

Everyone should be quick to listen, slow to speak.

JAMES 1:19 NIV

Someone quipped, "God gave us two ears and one mouth because we need to listen twice as much as we talk." Learning that means being "quick to listen, slow to speak." Good listening builds relationships. But good listeners aren't born, they're bred! So here are a few suggestions to improve your listening:

(1) Listen without interrupting. Resist the temptation to jump in and finish the sentence, or hijack the floor. Rein yourself in—just listen. *(2) Listen to understand.* Try to understand their point of view, feelings, thinking and needs. Good listening is hearing what they actually think, mean or feel, not what you imagine they do. Instead of guessing, ask, "Am I understanding you correctly? Do you mean...? Are you feeling...?" In other words, don't assume—verify. *(3) Listen without judging.* Don't rush to conclusions. If what they say doesn't quite add up, keep listening. "He who answers a matter before he hears it, it is folly and shame to him" (Pr 18:13 NKJV). When you hear more, it may make sense. *(4) Listen without correcting, countering or devaluing.* Saying, "That's not the way it was," or, "What did you expect? If you hadn't..." or, "You're just being too sensitive," puts people on guard and stops real communication. *(5) Validate the speaker.* Accept their perceptions and feelings as valid expressions of a valued person. "If I understand you correctly, you're thinking...feeling...Am I right?" Ask them to help get you on the same page with them. "Given what you've told me, I can see why you'd feel what you feel," is very validating and will increase their confidence and willingness to consider the solutions you may offer.

TODAY, ENCOURAGE SOMEBODY (1)

Anxiety in the heart of man causes depression,
but a good word makes it glad.

PROVERBS 12:25 NKJV

The nineteenth-century writer Walt Whitman struggled for years to get anyone interested in his poetry. In the midst of his discouragement he received a life-changing note from an admirer of his work. The note read: "Dear Sir, I am not blind to the worth of the wonderful gift of *Leaves of Grass*. I find it the most extraordinary piece of wit and wisdom that America has yet contributed. I greet you at the beginning of a great career." It was signed by Ralph Waldo Emerson. Whitman enjoyed a long career and is now considered one of the giants of American literature. But when times were tough he needed encouragement to keep going. And he's not alone. When we're on the brink of failure, the right word at the right time can keep us in the game. When we're too tired or discouraged to keep going, an act of compassion can give us new strength. Encouragement is one of the central themes of the Bible: "Anxiety in the heart of man causes depression, but a good word makes it glad." "Strengthen the weak hands, and make firm the feeble knees" (Isa 35:3 NKJV). "For I, the Lord your God, will hold your right hand, saying to you, 'Fear not, I will help you'" (Isa 41:13 NKJV). Encouragement doesn't deny the problem; it enables us to overcome it. It doesn't validate stubbornness or stupidity; it simply corrects and guides us in the right path. It doesn't leave us alone to carry the burden, it lets us know that God is present to help and strengthen us. So today, encourage somebody!

TODAY, ENCOURAGE SOMEBODY (2)

Anxiety in the heart of man causes depression,
but a good word makes it glad.

PROVERBS 12:25 NKJV

Henry Ford and Thomas Edison were friends; they met at a convention sponsored by Edison's company where Ford worked as an engineer. Someone introduced Ford to Edison as "a young man who has made a gas car." Ford and Edison talked a while about the automobile, then Edison banged his fist on the table with excitement. "You have it! Your car is self-contained and carries its own power plant." Ford later recalled, "No man up to then had given me any encouragement. I had hoped that I was headed right. Sometimes I knew that I was, sometimes I only wondered, but here, out of a clear sky, the greatest inventive genius in the world had given me complete approval." Sir Isaac Newton is best known for his Theory of Gravitation and description of the Three Laws of Motion. But Newton might never have published his work had it not been for Edmond Halley. A well-respected scientist in his own right, Halley visited Newton at Cambridge to discuss a problem he was working on, only to discover that Newton had already solved it. Halley encouraged Newton to publish his work, and even offered to do it at his own expense. The result was the publication of *Philosophiae Naturalis Principia Mathematica* in 1687, which laid the groundwork for the study of mathematics and changed the way people see the world.

Who can you encourage to do great things? Who has God put into your life to cheer on, raise up, or assist on their journey? When you help others to do the things God created them to do, you share in their achievement.

YOU ARE GOD'S CONDUIT

It is God who works in you.

PHILIPPIANS 2:13 NKJV

A conduit is a channel through which things like water and electricity move from one point to another. And you are God's conduit! You are designed to be a free-flowing channel for Jesus Christ Himself. God has chosen you to be His "change-agent" on the earth. In the Lord's Prayer the original Greek says, "Come thy kingdom. Be done thy will" (See Mt 6:10). Jesus no longer walks among us physically, but He has given us His mandate and all the power we need to carry it out. In other words, it's going to happen *through* you. In Deuteronomy 11:24 God promised His people that He'd give them every place on which they set the soles of their feet. *We* bring the influence and benefits of God's kingdom wherever we go. The problem is, our "receivers" don't always work. It takes faith to believe we actually *hear* God's instructions, just as it takes faith to believe an unseen radio wave is passing through our living rooms. Because we're confident of that reality, we tune in, receive and transmit.

Scientists tell us that the greatest metal conduit is pure gold. According to the Bible, that's our faith (See 1Pe 1:7). But certain obstacles can block our ability to receive and be conduits for God. If our hearts are hard, our wires are down, or if we're unaware of our identity as conduits, we go through life without tapping into the power God's given us. We must be full of the Word of God, and most importantly, spend time in intimacy with the Lord in order to be God's conduit.

THE ULTIMATE SOURCE OF WISDOM

The wisdom that is from above is...
JAMES 3:17

A s you go through life you discover there are many ways to gain wisdom, such as: (1) Writing down and reflecting on what you've learned through experience. (2) Gleaning from the collective knowledge of others. "By pride comes nothing but strife, but with the well-advised is wisdom" (Pr 13:10 NKJV). (3) Thinking outside the box. Statements like, "This is the way we do things around here" warrant scrutiny when they're used to defend ways that no longer work. (4) Not rushing to closure. Growth is always a work-in-progress. Creativity is untidy and unnerving. The ability to stay focused and faith-filled in the midst of change is a hallmark of maturity.

But the ultimate source of wisdom is God! A young executive told his secretary he'd an important meeting and didn't want to be interrupted. But his boss needed to see him and walked in. When he found the young executive on his knees praying, he withdrew quietly and asked the secretary, "Is this usual?" "Yes," she replied, "he does it every morning." "No wonder I come to *him* for advice!" said his boss. If you need wisdom, talk to God: "For the Lord gives wisdom; from His mouth come knowledge and understanding" (Pr 2:6 NKJV). "If any of you lacks wisdom, let him ask of God, who gives to all liberally...and it will be given to him" (Jas 1:5 NKJV). "The wisdom that is from above is first pure, then peaceable, gentle, willing to yield, full of mercy and good fruits, without partiality and without hypocrisy" (Jas 3:17 NKJV). "I will instruct you and teach you in the way you should go; I will guide you" (Ps 32:8 NKJV).

GOD'S INCREDIBLE LOVE FOR US

Take in...the extravagant dimensions of Christ's love.
EPHESIANS 3:18 TM

George Matheson was told by his doctor that he was going blind. Not to be denied, he pursued his studies, graduating from the University of Glasgow in 1861 at the age of nineteen. By the time he finished graduate seminary studies, he'd lost his sight. To make matters worse, his fiancée returned the engagement ring with a note: "I cannot go through life bound by the chains of marriage to a blind man." Matheson never married, and never fully recovered from his broken heart. He became a powerful and poetic pastor, led a full and inspiring life, yet occasionally the pain of loneliness flared up, as it did later at his sister's wedding. The ceremony brought back memories of the love he had lost. In response, he turned to the incredible love of God for comfort and penned these words on June 6, 1882: *O love that wilt not let me go, I rest my weary soul in Thee; I give Thee back the life I owe, that in Thine ocean depth its flow may richer, fuller be.*

Consider the stubborn love of Hosea for his wife Gomer. Hopping from one lover to another, she ruined his life. Destitute, she was placed for sale in a slave market. Guess who stepped forward to buy her? Hosea, who'd never removed his wedding band. God uses this story to illustrate His steadfast love for us. He told Hosea: "Love her the way I, God, love the Israelite people" (Hos 3:1 TM). God loves you with an incredible love. You can't win it being winsome, or lose it by being a loser. But you can be blind and resist it. Don't!

INFORMATION OVERLOAD! (1)

Many shall run to and fro, and knowledge shall increase.

DANIEL 12:4 NKJV

Technology lets us do things we've never been able to do, but it can be addictive. You can become tied to it in ways that are exhausting. One expert notes: "There's a strong tendency for humans to do everything they're able to. Combine that with constant connectivity, and the workday need never end. It's easy to contact anyone anytime, and with information always available on line you can keep clicking forever." Paul writes about "making the most of your time" (Eph 5:16 NAS). We say, "Time is money," but in actuality time is much more valuable, because it's a nonrenewable resource. Once spent, it's gone forever. Managing information overload means reestablishing boundaries that technology has demolished. So:

Recognize the signs: if you communicate with people all day yet you're still lonely, chances are, technology is dominating your life. *Take baby steps:* make yourself unavailable for short periods and see what happens. The wheels of industry won't grind to a halt! *Remember you have a choice:* people who think they should be available 24/7, exaggerate their own importance or the control others have over them. *Establish boundaries:* rein in the emails and instant messages. Do you really need all those "FYI's" about the same thing? *Give clear instructions:* tell people you answer emails at designated times throughout the day, and let them know who to contact for an immediate response. *Make a task list:* that way if you're interrupted you'll get back on track faster. *Stick to a schedule:* constantly dipping in and out on the computer is classic self-interruption. *Do a reality check:* after a few minutes of surfing the web ask yourself, "Should I be doing this *now?*"

INFORMATION OVERLOAD! (2)

The servant is not greater than his lord.

JOHN 13:16

When you're constantly multi-tasking, important things can fall between the cracks. A lawyer who negotiated an unbelievable deal in favor of his client was asked how he did it. He replied, "I was the only person at the meeting that day who didn't spend the whole time text messaging!" A respected researcher says we've trained our brains "to constantly flit around the universe of messages and information, seeking brief hits of excitement. Grazing ceaselessly, we never dig too deeply before moving on to the next distraction...and it ratchets up our stress levels in ways we're only starting to understand." Another expert says: "We get more information in seventy-two hours than our parents received in a month, and most people don't have the skills to deal with it. They let new things in, but don't get rid of old information they wanted to act on."

When was the last time you enjoyed some relaxed, uninterrupted down time? Can you even remember? We're so results-oriented that unless we're doing something that can be quantified, we think it's a waste of time. The fact is you *need* time away from the unrelenting onslaught of information to regroup, reflect and recharge. Jesus had a schedule to keep, people to minister to, disciples depending on Him, and a short time to do it all. Nevertheless, "He withdrew...into the wilderness, and prayed" (Lk 5:16). Now, since "the servant is not greater than his lord," do *you* think you're above all that? Are you wiser than He? Or more spiritual? Jesus said, "Come... apart...and rest a while" (Mk 6:31), because when you don't come apart, you fall apart!

"IT IS WELL WITH MY SOUL"

My peace I give you...Do not let your hearts
be troubled and...afraid.
JOHN 14:27 NIV

The peace Jesus gives brings a sense of assurance that no matter what happens, you know "it is well with my soul." He says to us: "My peace I give you. I do not give to you as the world gives. Do not let your hearts be troubled and...afraid." The peace Jesus gives doesn't depend on conditions and circumstances. It comes from knowing you're God's child and that your Father controls the universe, loves you and always has your best interests at heart. That's why people who've lost everything will often tell you they wouldn't trade what they've learned, even if it meant recouping all their losses. Joni Eareckson Tada discovered a supernatural peace when an accident confined her to a wheelchair, and Corrie ten Boom found it in a Nazi death camp. Missionary Elisabeth Elliot found it in ministering to the Indian tribe who massacred her husband. She wrote: "Only in acceptance lies peace...not in resignation." There's a big difference! Author Creath Davis points out that: "*Resignation* is surrender to fate. *Acceptance* is surrender to God. *Resignation* lies down quietly in an empty universe. *Acceptance* rises up to meet the God who fills that universe with purpose and destiny. *Resignation* says, 'I can't.' *Acceptance* says, 'God can.' *Resignation* paralyzes the life process. *Acceptance* releases the process for its greatest creativity. *Resignation* says, 'It's all over for me.' *Acceptance* says, 'Now that I'm here, what's next, Lord?' *Resignation* says, 'What a waste.' *Acceptance* says, 'In what redemptive way will you use this mess, Lord?' *Resignation* says, 'I'm alone.' *Acceptance* says, 'I belong to you, Lord.'"

IF YOU DON'T—WHO WILL?

Tell the next generation.

PSALM 78:4 NIV

What a father says to his children in the privacy of home isn't heard by the world, but it's clearly heard by posterity. A mega-church pastor writes: "Years ago I was invited to the White House to meet the President and a few key religious leaders. It was the first such invitation this country boy ever received. However, when I called home I discovered my son's basketball game was rescheduled for that weekend, and I'd already missed one. The question became one of simple priority, 'What's most important?' The government had been running without me for years, so I called the White House and said I wouldn't be coming. (They recovered from the news beautifully!) I went to the game and had the fun of seeing my son shoot the winning basket." Paul said, "Be…careful…how you live… making the most of every opportunity" (Eph 5:15-16 NIV). How you spend your time reveals your true values and priorities. Dad, are you spending quality time with your children?

Karl Marx said that to conquer a nation you just have to block the transfer of values, morals and beliefs between generations. Solomon said, "The righteous man walks in his integrity; his children are blessed after him" (Pr 20:7 NKJV). Before you know it they'll be gone, but what legacy will they take with them? Your kids are like mirrors, they reflect what they see. And it's hard for them to see God as their *heavenly* Father unless He's clearly visible in their *earthly* one. So: "Take them by the hand…lead them in the way of the Master" (Eph 6:4 TM). "Tell the next generation…of…his power, and the wonders he has done." If you don't—who will?

LITTLE CEDARS

The glory of Lebanon shall be given to it.

ISAIAH 35:2 NKJV

Solomon used the cedars of Lebanon to build the temple. When it was complete, the glory of God filled it. Let's look at four different types of cedars God still uses to build His church.

Little cedars. They were used to make fence posts for sheep pens. A guide tells of seeing a truckload of little cedars being transported over a road filled with potholes, twists and turns. Even though they weren't tied on, not one fell off. What a picture of consistency and stick-to-it-iveness! These folks have what it takes to survive the potholes and make it through the twists and turns of life. It's said that people don't determine their future, they determine their habits and their habits determine their future. And little cedars have habits like:

(a) Praying. They talk to God—then take time to listen: "Morning by morning, He wakens My ear to hear as the learned" (Isa 50:4 NKJV). (b) Bible reading. "Ezra...prepared his heart to seek the Law of the Lord, and to do it" (Ezr 7:10 NKJV). Do you approach God's Word with a prepared heart and a willingness to obey? (c) Witnessing. "You are My witnesses" (Isa 43:10 NKJV). The credibility of a witness in court determines which side wins. How credible is your testimony? (d) Tithing. "Honor the Lord with your wealth, with the first-fruits of all your crops; then your barns will be filled to overflowing" (Pr 3:9-10 NIV). You say, "But when I've paid my bills I don't have much left over." God wants to be first in your finances, not last. When you put Him first, His blessings will overflow into every area of your life.

FIRE CEDARS

The glory of Lebanon shall be given to it.

ISAIAH 35:2 NKJV

Another cedar Solomon used to build the temple was called the *fire cedar*. It's said that shepherds used it to make fires at night because it was saturated in oil, would ignite easily, and burn a long time. What a picture.

God gathered 120 fire cedars in the upper room, and: "Suddenly there came a sound from heaven, as of a rushing mighty wind, and it filled the whole house where they were sitting. Then there appeared to them divided tongues, as of fire, and one sat upon each of them. And they were all filled with the Holy Spirit" (Ac 2:2-4 NKJV). That day three thousand souls were won to Christ! The church was born in the fire and has been sustained by the fire—and we must not let that fire go out! Even in the days of the Old Testament tabernacle, God commanded His people to take the fire that burned on the altar and carry it with them wherever they went. Getting the idea? A lot that passes for "revival" or "renewal" today seems to be nothing more than "waves" that come and go. We are never more vulnerable than when we are spiritually hungry, because at that point we stand on the threshold of two spiritual realms. The way to discern true revival is to ask ourselves four questions: (1) Is it scriptural? (See Isa 8:20). (2) Does it magnify the person of Christ? (See Jn 3:30). (3) Does it demonstrate God's love? (See Ac 2:44-45). (4) Does it win souls and turn them into disciples? "By this My Father is glorified, that you bear much fruit; so you will be My disciples" (Jn 15:8 NKJV).

HUMMING CEDARS

The glory of Lebanon shall be given to it.

ISAIAH 35:2 NKJV

Picture the wind blowing through the cedars of Lebanon and some of them "humming" in response. And the greater the storm, the sweeter their song. These were called *humming cedars*. And God uses humming cedars to build strong churches. In Acts, a couple of humming cedars were incarcerated in a Philippian dungeon, their hands and feet locked in stocks, their backs flogged, the contempt of society heaped on them. How did they respond? "At midnight Paul and Silas were...singing hymns to God...Suddenly there was a great earthquake...the foundations of the prison were shaken; and immediately all the doors were opened and everyone's chains were loosed" (Ac 16:25-26 NKJV). One old preacher said: "God got so caught up in their praises that He began to tap His big foot. And when God taps His foot, you get earthquakes."

Praise breaks chains and opens doors; it's the strategy for victory. Satan will try to stop you from praising God because he knows: *(a) The importance of praise.* "Great is the Lord, and greatly to be praised" (Ps 48:1 NKJV). *(b) The healing effects of praise.* God's answer to "the spirit of heaviness" is "the garment of praise" (Isa 61:3). But like any garment, you must put it on. *(c) The power of praise in times of crisis.* When Israel was outnumbered by the enemy, God told them to put a choir in front of the army and march into battle. And it worked! "When they began...to praise, the Lord set ambushes against the [enemy]" (2Ch 20:22 NKJV). Don't wait until the battle is over to shout; go to war with the praise of God on your lips and watch Him turn your situation around.

TALL CEDARS

The glory of Lebanon shall be given to it.

ISAIAH 35:2 NKJV

Towering above the other cedars that grew on the mountains of Lebanon was the *tall cedar*. However, its strength was not in its height but in the depth of its root system. It's said that the tall cedar could bend almost to the ground without breaking, and come back stronger. Today God uses tall cedars to build great churches.

The new birth is only 5 percent of the process; the other 95 percent is growing up into spiritual maturity. "Though by this time you ought to be teachers, you need someone to teach you the elementary truths of God's word all over again. You need milk, not solid food! Anyone who lives on milk, being still an infant, is not acquainted with the teaching about righteousness. But solid food is for the mature, who by constant use have trained themselves to distinguish good from evil. Therefore let us leave the elementary teachings about Christ and go on to maturity" (Heb 5:12-6:1 NIV). Note the words "who by constant use have trained themselves [in the Scriptures]." You can't be like the old farmer who always testified at the Wednesday night prayer meeting: "I'm not making much progress, but thank God I'm established." One spring when his tractor was bogged down, its wheels spinning but going nowhere, the pastor happened to drive by. Rolling down his window, the preacher smiled and said: "Think of it this way brother; you may not be making much progress, but thank God you're established." No more excuses for immaturity! You must strive to be "mature and full grown in the Lord...becoming more and more in every way like Christ" (See Eph 4:13 NLT).

HANDLING YOUR ANGER THE RIGHT WAY

Don't sin by letting anger control you.
EPHESIANS 4:26 NLT

A guy's car stalled at an intersection, causing a chorus of honking horns from behind. He got out, walked calmly to the next car in line and said, "Sorry, I can't get my car started. If you'd like to give it a shot I'll sit here and honk your horn!" When you don't know how to handle your anger properly, two things happen: *(1) You stay angry.* You walk around with your thermostat at boiling point. Be realistic. More problems in life are forgotten than are ever resolved to our liking. *(2) You don't get angry even when it's appropriate.* Consequently, issues that could build character, end up creating vacillation and indifference. Express your anger the right way! When you lack the courage to confront your boss or an associate at work, you're more likely to explode at home. Jesus said, "If your brother sins against you, go and show him his fault, just between the two of you" (Mt 18:15 NIV). Sometimes we're supposed to get angry. Paul writes: "When Peter had come to Antioch, I withstood him to his face, because he was to be blamed...he would eat with the Gentiles; but when [the Jews] came, he...separated himself, fearing [them]...the rest of the Jews also played the hypocrite...so that even Barnabas was carried away with their hypocrisy" (Gal 2:11-13 NKJV). It's wrong to tolerate wrong when you can do something about it. Just do it the scriptural way. Say what you have to in kindness. This is called "speaking the truth in love" (Eph 4:15). Slamming doors and storming out are un-Christlike and counterproductive. Direct your anger toward the problem, not the person.

LESSONS FROM LAZARUS (1)

But even now I know.

JOHN 11:22 NKJV

Lesson one: *Jesus knows how you feel.* At Lazarus' funeral, "Jesus wept. Then the Jews said, 'See how He loved him!'" (vv. 35-36 NKJV). This story proves we serve a God who can not only raise the dead, but can "sympathize with [us]" (Heb 4:15 NKJV). So if you're grieving today turn to God and allow Him to comfort you. *Lesson two: Jesus can give you back what life's taken from you.* He can "restore to you the years" that life has stolen (Joel 2:25 NKJV). Claim that promise; take it to the place where you've lost so much, and ask God to replace and renew. Martha said, "Lord, if You had been here, my brother would not have died. But even now I know that whatever You ask of God, God will give You" (Jn 11:21-22 NKJV). Instead of saying "if only," pray "even now I know." It's not too late, God can move on your behalf. *Lesson three: Jesus can set you free.* "He cried…'Lazarus, come forth!' And he who had died came out bound hand and foot with graveclothes… Jesus said…'Loose him, and let him go'" (vv. 43-44 NKJV). God's Word is greater than the thing that has bound, limited or enslaved you. Even though your mind doesn't fully comprehend it, let your spirit respond to God. Pray with the Psalmist: "Give me understanding, and I shall keep Your law; indeed, I shall observe it with my whole heart. Make me walk in the path of Your commandments, for I delight in it" (Ps 119:34-35 NKJV). When you pray such a prayer your faith will grow, and the circumstances that seem impossible will be changed by God.

LESSONS FROM LAZARUS (2)

That the Son of God may be glorified through it.

JOHN 11:4 NKJV

Here are three more lessons from Lazarus:
(1) God has a bigger and better plan in mind. Lazarus was four days dead when Jesus arrived. When the Lord waits, it's for two reasons: (a) That He may be glorified. The Pharisees believed that your spirit left your corpse on the fourth day after you died. So if Jesus had intervened earlier they'd have said, "He wasn't really dead." Hence He told His disciples, "This sickness is...for the glory of God" (v. 4 NKJV). It's in looking back that we clearly see God's hand at work. (b) That our faith may be strengthened. Jesus said, "I am glad for your sakes that I was not there, that you may believe" (v. 15 NKJV). In life, crises come and go. Your next crisis will be different from your last one, but the thing that must remain strong is your faith. *(2) God will ask you to remove the hindrances and deal with the stench.* "Jesus said, 'Take away the stone.' Martha ...said to Him, 'Lord, by this time there is a stench, for he has been dead four days'" (vv. 38-39 NKJV). Are you praying for an answer in one area, while God's telling you to take away the stone and deal with a "stench" buried in another? Surrender, you can't win! When your heart's right with God your prayers will be answered. *(3) God wants to make you a living testimony.* Everywhere Lazarus went, without even speaking a word, his life declared that Jesus is Lord. And the same should be true of you. God has saved and raised you up to be a testimony to His grace and goodness.

WORK IN JESUS' NAME

Whatever you do, whether in word or deed,
do it all in the name of the Lord Jesus.

COLOSSIANS 3:17 NIV

John Ortberg writes: "We all work. We all create value—that's what work is. But what would it look like for you to work in Jesus' name? Well, first, work would become something you do *together* with Him. You were not meant to work on your own. So, tomorrow, take a moment at the beginning of your workday when you sit down at your desk or your computer or in your home, and invite Jesus to partner with you. Tell Him, 'Today, I'm not going to work by myself.' Any time throughout your workday when you have a tough problem, ask Him for help. When you have a difficult decision to make, ask Him for wisdom—then listen and be really open. When you find your energy flagging, ask Him for renewed strength. When you find your attitude turning negative, ask Him to reorient your heart. Put a symbol on your desk or wall where you can see it to remind you that today you and Jesus are partnering together in your work. Every few hours as you're working, pause for two or three minutes. Thank Him for His help. Hand Him your worries. Ask for His energy. Every moment is an opportunity to be with Jesus. When you forget—and you will, when you mess up—and you will, remember this really important rule: there's to be no beating yourself up! Every moment is another chance. God just keeps sending them. That's grace. Every moment of your workday is a new chance for you to be with Him."

ARE YOU LOSING YOURSELF?

There met Him ten men who were lepers.

LUKE 17:12 NKJV

Luke records: "There met Him ten…lepers…they lifted up their voices and said, 'Jesus, Master, have mercy on us!'…He said to them, 'Go, show yourselves to the priests.' And…as they went, they were cleansed" (vv. 12-14 NKJV). Leprosy was a slow, painful death. First you lost your fingers and couldn't work, then you lost your toes and couldn't walk, then it attacked your internal organs. Every day you lost a little more of yourself. Here are five helpful insights from this story: *(1) If you feel like you're "losing yourself," turn to Jesus.* He can restore what you've lost and give you back your peace and joy. *(2) "Lift up your voice."* Away with dignity and decorum! Desperate people do desperate things. God promises: "You will…find me when you seek me with all your heart" (Jer 29:13 NIV). *(3) Whatever He tells you—do it.* Don't lay down conditions to God. And don't seek an identical experience to somebody else. Jesus told the ten lepers, "Go, show yourselves to the priests." Why didn't He just speak to them or touch them like He did others? Don't question, obey! Faith doesn't demand explanations. *(4) Take a step of faith.* Luke records, "As they went, they were cleansed." You've got to walk it out; each step brings you one step closer. But nothing happens till you take that first step of faith. *(5) Start praising God!* Only one of the ten lepers returned to give thanks, and Jesus noticed it. You can go to God with confidence for your next answer, when you know you remembered to give Him thanks for your last one.

EXERCISE CONTROL, WITHOUT BEING CONTROLLING

The fruit of the Spirit is...self-control.
GALATIANS 5:22-23 NIV

There are two kinds of people: the controller and the self-controlled. Which one are you? Let's find out: *The controller* believes that "the Devil does it to them," or people, or circumstances, so they respond by blaming, resenting, or projecting frustration. They keep trying to manipulate people and circumstances to their advantage. But people and circumstances usually don't submit to our control, so their attempts only intensify their pain and turn their relationships into power struggles. The more they try to control the worse they feel; the worse they feel the more they try to control. Refuse to live that way. *The self-controlled* understand that the Devil can do nothing to them without their cooperation, and that they don't have to give it. They understand that people and circumstances aren't their problem either—how they deal with them is. So they respond by reminding themselves of three things: (1) The person I need to control is me. (2) Sometimes I must turn the people and circumstances in my life over to God and allow Him to deal with them. (3) I must draw daily on the Holy Spirit's power in order to control my reactions and follow the "sound mind" principles of Scripture for staying in charge of my life (See 2Ti 1:7). As a result they avoid engaging in blame-games, self-inflicted pain, and turning relationships into war zones. Knowing that "the fruit of the Spirit is...self-control" they understand that the Spirit won't control them, or help them control others and manipulate circumstances, but He will empower them to control themselves. Spirit-empowered people are freed from being part of the problem, and become part of the solution God is bringing about!

STAYING POWER!

Keep your mind on Jesus [and]...
you won't get discouraged and give up.

HEBREWS 12:3 CEV

It's difficult to endure hardship at the best of times, but when you don't know *why,* it can be frustrating. God doesn't give us lengthy explanations on how He works; He's used to creating worlds with a single sentence. So when you don't find an immediate answer in His Word or through prayer or the counsel of others, you're left wondering. And you wouldn't be the first. David repeatedly asks *why* in the Psalms, and God still called him "a man after My own heart, who will do all My will" (Ac 13:22 NKJV). So don't get discouraged. Bible commentator William Barclay pointed out that endurance isn't just the ability to bear a hard thing, but to use it for your growth and God's glory.

When the answers aren't forthcoming the question then becomes, "How do I get through this?" And the Bible addresses it by telling us Jesus endured "the shame of being nailed to a cross, because he knew...later on he would be glad" (Heb 12:2 CEV). Then it goes on to say: "Keep your mind on Jesus...you won't get discouraged and give up." The reason Jesus endured was because He was able to look ahead and envision the joy of pleasing His Father, building the church and saving a lost world. The Psalmist said, "I have set the Lord *always* before me...he is at my right hand, I shall not be moved" [discouraged, or thrown by the situation] (Ps 16:8). Staying-power is not denying reality, or white-knuckling it. It's keeping your eyes on Jesus and drawing from Him the strength you need to fight your way through to victory!

WEEPING AND REAPING

Those who sow in tears will reap with...joy.

PSALM 126:5 NIV

Friends can hold your hand and cheer you along, but shepherding a God-given dream to fulfillment always involves watering it with your own tears. Neither fellowship nor friendship can lower the price of personal sacrifice required. That's the not-so-good news. However, the better-than-great news is—there will be a harvest! "Those who sow in tears will reap with ...joy. He who goes out weeping, carrying seed to sow, will return with...joy, carrying sheaves with him" (vv. 5-6 NIV). But you must recognize what season you're in. There's:

(1) A time for weeping (See Ecc 3:4). This is not an excuse for passivity, or a posture of weakness that reduces you to tears because life's not fair and things are tough. Nehemiah was moved to tears over Jerusalem's ruins. Then he sought God, developed a plan, put together a team and rebuilt the city. What moves you? What do you feel passionate about? *(2) A time for reaping.* Everything in life has a season and a reason (See Ecc 3:2). Those who understand the reason and maximize the season are "like a tree planted by streams of water, which yields its fruit in season" (Ps 1:3 NIV). Note the words, "in season." Fruit won't grow before its time. That's why you must discern your life's changing seasons and adjust to them. Even restaurant menus remind us that certain dishes are only available in season. You need to know when it's time to stop weeping and start reaping, otherwise you'll miss your harvest. Tears are for the sower, joy is for the reaper. So when your season changes, harvest your fields with joy! You've paid your dues; now it's time to enjoy what God has promised you.

LONGING FOR HEAVEN (1)

They were longing for a better country—a heavenly one.
HEBREWS 11:16 NIV

Mel Blanc was the voice behind the Warner Brothers cartoon characters in *Looney Tunes*. At the end of every movie Porky Pig pops up with the same send-off: "That's all, folks!" Mel Blanc died a few years ago. Know what his family put on his tombstone? "That's all, folks!" But it's not, and deep down we know it. The Bible says God "set eternity in the hearts of men" (Ecc 3:11 NIV). It's a longing that won't go away. It's why the Egyptians built the Pyramids and the Greeks put a gold coin under the tongue of the departed so they could pay the ferryman to cross over the River Styx.

But our longing is not just for a longer life, particularly if longer just means more of the same. A Christian college once sent students door to door to talk to people about spiritual issues. Two of them knocked on one door to find a frenzied mother of three with a vacuum in one hand and a screaming baby in the other, food burning on the stove and a living room so messy it would have qualified as a Federal disaster area. "Are you interested in eternal life?" they asked. "Frankly, I don't think I could stand it," said the mom. We don't want just more of the same. We want what's wrong to be put right. We want suffering to stop. We want clean air, meaningful work, honest politicians, clear consciences, ceaseless beauty, and the end of loneliness and war. In other words, we want *Heaven*. And the good news is, when Christ is your Savior that's where you go when you die!

LONGING FOR HEAVEN (2)

They were longing for a better country—a heavenly one.
HEBREWS 11:16 NIV DEC. 12ᵗʰ 2021

A Christian art form that flourished in the sixteenth and seventeenth centuries featured paintings of common objects of beauty—a vase of flowers, a mandolin, a sideboard with fruit. Tucked somewhere in the paintings would be the two reminders of the passing nature of human existence: a skull and an hourglass. These paintings were called *vanitas* art. This word "vanitas" comes from the passage in Ecclesiastes: "Vanity of vanities; all is vanity…One generation passeth away, and another generation cometh" (Ecc 1:2-4). Now the symbols of the skull and the hourglass weren't intended to foster gloom; they were just a reminder that every possession and achievement we have is temporal, therefore not worthy of our heart's devotion. They were to prepare us for that moment when we meet God, the meaning and value of our lives weighed, and our eternal rewards given.

The Apostle Paul wasn't afraid to speak about death, specifically his own: "For to me, to live is Christ and to die is gain" (Php 1:21 NIV). The seventeenth-century bishop Jeremy Taylor wrote: "Since we stay not here, being people but of a day's abode, we must look somewhere else for an abiding city, a place in another country to fix our house in, whose walls and foundations are God, where we must find rest, or else be restless forever." Not only did Paul long for heaven, but the patriarchs and heroes of the Old Testament did too: "All these people were still living by faith when they died…they admitted that they were aliens and strangers on earth…they were longing for a better country—a heavenly one" (Heb 11:13-16 NIV). What a wonderful prospect!

GET MORE SLEEP

He gives His beloved sleep.

PSALM 127:2 NKJV

Illness, stress, family problems, job demands, etc., rob us of sleep. And when we constantly run on low battery power it shows up in our attitudes, our relationships and our performance. The Bible says: (1) "It is vain for you to rise up early, to sit up late, to eat the bread of sorrows; for so He gives His beloved sleep." (2) "I will both lie down in peace, and sleep; for You alone, O Lord, make me dwell in safety" (Ps 4:8 NKJV). (3) "When you lie down, you will not be afraid; yes, you will lie down and your sleep will be sweet" (Pr 3:24 NKJV).

Sleep is an act of trust: when you go to sleep the world is in God's hands, not yours. And it will get along very well, even if you're not awake to control things. When you awaken tomorrow morning, just like God giving Israel fresh manna, He will give you the grace needed. Jeremiah said, "After this I awoke and looked around, and my sleep was sweet to me" (Jer 31:26 NKJV).

Ever tried to pray when you were suffering from sleep deprivation? It's hard to do. Before Elijah was able to spend prolonged time in prayer the angel of the Lord made him take not one, but two long naps. Contrast that with the disciples in Gethsemane who couldn't pray because they kept falling asleep. Know what? It's hard to think, feel and act like Jesus when you lack sleep. That's why "He gives His beloved sleep." Maybe the most spiritual thing you could do is get to bed earlier and wake up refreshed so you're ready to fulfill God's purposes for your day.

WHAT TO DO WHEN THE SIZZLE FIZZLES (1)

You have left your first love.
REVELATION 2:4 NKJV

Nobody plans it, it just seems to happen. Romance runs head-long into reality, something gives, and it's usually romance. At first it's just two love-birds with no higher earthly priority than each other's happiness. Then comes the patter of tiny feet, and our well-ordered world gets turned upside down. Children don't fit neatly into our schedules and agendas. They can't and won't wait. Three kids, two jobs, one mortgage later, and romance seems to be a distant memory. Two overworked people wonder where they lost that romantic feeling and whether it will ever return. Some settle for marriage without the sizzle; some stay till the kids are older, then look for greener, more romantic pastures. But God offers a third, more exciting alternative: God's alternative—do what it takes to restore your "first love." (This Scripture was written to the church at Ephesus, but the principle also applies to building a good marriage.) So:

(1) Reexamine your perceptions. We think our current sizzle-free status is proof that romantic love is dead and the dream forever lost. That's because we confuse romance with love. Romance brings people together, but love keeps them together. People who love each other can make romance live again—at any age or stage. *(2) Realize that the sizzle wasn't lost, it was "left."* "You have left [behind] your first love." It didn't leave you. It didn't die. A new partner is not the solution. *(3) Retrace your steps.* You'll find romance where you left it: undernourished, crowded out, overlooked and seriously oxygen-deprived, but not dead. God created marriage. Talk to Him. Follow His instructions and your romance can live again.

WHAT TO DO WHEN THE SIZZLE FIZZLES (2)

You have left your first love.
REVELATION 2:4 NKJV

Here are three "R's" that work in our walk with God—and in our marriage. First: *Remember*. "Remember the height from which you have fallen!" (Rev 2:5 NIV). Not the depth, but the height. Not how bad it's become, but how great it once was. Not the worst of times, but the best. Recall when just being together was the highlight of your whole day? What were you doing *then* that you're not doing *now?* Do you remember when you phoned just to hear his voice? The gifts you couldn't afford, but bought her? The love notes you slipped into his lunch? Remember opening doors for her, pulling out chairs, walking to the outside of the curb, cooking his favorite dish although you were exhausted from working late, reading "1001 Ways to be Romantic," and trying them all twice? Remember quiet candlelit dinners when you shaved again and wore her favorite cologne, the one you hated? When intimacy wasn't all about *me?* "Our special" places, times, smells, looks, songs, poems? A rose on her tray with breakfast in bed because she had cried when she heard the song, "You don't bring me flowers anymore," and you vowed you'd never forget the flowers?

"Remember!" Remember what you did for love. The magic may seem to have appeared by accident, but it actually grew by action! *You* were the magic. What *you* did fueled the romance, then you stopped doing it and the flame subsided. But the pilot light still burns, and remembering "the heights" releases positive, faith-inspiring chemistry that can move you to actions that will fan the flame into a fire again!

WHAT TO DO WHEN THE SIZZLE FIZZLES (3)

You have left your first love.
REVELATION 2:4 NKJV

The second "R" for renewing your first love is *repent;* change your mind, direction, and actions. You can't solve a problem with the same thinking and behaviors that created it; new thinking and actions are required. If your relationship once sizzled, you still have what's needed to make it sizzle again. You've been remembering what you were doing at "the height" of the relationship. You've acknowledged that those actions made the relationship exciting and fulfilling, that you stopped doing them, and that you "left [behind] your first love." Now you're ready to repent (which means to turn around) and go back to where you were when the flame of love burned brightly.

The third "R" of renewal is *reenact;* "Do the things you did at first" (Rev 2:5 NIV). List the things you used to do when the relationship was great. Each of you should prayerfully and privately commit to doing a couple of the listed items, without telling your partner which ones you chose. Try to "catch" your partner reenacting "the things you did at first" and let them know how much it means to you that they cared enough to do it. You'll get more of what you reinforce by gratitude. But a word to the wise: at first it may feel strange, even unreal, when you begin to reenact those early behaviors. Be patient, that will change. Just keep doing it. And don't wait till you feel like it. You can *act* your way into new ways of *feeling,* even when you can't *feel* your way into new ways of *acting.* Do it till you feel it, till the joy of your first love reignites!

HONORED, BUT NOT EXALTED!

We have this treasure in earthen vessels.

2 CORINTHIANS 4:7

When God calls you to do something, it means you're called to a higher level of accountability. Jesus said, "Unto whomsoever much is given, of him shall be much required" (Lk 12:48). But this is where we get it wrong. We think those who are called are not cut from the same bolt of cloth as others. Wrong! Just because someone prays powerfully and delivers God's Word skillfully, doesn't mean they don't struggle in certain areas. Their struggles may be unseen, but they're still real. We must be careful to make the distinction between the treasure and the vessel. If you're a leader, never allow anyone to expect *you* to be the treasure. Keep your ego in check. Paul says: "We *have* this treasure," he didn't say we *are* the treasure!

Let's face it, God uses people we wouldn't use, like Rahab, working the red light district of Jericho. But when she placed her faith in God He used her to win the battle of Jericho, then included her in the family of Christ. Or how about Jephthah who was born to an unwed mother, rejected by his family, and lived in a cave with his own gang of private mercenaries? God used him to deliver Israel and become the nation's youngest judge. Isn't grace amazing?

God specializes in restoring broken vessels. He takes things that aren't productive—marriages that don't work, people with "issues"—and teaches them how to be victorious and fruitful in His service. Knowing this gives us the strength and tenacity to face whatever comes, because we know that when God places His treasure within us, He prizes, protects and prospers it.

BUILD UP YOUR FAITH!

Taking the shield of faith.
EPHESIANS 6:16 NKJV

A Roman soldier's shield protected him from head to toe. It was made of iron, upholstered in thick layers of fabric, and saturated in water when going to battle. Consequently the flaming arrows of the enemy fizzled on contact. Getting the idea? Paul writes: "Take up the shield of faith, with which you can extinguish all the flaming arrows of the evil one" (NIV). Satan can't penetrate a heart that's pure, saturated in Scripture and fortified by faith. That's why Jesus told Peter, "I have prayed for you, that your faith should not fail" (Lk 22:32 NKJV). It's your *faith* that's under attack; it's your *faith* that needs to be fed and nurtured; it's your *faith* that sustains you in life's battles! Jesus said, "Have faith in God" (Mk 11:22). Note, He didn't just say, "Have faith in something bigger than yourself." No, He said, "Have faith in *God.*"

If you're under attack today claim this promise: "He gives power to the weak, and to those who have no might He increases strength. Even the youths shall faint and be weary, and the young men shall utterly fall, but those who wait on the Lord shall renew their strength; they shall mount up with wings like eagles, they shall run and not be weary, they shall walk and not faint" (Isa 40:29-31 NKJV). God gives each of us a "measure of faith" (Ro 12:3 NKJV). But Jude says you must develop it by "building yourselves up on your most holy faith" (Jude v. 20 NKJV). Faith under attack is faith under construction. It's in the battles of life that you discover whether you have *nurtured* faith or *neglected* faith!

THUMPS

Count it all joy.

JAMES 1:2 NKJV

Max Lucado writes: "When a potter bakes a pot he checks its solidity by pulling it out of the [furnace] and thumping it. If it 'sings,' it's ready. If it 'thuds,' it's put back in. Character is also checked by thumping…Late night phone calls…grouchy teachers…burnt meals…flat tires…you've-got-to-be-kidding deadlines. Thumps trigger the worst in us…They aren't big enough to be a crisis, but if you get enough of them, watch out. Traffic jams…long lines…empty mailboxes…dirty clothes on the floor…Thump. Thump. Thump. How do *you* respond? Do you sing or do you thud? Jesus said, 'People speak the things that are in their hearts' (Lk 6:45 NCV), and there's nothing like a good thump to reveal the true nature of a heart…it's not in momentary heroics, but in the thump-packed humdrum of day-to-day living. If you've a tendency to 'thud' more than you 'sing,' take heart. There's hope for us 'thudders.' Begin by thanking God…not a half-hearted thank-you…but a rejoicing, jumping-for-joy, thank-you from the bottom of your heart. James says: 'Count it all joy when you fall into various trials…the testing of your faith produces patience.' God's doing the thumping… for your own good…You're going to be tested…you might as well learn from the thumps. See it as an opportunity to develop patience and persistence. Each thump helps or hurts you, depending on how you use it. Be aware of 'thump-slumps'…For all of us there are times during the week when we can anticipate an unusual amount of thumping. Handle them head on…bolster yourself with extra prayer…don't give up…and remember no thump is disastrous. All thumps work together for good when you love and obey God."

BEING REAL!

You are like whitewashed tombs.

MATTHEW 23:27 NKJV

Marybeth Whalen writes: "The painters painted the wall leading downstairs...A week later I discovered while the wall had been repainted, the habits hadn't changed. The kids were still...dragging their dirty hands behind them, making what was white and clean, gray and dirty...Like that wall, if I'm not careful I can cover up what's there...wear the Christian tee shirt, carry my Bible, smile like everything's great, and talk a good game about my walk with the Lord. But deep inside the ugly old habits are...waiting to be revealed the moment life gets messy...I can become a modern-day Pharisee who focuses on the whitewash...and ignores the dirty stuff underneath."

In Bible times tombs were whitewashed on the outside to disguise the death and decay inside. Jesus told the Pharisees: "People look at you and think you're saints, but underneath... you're total frauds" (v. 28 TM). Acting like a Pharisee saying, "I thank you, God, that I am not a sinner like everyone else" (Lk 18:11 NLT), precludes grace, mercy and compassion. We live in an appearance-driven society and Jesus understood the danger that comes from focusing on looks instead of your spiritual condition. So, how do you stop it from happening?

(a) Follow Jesus' example. He specialized in ministering to the broken, the forgotten, the lost and the lonely. (b) Never forget that while you may be a Christian, you'll still struggle in certain areas. (c) Ask God to reveal behavior patterns that are appearance-oriented instead of heart-oriented. (d) Surround yourself with transparent people who lift you when you fall and encourage you to be real.

"I WANT IT NOW!"

Don't be greedy, for...the things of this world.

COLOSSIANS 3:5 NLT

A big credit card company has a TV commercial with the slogan, "You can have it all *now!*" Sound familiar? Not much has changed. Satan said to Adam and Eve, "If you want that apple, take it." Leave payday till "some day." Go ahead; put it on your credit card. Better yet, get this new, low-interest card and pay nothing for one year. That's right, folks, no interest and no payments for one full year." If you're the typical overextended family carrying a per capita credit card debt of $10,000 to $20,000, don't take the bait. It's time for getting out of debt, not deeper into it. If you want help, try using these four Bible principles:

(1) "Don't be greedy for the good things of this life, for that is idolatry" (See Col 3:5 NIV). Stop craving things you don't need. Instead, try enjoying what you've got. (2) If you're not tithing, start *now!* You'll be switching from the world's faltering economy to God's fail-safe economy. When you tithe He promises to protect your interests and send blessings "there shall not be room enough to receive" (See Mal 3:8-12). (3) "The earth is the Lord's, and everything in it" (Ps 24:1 NIV) and He guarantees to "supply all your need[s]" (Php 4:19). So before you go shopping, try praying! Ask God for what you need, then wait for Him to respond. (4) Begin giving away some of what you've got. "It is possible to give away and become richer...[and] to hold on too tightly and lose everything... the liberal man shall be rich" (Pr 11:24-25 TLB). Go ahead, do it! Obey God, be patient, and watch what happens.

LET'S KEEP THE FAITH

Contend earnestly for the faith.

JUDE V. 3 NKJV

The Bible says: "We must give the more earnest heed to the things we have heard, lest we drift away" (Heb 2:1 NKJV). The word "drift" should set off alarm bells. Jesus pointed out that while the harvesters slept an enemy sowed weeds among the wheat. When they finally wakened they said, "An enemy has done this" (Mt 13:28 NKJV). Cancer begins with one unidentified, unchecked cell, and if left un-dealt-with it can destroy your whole body. Hence Jude writes: "Contend earnestly for the faith which was once for all delivered to the saints. For certain men have crept in unnoticed, who long ago were marked out for this condemnation, ungodly men, who turn the grace of our God into lewdness and deny the only Lord God and our Lord Jesus Christ" (vv. 3-4 NKJV). Note the words "the faith which was once for all delivered to the saints." Our methods may change, but our message never changes. Paul writes: "The time will come when they will not endure sound doctrine" (2Ti 4:3 NKJV). Study the progression in the lives of Abraham, Isaac and Jacob. Abraham's blessings came through a personal relationship with God. Isaac inherited his father's blessings. Not until the Philistines attacked him, did he go back and dig again the wells of his father Abraham and build an altar to the Lord. Finally Jacob, the third generation, came along and tried schemes and shortcuts to obtain God's blessing. Only when he had a life-changing encounter with God at Peniel, did he reestablish his life on the foundations laid by Abraham and Isaac. Let's keep the faith; let's give our children "the truth, the whole truth, and nothing but the truth."

FIND A WAY TO SAY "THANK YOU"

I thank my God upon every remembrance of you.
PHILIPPIANS 1:3

Author Barbara Glanz tells about a successful business man who remembered his eighth grade literature teacher. He wrote to her and received this reply: "You'll never know how much your letter meant. I'm eighty-three and living alone. My friends and family are all gone. I taught school for fifty years and yours is the first thank-you I've ever gotten from a student. Sometimes I wonder what I did with my life. I will read, and reread your letter until the day I die." Ironically, she was the teacher students talked most about at class reunions, but nobody ever told her.

Paul was uncompromising on the truth, but his sensitive side also shows up in his writings. Knowing our need for appreciation he opens his Epistles with words like: "I make mention of you always in my prayers" (Ro 1:9 NKJV). "Therefore I also, after I heard of your faith in the Lord Jesus and your love for all the saints, do not cease to give thanks for you" (Eph 1:15-16 NKJV). "I thank my God upon every remembrance of you...for your fellowship in the gospel from the first day until now, being confident of this very thing, that He who has begun a good work in you will complete it until the day of Jesus Christ" (Php 1:3-6 NKJV). "We...boast of you among the churches of God for your patience...in all your persecutions and tribulations that you endure" (2Th 1:3-4 NKJV).

In our busy, self-centered world, we need to remember those who have made a difference in our lives, and when they come to mind, pray for them, and find a way to say "thank you."

AMAZING!

They spread the word...about this child.
LUKE 2:17 NIV

It's almost Christmas! Time for parties, pageantry, and presents. But the real story is about:

(a) The shepherds. Sheepherders had so little status in first-century Palestine that they weren't even deemed reliable enough to testify in court. Yet God chose them to announce His Son's arrival, and they in turn went out and told it to the world! Amazing! Luke records, "When they had seen him, they spread the word." Here's your answer to: "Could God use someone like me?" You don't need to be a seminary graduate. Just tell folks what you've seen, heard, and the change Christ has made in your life. Share the Word and God will do the rest!

(b) Those who heard their story. "All who heard it were amazed" (v. 18 NIV). God's grace still amazes people; "God was reconciling the world to himself in Christ, not counting men's sins against them. And he has committed to us the message of reconciliation" (2Co 5:19 NIV). What a message! "Your sin-debt is cancelled, your books are reconciled, now you can have a personal relationship with God by simply trusting in Christ." Amazing!

(c) Mary. Luke writes: "Mary treasured up all these things and pondered them in her heart" (Lk 2:19 NIV). She wanted to understand what God was doing and how it related to her. And you need to do that too. God doesn't change—but He moves. And you need to stay in step with Him. If you do He will use you and bless you in ways that are—amazing!

LET GOD USE YOU

Mary said...be it unto me according to thy word.
LUKE 1:38

When God told Mary she was going to have a child, she asked how it could be possible. Perhaps God's been telling you things He wants to do through you, but you're looking at yourself and asking, "How will this be?" (Lk 1:34 NIV). You're telling God, "I don't have the training, the experience, the skill or the connections. And I certainly don't have the strength to accomplish it alone." Like Mary, you're thinking only in the natural, that you must have man's help to do it. If you've been wondering how God will make things come to pass in your life, remember, *He* will accomplish the task. No man will get the credit for your deliverance. God told Mary, "The Holy Ghost shall come upon thee" (v. 35). The Holy Spirit can impregnate you with a vision, inspire you with creative ideas, introduce you to the right people, and empower you to do the job. God had a special plan for Mary, and He has one for you too. You aren't privileged to see the future. You don't know all that He has in store for you. But He has a plan. After the angel spoke to Mary do you know what she said? "Be it unto me according to thy word." Not according to my marital status, or my job, or my finances, or what I deserve. No, "Be it unto me according to thy word!" Was that easy to say? No, she was taking an extreme risk. To be pregnant and unmarried brought dire consequences in those days. Yet she gave herself willingly to God —and the results were truly miraculous! So, let God use you!

TAKE UP YOUR CROSS (1)

Let him...take up his cross daily.

LUKE 9:23 NKJV

We tend to equate our cross with things like a difficult mate, a headstrong teen, a bedridden loved one, or too much month left at the end of the money. One author writes: "We think God passes out crosses like a warden handing shovels to a chain gang. No one wants one. Each one gets one...[But] the cross means much more. It's God's tool of redemption...proof of His love. To take up the cross...is to take up Christ's burden for...people." Jesus said, "The load I give you to carry is light" (Mt 11:30 NCV). The cross you're called to bear won't break your back, it will awaken and develop in you areas of strength which are lying dormant or being used for less worthy purposes. When you recognize this you'll stop praying for a lighter cross and ask God for a stronger back. When Paul began praying this way, God said, "My grace is sufficient for you" (2Co 12:9 NKJV).

When a badly burned infant dressed in funeral clothes was left to die in a field, attorney John Bentley and his wife nursed him back to health and adopted him. Today the Bentleys oversee an orphanage. Instead of walking away, they're shouldering the cross for China's children. Michael Landon, Jr. was nineteen when he accepted Christ and started impacting Hollywood by making redemptive films instead of the usual garbage. The son of an acting legend, Landon is uniquely qualified to carry the cross for the entertainment industry. But remember, the cross calls for dying to self-interest and crucifying the desires of your flesh so that the life of Christ can be seen in you.

TAKE UP YOUR CROSS (2)

Let him...take up his cross daily.

LUKE 9:23 NKJV

Here are three questions that will help you to identify your cross:

(1) What direction is God leading me? If you think your background doesn't matter, think again. It can be a roadmap to your future. Consider the experiences and the kind of lifestyle you've been exposed to. Growing up in Egypt prepared Moses to stand before Pharaoh. David's years leading sheep, groomed him to lead a nation. Paul's distinction as a Hebrew scholar and Roman citizen qualified him uniquely to minister to both religious and nonreligious people. *(2) What burdens has God laid on my heart?* Paul says: "My heart's desire and prayer to God for Israel is that they may be saved" (Ro 10:1 NKJV). Paul was driven by a passion to see his people saved. What drives and inspires you? Building shelters for the homeless? Standing against abuse and neglect? Try visiting a nursing home and see if you don't leave feeling uplifted. Or spend time with a group of special-needs kids; they'll teach you more than you teach them! Fulfillment comes from the desires of your heart, not just the ideas in your head. *(3) What areas utilize my talent?* The Bible says God "has given each one of us a special gift" (Eph 4:7 NLT) and although He "works through different [people] in different ways...the same God...achieves his purposes through them all" (1Co 12:6-7 PHPS). How can you tell the difference between a self-generated and a God-generated idea? Solomon said, "Many are the plans in a man's heart, but it is the Lord's purpose that prevails" (Pr 19:21 NIV). Man-made ideas have a short shelf life, divine direction persists; it has longevity.

FREQUENT ENCOUNTERS WITH GOD!

These are the Scriptures that testify about me.

JOHN 5:39 NIV

Here are two compelling reasons for saturating your mind in the Scriptures:

(1) To know who God is. One day in school, a little girl was asked by her art teacher what she was drawing. "A picture of God," she replied. The teacher said, "But nobody's ever seen Him." Confidently the little girl replied, "They will when I'm finished!" Till Jesus came, all we had were glimpses of God. Then Jesus announced, "He that hath seen me hath seen the Father" (Jn 14:9). If you want to know who God is, what He thinks and how He acts, start spending more time with Jesus. *(2) To know who you are.* When God called Moses to deliver Israel, Moses told God two things: (a) "When I...say to them, 'The God of your fathers has sent me to you,' and they say to me, 'What is His name?' what shall I say?'...God said to Moses ...'say...I AM has sent me to you'" (Ex 3:13-14 NKJV). In order to know who *you* are you must know who *God* is; then you'll have credibility, confidence, direction and purpose. (b) "'But suppose they will not believe me'...So the Lord said to him, 'What is that in your hand?' He said, 'A rod.' And He said, 'Cast it on the ground.' So he cast it on the ground, and it became a serpent" (Ex 4:1-3 NKJV). Moses already had what he needed, he just didn't recognize it or know how to use it until God showed him. Getting the idea? In order to know who you are and who God is, you must have frequent encounters with Him.

YOU'RE GROWING UP SPIRITUALLY WHEN...

Let us...go on to maturity.

HEBREWS 6:1 NIV

When Jamie's thirteen-year-old brother died in a skating accident, his mother locked herself in her bedroom for days on end. That's when six-year-old Jamie decided he'd have to replace his brother, and the threads of an intricate fantasy were woven. He became obsessed with imitating his brother's personal characteristics; he wore the same clothes and learned to whistle like him. He became his mother's constant companion, deciding that to stay a child meant freedom from sorrow and responsibility. Jamie continued to resist adulthood, and it was as if his physical body joined in the resistance. At age seventeen he was barely five feet tall, and in later years children were among his closest friends. And no wonder—since age six he'd idealized childhood, rejecting maturity. In fact, the boy who sought eternal youth as a defense against tragedy never did grow up entirely. Instead he became famous for creating Never-Never Land, that ageless island of dreams where little boys never grow up. That's because Jamie eventually became Sir James Barrie—author of the children's book *Peter Pan*.

What's the lesson here? You're growing up spiritually when: (1) You have the ability and discipline to feed yourself spiritually. (2) You know you were not born to be served, and that only in serving others do you serve the Lord. (3) You understand that your feelings are fickle, so you walk by faith and stand on God's Word. (4) You realize you'll be tested, so you commit yourself to living by scriptural principles and not human impulses. (5) You know that true satisfaction comes only from discovering and doing God's will.

"WHERE'S MY HEART?"

Where your treasure is, there your heart will be.
MATTHEW 6:21 NIV

William Randolph Hearst lived in Hearst Castle. It was 90,000 square feet sitting on 265,000 acres. At one time he owned fifty miles of California coastline. And he collected stuff for eighty-eight years. He had 3500-year-old Egyptian statues, medieval Flemish tapestries, centuries-old hand-carved ceilings, and some of the greatest works of art of all time. After eight decades of collecting stuff William Hearst died. Now people go through his house by the thousands and they all say the same thing: "Wow, he sure had a lot of stuff."

We go through life, get stuff, then die, leaving all our stuff behind. And what happens to it? Our kids argue over it. Our kids, who haven't died yet, go through our stuff. Like vultures, they decide which stuff they want to take to their houses. They say to themselves, "Now this is my stuff," then they die and new vultures come to get it. Nations go to war over stuff, families are split apart over stuff. Husbands and wives argue more about stuff than any other single issue. Prisons are full of street thugs and CEO's who committed crimes to acquire it. Why? It's only stuff. This is what Jesus was addressing when He said: "Do not store up for yourselves treasures on earth, where moth and rust destroy, and where thieves break in and steal. But store up for yourselves treasures in heaven, where moth and rust do not destroy, and where thieves do not break in and steal. For where your treasure is, there your heart will be also" (vv. 19-21 NIV). Now, having read those words, ask yourself the question, "Where's my heart?"

FACING THE NEW YEAR WITH COURAGE!

Be strong and courageous.

DEUTERONOMY 31:6 NIV

When you try something for the first time, or something you've already failed at, you need courage. Remember learning to walk? First you tried standing on shaky limbs, smiled in short-lived triumph, fell down, cried in frustration, and kept getting back up until you mastered the art of standing. Something inside you told you that you were meant for more than just lying in a crib. Then came the next stage—walking. Sounds simple enough, but it wasn't. That's because wobbling always precedes walking. And that's the difference between adults and infants. As an infant you weren't image-conscious. You just saw arms outstretched toward you and heard a loving voice saying, "Come on, you can do it!" And you've been walking ever since! That's why God says to anyone stepping into unknown territory, "Be strong and courageous." The word "be" really means "become." Courage is a quality you grow into, like filling bigger shoes. The more you walk in them the more comfortable they get. It's not like a software program where you simply enter your password and "hey, presto," you're courageous! Courage comes from spending time with God, seeing His arms outstretched toward you and hearing Him say, "Come on, you can do it, I'm with you!"

On New Year's Eve the late King George read these wonderful words to the British people: "I said to the man who stood at the gate of the year, 'Give me a light that I may tread safely into the unknown' and he replied, 'Go out into the darkness and put your hand into the hand of God. That shall be to you better than light and safer than a known way!'"

ACKNOWLEDGMENTS

Abrashoff, Michael. *It's Your Ship*. (New York: Warner Bros., 2002)

Aurandt, Paul. *More of Paul Harvey's The Rest of the Story*. (New York: Bantam Books, 1981)

Beattie, Melody. *More Language of Letting Go*. (Hazelden, Minn.: 2000)

Blackaby, Henry T. & Richard Blackaby. *Experiencing God Day-by-Day*. (Nashville, Tenn.: Broadman & Holman, 1998)

Campbell, Micca Monda. "Your Heavenly Referee." Posted August 7, 2008. *encouragementfortoday@crosswalkmail.com*

Carlson, Richard, Ph.D. *Don't Sweat the Small Stuff with Your Family*. (New York: Hyperion, 1998)

Chambers, Oswald. *My Utmost for His Highest*. (Grand Rapids, MI: Discovery House, 1992)

Cowman, L. B. *Streams in the Desert*. (Grand Rapids, Mich.: Zondervan, 2006)

Davis, Verdell. *Riches Stored in Secret Places*. (Nashville, Tenn.: W. Publishing Group, 1994)

Evans, Tony. *Life Essentials*. (Chicago: Moody, 2007)

Evans, Tony. *Time to Get Serious*. (Wheaton, Ill.: Crossway Books, 1995)

Geraci, Ron. *Get a Grip*. (Reader's Digest: January 2008)

Gray, Alice. *Stories for the Heart*. (Portland, Ore.: Multnomah, 1996)

"Have a Good Day!" June, 1978. *Christian Service Songs*. (Wheaton Ill.: Tyndale House, 1978)

Kennedy, D. James, and Jerry Newcombe. *New Every Morning*. (Colorado Springs, Colo.: Multnomah, 1996)

Leonard, Dennis. *Happiness Matters*. (Denver, Colo.: Legacy Publishers International, 2006)

Lucado, Max. *3:16 The Number of Hope*. (Nashville, Tenn.: Thomas Nelson, 2007)

Lucado, Max. *Cast of Characters*. (Nashville, Tenn.: Thomas Nelson, 2008)

Lucado, Max. *Cure for the Common Life*. (Nashville, Tenn.: Thomas Nelson, 2006)

Lucado, Max. *Every Day Deserves a Chance*. (Nashville, Tenn.: Thomas Nelson, 2007)

Lucado, Max. *Facing Your Giants*. (Nashville, Tenn.: Thomas Nelson, 2006)

ACKNOWLEDGMENTS

Lucado, Max. *God's Inspirational Promise Book*. (Nashville, Tenn.: W. Publishing Group, 1999)

Lucado, Max. *The Inspirational Bible*. (Nashville, Tenn.: W. Publishing Group, 1991)

Mason, John L. *Let Go of Whatever Makes You Stop*. (Tulsa, Okla.: Insight International, 1994)

Mason, John L. *You're Born an Original, Don't Die a Copy!* (Tulsa, Okla.: Insight International, 1984)

Maxwell, John C. *Encouragement Changes Everything*. (Nashville, Tenn.: Thomas Nelson, 2008)

Maxwell, John C. *Leadership Gold*. (Nashville, Tenn.: Thomas Nelson, 2008)

Maxwell, John C. *Talent Is Never Enough*. (Nashville, Tenn.: Thomas Nelson, 2007)

Meyer, Joyce. *Approval Addiction*. (New York: Warner Faith, 2005)

Nouwen, Henry. *Here and Now: Living in the Spirit*. (Chestnut Ridge, N.Y.: Crossroad Publishing, 2006)

Ortberg, John. *God Is Closer Than You Think*. (Grand Rapids, Mich.: Zondervan, 2005)

Sala, Harold. *Guidelines for Finding Your Way*. (Uhrichville, Ohio: Barbour, 2003)

Sample, Stephen B. *The Contrarian's Guide to Leadership*. (Hoboken, N.J.: Wiley, 2003)

Swindoll, Charles R. *The Grace Awakening*. (Nashville, Tenn.: W. Publishing Group, 1998)

Swindoll, Charles R. *Perfect Trust*. (Nashville, Tenn.: J. Countryman, 2000)

Tenney, Tommy. *The Daily Chase*. (Shippensburg, Pa.: Destiny Image, 2000)

Walker, Jon. "Forgiving in an Unhealthy Situation." (The Purpose Driven Life Devotional Online. December 10, 2007)

Warren, Rick. "How Do You Recover from Disaster?" Posted Oct. 29, 2007. The Purpose Driven Life Daily Devotional Online.

Warren, Rick. *Bible Study Methods*. (Grand Rapids, Mich.: Zondervan, 2006)

Whitwer, Glynnis. "The Adventure of Obedience." Posted June 25, 2008. *www.crosswalkmail.com*

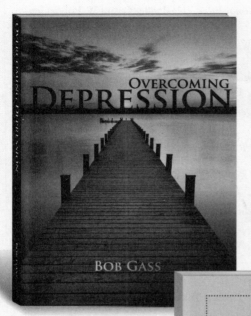

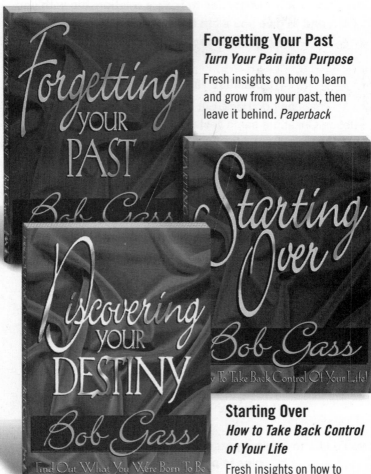

THREE REASONS WHY YOU NEED JESUS

Jesus loves you! He desires to have a relationship with you, and to give you a life full of joy and purpose. Why do you need Him in your life?

1. BECAUSE YOU HAVE A PAST.

You can't go back, but He can. The Bible says, "Jesus Christ the same yesterday, and today, and for ever" (Hebrews 13:8). He can walk into those places of sin and failure, wipe the slate clean, and give you a new beginning.

2. BECAUSE YOU NEED A FRIEND.

Jesus knows the worst about you, yet He believes the best. Why? Because He sees you not as you are but as you will be when He gets through with you. What a friend!

3. BECAUSE HE HOLDS THE FUTURE.

Who else are you going to trust? In His hands you are safe and secure—today, tomorrow, and for all eternity. His Word says, "For I know the plans I have for you... plans for good and not for evil, to give you a future and a hope. In those days when you pray, I will listen" (Jeremiah 29:11–12 TLB).

If you'd like to begin a personal relationship with Jesus today, please pray this prayer:

Lord Jesus, I invite You into my life.

I believe You died for me and that Your blood pays

for my sins and provides me with the gift of eternal life.

By faith I receive that gift,

and I acknowledge You as my Lord and Savior.

———— **AMEN** ————